THE TRADITIONAL BOWYER'S BIBLE

Volume Three

Tim Baker
Paul Comstock
Gabriela Cosgrove
Jim Hamm
Gene Langston

Jay Massey
Jay St. Charles
Jeff Schmidt
Scott Silsby
David Tukura

·BOIS·
d'ARC
PRESS

DISTRIBUTED BY

Lyons & Burford

31 West 21 Street New York, New York 10010

EDITOR'S NOTE

When we first envisioned the *Bowyer's Bibles*, we never dreamed they would take on such a life of their own (that first volume "sat up on the operating table", as Tim Baker so aptly put it). Now, as we complete this final book, many thousands of readers have begun making, shooting, and hunting with weapons they've crafted for themselves, a result the authors would have found unimaginable when we started the project only a few short years ago. We can only hope that you have found the *Bowyer's Bibles* as enlightening as those who wrote them.

Jim Hamm
Spring, 1994

ACKNOWLEDGEMENTS

The authors of this volume are indebted to Doug Elmy, Dr. Errett Callahan, and Dr. Bert Grayson. Joe St. Charles kindly provided the photos taken by Arthur Young. Steve Allely once again contributed his peerless artistic talents. Robert Ranley, Steve Honnen, Pat Mahan, and Bill Holme offered access to their collections as well as insight into Plains weapons.

✧ ✧ ✧

The authors would especially like to
remember their colleague

Glenn Parker
(1947-1993)

The world in general and archery in particular
are better for his having paused here.

ABOUT THE AUTHORS

Tim Baker, like many others, first became interested in archery after reading about Ishi and the remarkable weapons he made with only stone tools. Upon reading the available archery texts, it became clear to Tim there was a great deal of contradiction and confusion about wooden bows and their design. He decided the only way to get reliable information was to make every conceivable type of bow of every conceivable material while keeping complete statistics on each one. By comparing stats, the qualities which produce superior bows slowly became apparent. Based upon his research, he has written articles on wooden bows and their construction, as well as teaching at archery meets and primitive skills workshops. Tim can be contacted at 6609 Whitney, Oakland, CA, 94609.

Paul Comstock never used a hunting weapon he really liked until he started carrying a wooden bow. He earlier tagged whitetails and black bears using a center-fire rifle, muzzleloader, shotgun, compound bow, and glass-laminated recurve bow. Since switching to wooden bows, he has abandoned modern hunting weapons entirely. Where legal, he also uses stone-tipped arrows exclusively. His largest game so far with a wooden bow is a 300-pound black bear.

He began making wooden bows in 1984. From the outset he began experimenting with woods other than yew and Osage orange, curious because old bowmaking books ignored these woods almost completely. In 1988 he published the first edition of *The Bent Stick*, the first bowmaking manual to describe in comprehensive detail how to get the best results from some of North America's most common trees. Paul sells *The Bent Stick* for $11 a copy, postpaid, and *Hit the Mark! Shooting Wooden and Primitive Bows* for $7, postpaid. He can be reached at P.O. Box 1102, Delaware, OH 43015.

Gabriela Cosgrove began making wooden arrows professionally in 1982 when she and her husband, Tim, bought Kustom King Arrows. What began as a small operation has since ballooned into a full-fledged business that carries quality traditional archery equipment such as bows, arrows, leather goods, books, and videos. Gabriela, today recognized as one of the finest arrowmakers in the country, has always had an interest in the outdoors and in keeping things as natural and uncomplicated as possible (she also enjoys baking bread and gardening). For information on her arrows or other traditional archery products, contact her at Kustom King Arrows, 1260 E. 86th Pl., Merrilville, IN 46410.

Jim Hamm was born in Texas in 1952, and practically grew up with a bow in his hands, graduating from small game to deer hunting when only twelve. His interest in archery never faded, and about the time he married discovered bows made entirely from wood, a discovery which was to consume his adult life. Though spending his early years operating heavy equipment, working freight docks, and "becoming a promising young executive", Jim finally went into archery full-time. He has been, as he puts it, "self-unemployed" for the past fifteen years: making bows, researching, writing about bows, and recently, teaching others the age-old skill of wooden bowmaking through intensive, hands-on seminars conducted at his home. He also owns and operates Bois d'Arc Press, publishing archery books both old and new. Jim's first book, *Bows and Arrows of the Native Americans*, is available for $16.95 postpaid. To order books write; Bois d'Arc Press 4, PO Box 233, Azle, TX, 76098.

Gene Langston was born in Rome, Georgia, not far from the home of the Thompson brothers. When he was nine years old, he was given a hickory longbow set for Christmas, complete with a tab, an armguard, a target, and three cedar arrows, which started a life-long love affair with archery. "I've got a picture of me in a Davy Crockett outfit, shooting that bow," he says. "Pretty good form, too." Like many others, he changed to fiberglass recurves and had a brief flirtation with a "faux bow," but inevitably returned to his first love, the wooden bow.

Gene has done many things. As an Army Ranger, he led a recon platoon in Viet Nam in 1968-69; he worked his way through college as a conservation officer; he was a police detective, working in undercover investigations for nearly nine years before retiring for health reasons. He is also a widely published fiction writer, with stories in major literary journals throughout the country. He now lives in North Carolina, where, in addition to making bows, arrows, and linen strings, he teaches creative writing in the adult education programs of three colleges. He has a freelance fiction editing service and has recently been named Associate Editor of the newly-organized Inheritance Press of Chapel Hill, North Carolina, a small book publishing concern.

A native of Oklahoma, **Jay Massey** has lived in Alaska for the past 23 years and is a registered guide/outfitter and a former member of the Alaska Board of Game. He operates an outfitting business, Moose John Outfitters, which caters to archery hunters, wilderness enthusiasts and salmon fishermen. He has written four archery books and is currently at work on a fifth which will combine fiction with fact to dramatize significant archery-related events of medieval England, the Steppes of Asia and pre-contact Indian America.

Jay's other books can be ordered through Bear Paw Publications, P.O. Box 429, Girdwood, AK 99587: *Bowhunting Alaska's Wild Rivers* ($15.95); *A Thousand Campfires* ($14.95); *The Bowyer's Craft* ($16.95); and *The Book of Primitive Archery* (18.95). Add $2 for postage and handling.

Raised in a family very active in archery and the outdoors, **Jay St. Charles** had his first bowhunting experiences in the company of his father, Glenn, in Washington State's Cascade Mountains in the early 1950's. Those early experiences served to shape his life, with much of his time having been spent in various archery and bowhunting involvements, and in "sabbaticals" in the wilderness areas of North America. Jay, age 44, is currently employed as a bowyer, and lives with his wife and son near his shop south of Seattle, Washington.

"I have always been attracted to simplicity and portability in any equipment I use in the outdoors. When I began working with wooden bows in earnest in the early 1980's, my thoughts were directed back to the basic sleeve and socket takedown bows used by my father and his hunting partners in their early days of bowhunting in the Northwest. I encourage other bowyers to try this option." Jay can be contacted at 19807 First Ave. South, Seattle, WA, 98148.

Jeffrey Schmidt is a professor of physics at the University of Wisconsin — Parkside Campus. He has been interested in archery and in particular composite bows for almost thirty years. In the last four years, he has constructed more than two dozen Asiatic composite bows, focusing primarily on designs from the Middle East. In collaboration with John McPherson, a video *How to Construct the Asiatic Composite Bow* was produced in 1993 and is available from Prairie Wolf, PO Box 96, Randolph, KS, 66554. The two are currently writing a comprehensive book on the subject which will also be available via Prairie Wolf.

Scott Silsby is a retired career Naturalist who now conducts workshops on a wide range of "old time" and Prehistoric skills at his home in the Shenandoah Valley. After forty years, he has perfected the production of an entire archery system with Stone Age tools and is a co-founder of the Society of Primitive Technology. He markets replica points of many types as well as Greenstone in rough, preform, and finished form. Contact him about workshops, replicas, or Greenstone at Flintworks, Rt. 1 Box 2426, Front Royal, VA, 22630.

David Tukura was born in Nigeria in 1960 and as a young boy began shooting a wooden bow in the African bush. As he grew older, he not only continued using a bow for hunting but began researching the use and application of the bow in the context of historical warfare by his people, the Bassa.

David recently received his doctorate in sociology from MacMaster University in Canada. His research into archery continues, and his present ambition is to combine North American bowmaking techniques with those of Africa.

DEDICATION

V

To all of those in the coming centuries

who will help preserve this ancient art of the chase.

May a bent stick bring you the same joy

it has brought us, as well as

teach the same humbling lessons —

joy and knowledge not of time or place

but of humankind.

© 1994 by Bois d'Arc Press

ISBN #1-55821-311-2

Printed in the United States of America

Graphics Production – LeWay Composing Service Inc., Fort Worth, Texas

TABLE OF CONTENTS

TRADITIONAL ROOTS

Jay Massey

In America, the cornerstone of traditional archery was set in place more than one hundred years ago with the publication of Maurice Thompson's book, *The Witchery of Archery*. That memorable book formed the basis for nearly everything which was to come later. The rich tradition of archery had been kept alive in England, of course, since the Middle Ages. And during the same period it was being quietly passed down through the generations by Native Americans — Indian, Eskimo, and Aleut — even as the bow and arrow was being replaced by gunpowder.

But it was the publication of Thompson's classic work, more than word-of-mouth, that really brought the archery tradition back to life in this country. As Dr. R.P. Elmer wrote, "That wonderful little book has as much effect on archery as Uncle Tom's Cabin had on the Civil War!"

Come to think of it, the Civil War was precisely what provided the incentive for Maurice Thompson and his brother, Will, to take up archery. As Confederate veterans, they were prohibited from owning firearms after the War Between the States. As a result, they turned to the more primitive bow and arrow.

The Thompson brothers were archery romanticists; to them, archery was a pursuit which recalled simpler, more heroic times when survival depended more on the strength of one's muscles than the strength of his financial ledger. Throughout the book are passages and poems which clearly indicate the Thompson's longings for a more heroic era.

Consider, for example, the opening lines of one chapter in *The Witchery of Archery:*

> Cheerily blow the bugle horn
> In the cool green woods of morn;
> Loose the hounds and let them go,
> Wax the cord and bend the bow.

Or the words in this sonnet, written by John Hamilton Reynolds and reprinted in Thompson's book:

> The trees in Sherwood Forest are old and good;
> The grass beneath then now is dimly green;
> Are they deserted all? Is no young man
> With loose-slung bugle met within the wood;
> No arrow found, foiled of its antlered food,
> Struck in the oak's rude side?

The poetic writings of Maurice Thompson left a marked impression on count-less Americans, including two young men who would follow in the Thompson brother's footsteps — Saxton Pope and Arthur Young. In his book, *Hunting with the Bow and Arrow,* Pope paid tribute to the Thompson brothers by writing: "In America our hearts have heard the low whistle of the flying arrow and the sweet hum of the bow-string singing in the book, *The Witchery of Archery* by Maurice Thompson. To Will and Maurice Thompson we owe a debt of gratitude hard to pay. The tale of their sylvan exploits in the everglades of Florida has a charm that border on the fay [magical]. We who shoot the bow today are chil-dren of their fantasy, off-spring of their magic. As the parents of American archery, we offer them homage and honor."

Throughout his first book, Pope refers again and again to the Thompson brothers, even reprinting a poem Will Thompson wrote in memory of his late brother:

AN ARROW SONG

A song from green Floridian vales I heard,
Soft as the sea-moan when the waves are slow;
Sweeter than melody of brook or bird,
Keener than any winds that breathe or blow;
A magic music of our memory stirred,
A strain that charms my heart to overflow
With such vast yearning that my eyes are blurred.
Oh, song of dreams, that I no more shall know!
Bewildering carol without spoken word!
Faint as a stream's voice murmuring under snow,
Sad as a love forevermore deferred,
Song of the arrow from the Master's bow,
Sung in Floridian vales long, long ago.

-Will H. Thompson

Although Saxton Pope undoubtedly received his inspiration for archery from the Thompsons, he acquired much of his practical knowledge about bowmaking and hunting from Ishi, the last Yana Indian who was discovered in 1911 still liv-ing a Stone Age existence in the Mount Lassen area of California. As Ishi's physician, Pope became his friend and hunting companion and was with him when he died of tuberculosis in 1916. But before his death, Ishi passed on much of the lore of the bow and arrow to both Saxton Pope and Arthur Young.

In turn, the archery adventures of Saxton Pope and Arthur Young and the public attention they received — Pope wrote several books on archery and hunt-ing and Young became a noted lecturer — encouraged thousands of other Americans to carry on the archery tradition.

According to Howard Hill, it was reading *The Witchery of Archery* which caused him to abandon golf as a profession and make a lifelong commitment to archery. In his book, *Hunting the Hard Way,* Hill refers to the Thompson brothers at length and writes of Maurice Thompson, "A marvelous archer and a writer of no mean ability, he painted a picture of the Everglades and Sub-everglades around Lake Okeechobee and Kissimmee River country that is vivid enough to keep anyone on edge who has a heart for the bush."

And in the introduction to the book, *Fred Bear's Field Notes,* Fred Bear flatly states, "My interest in archery and bowhunting began in 1925 after seeing a film of Arthur Young hunting with a bow in Alaska."

In another of his books, Bear wrote, "The revival of bowhunting as a popular sport in America was due in large part to four men." He went on to describe how Maurice and Will Thompson, Saxton Pope and Art Young had passed on the tradition to him and others of his generation, which included such archers as Earl Ullrich, Gilman Keasey, Dr. Charles Grayson, Glenn St. Charles and countless others.

These archers, in turn, passed the tradition on to my generation and now — with the tremendous revival of interest in traditional archery — it appears there will be another generation to carry the torch.

Twenty years ago, I would never have imagined the ground swell of excitement that is currently building for traditional archery. I would not have dreamed that, as we approach the year 2000, tens of thousands of archers would be enthusiastically taking up the time-tested longbow and recurve, and that many of them would even be hand-crafting their own bows and arrows. During the 1970's, for example, droves of archers were starting to abandon the recurve bow in favor of the mechanical compound device. Back then, if you ran across a guy shooting a longbow, you knew immediately that here was a guy with grit, a man strong enough to swim against the tide.

That was precisely my reaction to Alaskan archer Dick Hamilton when I met him at an indoor archery range on Elmendorf Air Force Base near Anchorage, Alaska. I'd hunted with longbow and flatbow for my first two years, then switched to building and shooting laminated recurves. Still, I had fondness for the longbow, and when I met Hamilton I knew that here was a man who was willing to forgo the new developments in archery in order to experience the true essence of "hunting the hard way." Hamilton was a dyed-in-the-wool Howard Hill fan, preferring a Hill bow, a Hill backquiver, armguard, and glove. He was an oddity at the local archery range, where the high-tech archers would smirk at the sight of his longbow. Hamilton didn't care. He was fiercely independent and twice as strong — both mentally and physically — as the compound advocates who quietly derided him behind his back.

Dick and I became good friends and hunting partners. It took me several years to come back around to using longbows and flatbows because frankly, I liked the speed and accuracy of my heavy-handled recurved bows and the hunting success that came with them. But during the entire time, Hamilton stayed with the longbow, never changed his equipment, but always strove to perfect himself and his technique.

An interesting fact about Hamilton — who grew up in West Texas and worked as a driller and roughneck while attending college — is that he developed a design for a pulley-equipped mechanical bow back in the 1950's, long before anyone else came up with the idea for the compound device. He worked out the design on paper, and I believe, even built a crude prototype, but discarded the idea as unthinkable because he thought the device was not real archery.

That is but one reason I've had such respect for Hamilton and why I've always seen him as representing the true spirit of traditionalism. Here was a man who could have taken the easier way, but didn't. While others of our generation were searching for technological shortcuts, he steadfastly refused to compromise. To heck with what everyone else was doing — that was his attitude.

One cannot help but admire such an attitude: stubborn, hard-headed, honest, and straight-forward, an absolute refusal to compromise one's principles. Those are Early American qualities — and many of our other public and social institutions would do well to revive and emulate them.

Thinking about Dick Hamilton, an incident from the late 1970's comes to mind. I shot a roll of color film of Hamilton and sent the transparencies off to *Archery World Magazine* for possible use as a cover photo. The photos were taken on a bright autumn afternoon and they depicted Hamilton hiking up a ridge of the Chugach Range into Dall sheep country. He was carrying his Howard Hill longbow and backquiver. Several of the photos, I felt, filled all the requirements of a good magazine cover shot: a dramatic pose of an archer in spectacular game country, sharp detail and good color range and saturation. Plus, they were shot in vertical format, with a magazine cover in mind.

However, the editor of *Archery World Magazine* quickly returned them to me with a "thanks, but no thanks," note. "Those are great shots," he wrote, "but that bow the guy's carrying really looks like an oldie."

In other words, the photo of Hamilton with his Hill longbow and backquiver looked like an anachronism — outdated, out of style.

I'd like to have seen the look on that editor's face had he traveled to the Great Lakes Longbow Invitational in Michigan this past summer — where there were well over one thousand registered longbow shooters!

The Michigan longbow shoot typifies the resurgence of archery traditionalism. It is but one of many big traditional and longbow archery events which are held annually across the U.S. and Canada. The attraction is simple: the emphasis is on fun, with little of the back-stabbing, belly-aching and "sandbagging" that seems to characterize modern archery shoots. Folks go to the traditional events to have a good time, not to win money. You'll rarely see a traditionalist puffing out his chest and acting "macho" either, for the simple reason that there are so many competent archers, bowyers, and bowhunters at the traditional shoots that he'd simply be laughed down if he were to strut around like a tom turkey in the spring woods.

Another wonderful thing about the traditional shoots is that you'll find the best hunters, archers, and bowyers in the country fraternizing face-to-face with absolute novices. It's a great place for the neophyte to obtain first-hand knowledge from long-time traditionalists.

Some of the old-time archers one meets at these events — be they Glenn St. Charles, Dr. Charles Grayson, Floyd Eccleston, or whomever — almost certainly obtained their knowledge directly from some pioneer like Hill or Bear or Compton or Pope or Young — archers whose names belong in the Traditional Archery Hall of Fame, if there were such a place.

A few high-tech archers have accused traditionalists of being "elitist", but the spirit that exists at the traditional events indicates the exact opposite. The attitude of the archers there do not represent vanity, conceit, egotism, and materialism; these things seem more typical of the results-oriented high-tech archery. What we see instead are such positive attributes as cheerfulness, generosity, laughter, good sportsmanship, and good old-fashioned fun.

The essence of the traditional archery get-togethers is strikingly similar to the things Maurice Thompson, Saxton Pope, and other archers wrote about during their time. It is the revival of the traditional attitude that gives me satisfaction, knowing that whatever small contribution I may have made is helping keep traditional archery alive. May we always have archers willing to carry it on!

TOOLS

Paul Comstock

"The right tool for the right job," went a saying I used to hear as a boy. This phrase also has value for those making wooden bows. Unless he has some woodworking experience, the novice bowyer is often at a loss as to what kinds of tools can help him. At the other extreme are veteran woodworkers so skilled they deserve to be called artists. When such men take up bowmaking, their long experience with tools usually allows them to produce sophisticated weapons in short order. Many of us lie somewhere in the middle. A person does not need prior woodworking experience to become a bowyer. If he is coordinated enough to tie his shoes, he should be able to handle bowmaking tools. However, our level of experience will determine which tools work well for us. Some tools are best for green beginners while others work better for those with lots of experience.

Tools can also be classified as those that remove wood quickly and those that remove wood slowly. Tools that remove wood quickly must be used with special care because they can butcher a bow stave in a single second of inattention. Beginners must be particularly cautious with tools such as the draw knife, axe, and any power saw.

Tools which remove wood slowly are particularly valuable for making wooden bows. They make it easier for the beginner to avoid mistakes. Unlike most tools that remove wood quickly, slow-working tools do not leave a ragged, gashed, irregular surface. This makes slow-working tools valuable in the final stages of producing a bow, as control is much easier.

Some bowyers are quite opinionated about tools. Some despise power tools, saying a bow cannot possibly be "primitive" when such monstrosities are used. Thousands — probably millions — of wooden bows were made in the first half of this century with power tools. Wooden bows were the only type available then. And their authenticity was not besmirched by the touch of electricity.

While power tools can vastly reduce the amount of time needed to make a bow, they are not mandatory. A person need not think he must possess thousands of dollars worth of power tools and an elaborate workshop.

If you are limited on space and resources, you can make beautiful bows with nothing but hand tools. You can do it in your garage, in your basement, or sitting on your back porch.

Until the Bronze Age, all bows were made with tools of stone or natural material. Such tools also make bows today and very effectively.

If you have made a number of bows, you have probably discovered favorite tools for any given task. It can also be quite effective to use tools in combinations. For example, in the early stages of making a bow, I usually switch back and forth between a rasp, scraper, spokeshave, and bandsaw in rapid succession.

WOOD REDUCTION STRATEGY

A bowyer is often well-served by developing a wood-reduction strategy, and relying on different tools during different phases of reduction.

We must give some thought to the hacking and chopping that precedes the tillering process, since it is possible to ruin a good stave if one is careless.

My wood reduction strategy is fairly quick while at the same time being fairly foolproof. It makes it easy to avoid mistakes and to correct any mistakes I do make.

Starting with a split log (Figure A), I first draw a starting outline on the back, and cut the log to the outline (Figure B). This can be done with a fast-working tool, as long as the tool is under control. This fast-working tool could be a circular saw, band saw, draw knife, or a small ax.

Next, I draw a beginning limb thickness on both sides of each limb. I usually make this beginning thickness about a quarter of an inch more than what I would guess the final limb thickness will be. Then, using a fast-working tool, I make the cuts shows in Figure C. This leaves the edges close to their final thickness, while the middle of the limb remains quite deep.

Using a fast-working tool, I next make the belly flat or nearly flat (Figure D).

It is extremely dangerous to omit the step of Figure C and try to jump from Figure B to Figure D. If someone of average ability tries it, odds are high he will make the limb too thin in spots if he uses a fast-working power tool. He could also accidentally cut the limb in two.

The next step is to draw new lines on the limb sides that will be the thickness used for the initial tillering bends. Then, using a slow-working tool, I reduce the corners to meet my new lines (Figure E). Still using the slow-working tool, I next flatten the belly (Figure F). Then I give the bow its first bend. From this stage on, only slow-working tools are used.

This strategy is also what I have used with good effect when making rounded-belly English longbows. On such bows, the next step after Figure F is to round off the square corners.

HAND TOOLS
The Minimum Tool Kit

What is the minimum a bowyer needs to produce a good bow quickly?

A sharp hand axe, a wood rasp, and a scraper. Some would say, "a draw knife, a wood rasp, and a scraper." However, a draw knife requires the use of a vise or a woodworking horse. The axe does not.

A good bowmaking axe has a blade nearly as sharp as a knife. The easiest way to sharpen the hatchet is with a sharp, flat mill file. When removing wood quickly, the bowyer can swing the axe at a slight angle to the stave. Hitting the

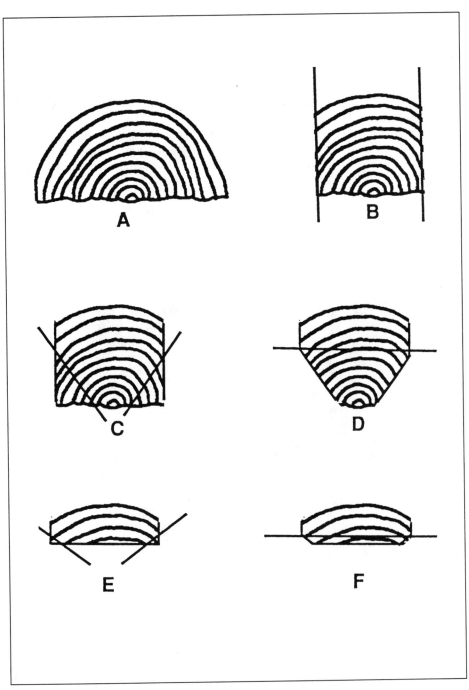

Wood reduction strategy.

stave with authority will usually start a long split in the wood. If this split piece does not fall off by itself, I typically remove it by chopping its attached end off with the axe.

Once the bowyer begins to get close to the desired dimensions, he can use a different axe technique for more control. This involves holding the axe only halfway down the handle, while directing a series of small V cuts directly into the sides of the stave. By making a few light chops angled to the left, followed by a few more angled to the right, he can remove wood fairly quickly without accidentally splitting off the wood he wants to keep. This gives the axe-user an advantage difficult to obtain with a drawknife. When using the average drawknife, it is difficult to remove wood slowly without splitting the wood. When you get close to your final dimensions, accidental splitting is the last thing you need.

Another effective tool for roughing out a bow is a sharp machete. In his bow-making video, primitive technology mentor John McPherson uses a large knife to chop on a bowstave. Inspired by the example, I tried a machete and found it

Elements of the minimum tool kit can include a sharp hatchet (top) and (from left) a splitting wedge, a Nicholson rasp, a woodworker's rasp, a Japanese rasp assembled from saw blades, a Stanley Surform, a knife scraper, a paint scraper, a cabinet scraper, a goose-neck scraper, and Richard Baugh's Bowscraper.

as effective as a hatchet. The machete was particularly successful at following the grain when working down the belly of a wide, flat limb.

Available in most hardware stores is a four-sided rasp made by Nicholson. It has a rounded side and a flat side. Each side has a rasp and file surface. The rounded rasp removes wood the quickest. The flat rasp removes wood more slowly. The rounded file removes wood slower still. The slowest cutting surface is the flat file side. The rasp teeth on this tool are fairly large, while more expensive woodworking rasps usually have smaller teeth, which slow stave reduction in the early going when there is still far too much wood present. An interesting rasp imported from Japan uses saw blades fastened together. It has a coarse-cut side and fine-cut side.

The only time I use a small-toothed rasp is in the final stages of tillering, but the flat side of the Nicholson rasp works just as well. For fast wood removal, the round-rasp side of this tool works well. When really taking off wood, I hold it so the teeth on the side of the round rasp dig in deeply. A great advantage to the Nicholson, or any other type of rasp, is it removes wood without snagging the grain. When a spokeshave hits a dip in the grain, it snags and tears out pieces of wood.

Keeping a smooth surface on the belly is important during the final stages of tillering. The rough surface left by the round rasp can be quickly flattened by the flat rasp side. Using the round file side next will leave the surface flat enough to be completely smoothed by a scraper.

Nicholson and other companies also make farrier's rasps. (In case you need to grab the dictionary, a farrier is someone who shoes horses.)

As great as the smaller Nicholson is, a farrier's rasp can remove wood twice as fast because the tool is quite large (usually at least 1.5 inches wide by more than a foot long) with large teeth. It also has smaller teeth on the flip side.

If you know anyone who owns horses, ask who their farrier is. Then call the farrier and ask where he gets his rasps. When you see how quickly a farrier's rasp can chew through Osage and hickory, you'll be mighty glad you own one. After obtaining a farrier's rasp, I wondered how I ever got along without one.

The most basic scraper is a sharp knife. Hold the blade at a right angle to the wood and scrape along the surface. The sharper the knife, the better it works as a scraper. It is a good plan to keep a whetstone handy, so you can pause occasionally and touch up the blade.

The biggest disadvantage of the knife scraper is that it can bounce or skip on the wood, leaving a surface that looks like a washboard. This usually happens when the knife blade is held at a 90-degree angle to the edge of the limb, as shown in Figure A (next page), viewed from above. If the knife is turned slightly (Figure B), bouncing can be reduced. If skipping does start, it can be quickly scraped off by changing the angle from Figure B to Figure C, or vice-versa.

Holding the tool at an angle and switching the angle frequently is effective with all kinds of scrapers, as well as the spokeshave.

If you can't scrape a washboard surface flat, use coarse sandpaper wrapped around a block for the job. Or use the flat file side of a rasp.

One tool with a long history is the cabinet scraper. This rectangular piece of metal works well for those adept at sharpening it. My friend Dean Torges, an

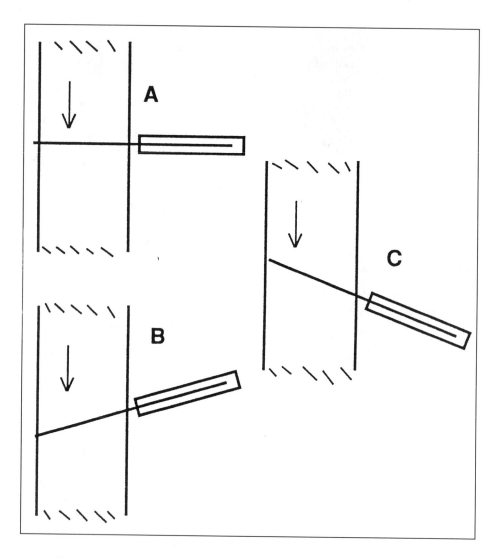

experienced woodworker, says a well-sharpened cabinet scraper will keep its edge far longer than a knife. The trick to sharpening a cabinet scraper is to roll a burr on each side of the square blade's edge. The first step is to place the scraper in a vise and lightly file the edge quite square and sharp, exposing all new metal on the edges. Next, grab a piece of hard, polished steel. Torges uses the back side of a chisel. He oils the back of the chisel to avoid snagging the scraper's edge. Holding the chisel five degrees from a right angle with the scaper's edge, lightly wipe the top side of the edge you just ground 20 or 30 times in one direction. Avoid pushing too hard or rocking the chisel. Flip it over and repeat the process on the other side. This pushes the burr away from the square edge, and creates a tiny hook along the length.

This is a good way to roll back the burr on the edges of a cabinet scraper.

Cross-section of the scraper's edge, showing burr.

A similar tool is the goose-necked scraper. I rarely bother to pick up a cabinet scraper, but find lots of uses for the goose-necked scraper's curved edge. I most commonly use it to remove tool marks from a nearly finished bow.

Broken glass can also work as a scraper. But broken glass dulls quickly and creates tiny glass chips that go everywhere. Broken glass is hardly worth the bother compared to a sharp knife.

Some hardware stores sell paint scrapers that must be pulled along the wood's surface. These tools also work well on bows if the sharp corners of the blade are rounded off.

Richard Baugh of Palo Alto, Calif., is a bowmaker who did all of us a favor by inventing the Bowscraper. This tool was made exclusively for the production of wooden bows. Anybody who owns a Bowscraper will use it a great deal. For me, its greatest asset is it will remove rasp marks with great speed. It will also remove wood faster than a routine scraper.

Used in combination, the rasp and scraper form a great team for reducing a bow's draw weight without changing the tiller. This is a touchy job for most tools. The trick is to remove wood evenly from the belly. If you use some other tool, such as a spokeshave, the danger is you will remove too much wood from one spot without noticing what you are doing. This will weaken the limb and change the tiller. Which can ruin the bow.

I once watched a bowyer of vast experience, working before an impressed and expectant crowd, lighten a bow with a spokeshave. To his embarrassment, he strung the bow only to find he had given one spot too many passes with the spokeshave. The limb hinged viciously and the bow was converted to a useless piece of scrap before a host of witnesses. This tragic tale is repeated here as a lesson for the rest of us: reducing the weight of a bow must be done carefully.

With a rasp and scraper, the job is not too tough. Starting with a smooth belly, the first step is to simply rough up the entire belly surface with the rasp. It is easy to tell where you have been because the wood is now rough and easy to tell where you haven't been, because the wood is still smooth. Once the entire belly is evenly roughed, scrape it smooth. You can tell where you have scraped because the surface is smooth. You can tell where you haven't scraped because the surface is still rough.

This is not a terribly fast procedure. Each combined pass of the rasp and scraper will knock only a pound or two from the draw weight. But a good tiller is a precious thing. You must protect it at all costs. If you are working on a $100 piece of yew or Osage orange, you'll be sick for a month if you ruin the bow.

Aggressive work with the rasp, combined with the scraper, could drop a 67-pound bow to a 64-pound bow in a single pass. Just make sure the rasping is done evenly and don't rasp too deeply in a single spot. Using long strokes as much as possible will help prevent this. Check the tiller after each series of passes with the rasp and scraper. If a problem develops, the faster you know it, the better.

Hammer and Wedges

For the bowyer cutting his own trees, a sledge hammer and splitting wedges are also part of the minimum tool kit.

Most will probably want to use a long-handled six or eight-pound sledge hammer. But a small sledge held with only one hand works well on all but the largest logs.

Splitting wedges, like sledge hammers, are sold in almost every hardware store. For the aboriginal purist, antler and wooden wedges can be hammered into a log with a rude wooden club.

A useful old-time splitting tool is a froe. It has a long blade with the handle sticking up at a right angle. The froe is used to split the wood between growth rings, lengthwise with the log or stave.

Draw Knife

To use a draw knife, you need a vise or some other device to secure the wood.

Draw knives are not particularly common or easy to obtain. The best bets for finding one are woodworking supply catalogs, woodworking stores in large cities, antique stores, or flea markets.

A draw knife will have a curved or straight blade. I use a draw knife with a straight blade to remove bark. The blade is not particularly sharp. This helps prevent cutting through the outer ring, which would be a significant mistake.

I prefer a curved-blade for reducing the sides or belly of a bow. This blade is very sharp. The curved edge makes it easier to control the cut and helps prevent unwanted splitting. Holding this drawknife at varying angles, similar to the scraping technique, also helps the process.

Jim Hamm and other veteran users of Osage orange like to use draw knives to work the Osage back down to one ring. Hamm attributes his success to a dull drawknife blade which tends to pry wood apart between the rings, rather than cutting it. And he recommends dry Osage for drawknifing.

A safer method for a novice might be a spokeshave. If the Osage rings are particularly thin, I would use a rasp and scraper.

When reducing a bow's belly and sides, the draw knife works best when the grain is straight. It works particularly well with straight-grained yew and most of the white woods. Many oak, maple, birch, ash, and hickory trees grow with very straight grain.

If an Osage stave has many knots and ripples in the grain, a draw knife will snag and tear out large pieces of wood. Another poor candidate for the draw

Here are two good draw knives, one with a curved blade and the other with a straight blade.

knife is elm, particularly elms made of mostly white sapwood, such as American elm. These trees have interlocking grain that create a nightmare for someone trying to use a draw knife.

The novice intrigued by the draw knife should be encouraged to practice with scrap pieces. Beginners will probably find they get better results with a small axe.

Spokeshave

For the novice, the spokeshave can be a difficult tool. It is not always easy to find and can also be difficult to sharpen. It will gouge wood when the grain dips or around a knot. The best spokeshaves work poorly when the grain is rippled, or on the interlocking elm grain.

Perhaps the easiest spokeshave to find is that manufactured by Stanley. In the hands of an experienced woodworker, they are quite effective. In the hands of a beginner, they are often next to useless. I have heard a number of new bowyers complain they could accomplish nothing with a spokeshave.

Success with a spokeshave depends on a number of variables. Here are some examples:

I purchased a new Stanley spokeshave and could not find one worthwhile application for it. Dean Torges then sold me a Stanley spokeshave that he had modified. He had ground the blade to resemble a curved drawknife, with the highest part of the curve in the middle of the blade. Here was a tool I could use, providing the grain did not dip and the original limb surface was fairly smooth.

Torges uses a jig he made, combined with a grinding wheel, to sharpen spokeshaves. I know other people who use fine grit belts on a belt sander to sharpen their blades. Others hire woodworkers to sharpen their spokeshaves.

Also useful is a small spokeshave made by Kurz of Germany. The German spokeshave has a curved surface that rests on the wood. This tool does a very good job of taking off rough, irregular wood left behind by the band saw. The Stanley's flat surface cannot match the German spokeshave at this job. For

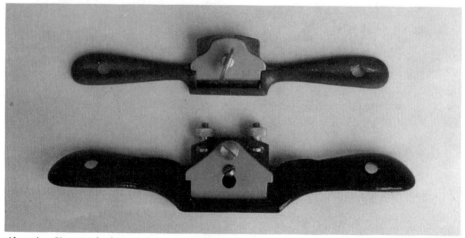

Above is a Kurz spokeshave, below is a Stanley.

reducing an already flat surface, the German spokeshave works reasonably well, but the Stanley is better because the blade is much sharper.

Your success with a spokeshave will probably depend on the tool and the particular piece of wood with which you are working. If you run into problems with this tool, switch to a rasp.

Assuming you have a spokeshave you can use, it is probably best to only use it before tillering starts. My advice to beginners is to put the spokeshave aside and don't touch it once you start bending the bow. It will gouge and gash many pieces of wood, creating an unsightly bow. It is very easy to remove too much wood with a spokeshave. It is much easier to avoid mistakes if you use a rasp.

If you try to lighten a bow with a spokeshave, cover the belly with pencil marks first. It will help keep track of where you have worked and where you haven't. And check the tiller frequently.

Plane

Carpenter's planes have limited application in bowmaking because they require a perfectly flat surface. Odds of success will be higher with a small plane and straight wood. The Stanley Surform tools work well but will gouge wood where the grain dips.

Better results can be expected with a toothing plane. This tool was endorsed by old-time bowyer James Duff in his book *Bows and Arrows.* Duff explained that

Dean Torges using a toothing plane.

A toothing plane left small, parallel tool marks in this piece of Osage, which can be easily removed with a file or scraper.

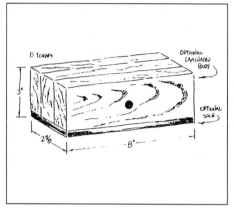

Select durable stock for plane body, beech, hard maple or some stable dense tropical wood. If necessary, glue up thinner stock to achieve dimension thickness. Square up stock to 2 5/8 inches wide by 3 inches high by 8 inches long. Drill a half-inch hole through center of plane side.

With band saw, rip 1/4 inch strips from each side of plane body. Clean kerf marks from wood. Lay out escapement, plane iron bed angle, mouth and throat, then band saw. Bedding must be perfectly flat to receive iron securely. Keep waste block to provide wedge for securing blade.

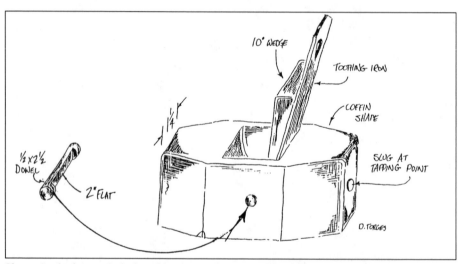

Glue strips back to main body, taking care to keep assembly aligned and mouth opening no more than 1/4 inch. After glue dries, belt sander may be used to insure sole is perfectly flat. Cut a two-inch wide flat halfway through a 1/2 by 2 1/2 inch dowel. Position through cheeks so flat faces iron blade. Dowel will rotate to accomodate wedge angle. Shape plane body for comfortable grip. To adjust depth of cut, tap plane body on toe to lower the blade, on the heel to raise it. You may wish to place metal slugs (such as roofing nails with lead flashing) at these tapping points to protect the plane body.

the flat surface of the plane helps remove faint dips and ripples in the belly.

Dean Torges let me try one of his toothing planes. It will not gouge wood where the grain dips. The cut can be adjusted to allow the plane to remove wood quickly or slowly. These characteristics make the toothing plane a good bet for the average bowyer.

No one sells toothing planes. You'll have to make your own. But you can buy the blades you need.

Calipers

In my tool box is a large pair of very old outside calipers, left to me by my late father who was a mechanic. These calipers are my secret weapon, the single most important bowmaking tool I own. They allow me to virtually guarantee the limbs of the bows I make will never break, split, fret, or chrysal. Such problems usually happen to me only when the wood has suffered some sort of deterioration that escaped my attention. Before using the calipers, I could never be completely sure the bow would stand up to the strain of hard shooting over many months. Some would, and some wouldn't. After I started using the calipers, my bow failure rate fell dramatically.

What the calipers do is let me obtain perfect tapering of the limb thickness. Which is very important for making durable wooden bows.

Consider a time-honored technique often advocated by old-time writers: Start with a piece of wood with perfectly straight grain, and a perfectly straight back. Taper the limb so the feathered rings on the belly each point toward the limb nocks. Tiller the bow well and it lasts for years.

In this context, the old-timers' advice is correct. What they were actually doing was making sure the limb thickness grew gradually thinner from the handle to the nocks. This is important because an uneven taper, with a thick or thin area in the limb, will often break the bow eventually. In many other cases, it causes fretting of the belly.

By always feathering the grain toward the nock, the old-timers were making sure their straight-grained limbs had the correct thickness taper. For this reason, some bowyers demand their staves have perfectly straight grain. If the back has curves, bumps, and hollows, some of these bowyers will not use the wood. They believe a durable bow cannot be obtained from such wood, because their feathering-grain technique cannot be relied on with such wood.

These bowyers have been deceived. By itself, feathering rings toward the nocks means nothing. Repeat: Nothing. What counts is that the limb thickness must be evenly and gradually tapered from handle to nock.

Do you have a lumpy-backed stave? Allow a set of outside calipers to come riding to the rescue. Used correctly, the calipers will ensure the lumpy-backed bow is extremely durable.

Here's how it's done: Tighten the calipers on the back and belly near the handle. Tighten them so the calipers grip the wood slightly when the calipers are moved from one side of the limb to the other. Then slide the calipers toward the nock by three or four inches. At this spot the limb should be slightly thinner, so the calipers can move from side to side without gripping the wood. Continue to move toward the nock, checking the thickness every three or four inches. If each

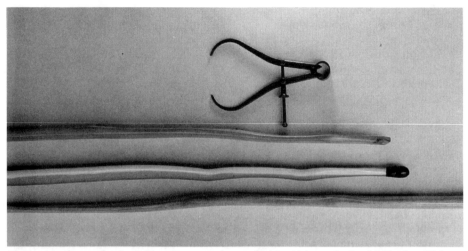

Used correctly, a pair of outside calipers can be a valuable aid in producing highly durable bows from lumpy character wood.

new spot is thinner than the wood on the side toward the handle, you have a good thickness taper.

In some spots, a section of the back may curve gradually toward the belly. This section of limb should be tapered as if it were perfectly straight.

Other sections of the limb may have a lump in the back, often no more than an inch long. This lump should be left thicker than the wood on the handle side. Tighten the calipers next to the lump, on the handle side. Then check the other side of the lump, on the nock side. If the nock side is slightly thinner, the taper is correct for that section of limb. Any such hump less than half an inch tall can be dealt with using this method. Any hump in the back results in a little extra limb thickness. Without extra thickness such a humped spot can easily be bending too much in comparison to the rest of the limb.

If we made wooden bows from nothing but boards, the advantage of calipers would be reduced to one of slight convenience. But most trees do not grow like boards. Most trees have humps and contours in the surface wood. The man who can succeed with such "character wood" will be making bows while the fellow who demands perfectly straight grain is still in the forest looking for something to cut down. Outside calipers are the great equalizer when using character wood.

By itself, a good thickness taper is not enough to guarantee good durability. All other requirements of correct tillering must be met. If the well-tapered limb is badly tillered, it can still fret or break. You need both a gradual thickness taper and a proper tiller.

File

The time required to put the finishing touches on a bow dropped for me when I started using a file. I learned a file can remove small blemishes and tool marks quicker than sandpaper.

A file that has been used on metal will not do the job. A brand new flat mill file, used only on wood, works well. It is a good plan to buy a small brass brush to clean the file.

If I encounter a rough spot not easily smoothed with sandpaper, I grab the file. I go over the spot with a corner edge of the file. When the blemish seems gone, I next use the flat side of the file to smooth the wood. After that, 100 grit sandpaper will easily smooth the spot.

Sandpaper

Making a wooden bow smooth, glassy, and shiny takes sandpaper. Often, it takes a lot of sandpaper. Sandpaper can dull quickly, and the job goes faster with new, sharp paper. It can easily take two hours to sand a bow properly.

Sixty-grit is a good paper to start with. It will remove many small tool marks. Wrapping 60-grit around a block is a good way to remove any small ripples in the belly. These ripples can cause chrysalling or fretting on the belly when construction is marginal or strain on the limbs is high. Such ripples are usually easiest to spot after the bow has been smoothed and polished. Point the limb tip at some light source and hold the bow so the handle is close to your eye. This makes ripples very easy to spot.

It is my habit to always go over a bow thoroughly with 60-grit paper wrapped around a block. This step goes a long way toward making the bow smooth and even.

After using 60-grit paper, I next go over the bow with 100-grit wrapped around the block. Stubborn tool marks usually reveal themselves under 100-grit paper, which sends me reaching for the file or goose-neck scraper.

Is the bow now smooth and even all over? If so, time to do it all again, this time with 150-grit.

After 150-grit, some would continue using finer sandpaper, down to 250-grit. After using 150-grit, I prefer to switch to 00 or 000 steel wool. The wood will be very smooth and glassy by the time I've finished.

Some have said sanding a bow will remove a pound of two from the draw weight. I have not had this experience in bows pulling 55 pounds or more. One reason may be that combined use of the rasp and the Bowscraper assures my bow will be quite smooth before sanding begins.

Burnishers

Wood is burnished by rubbing it with something hard and smooth, usually glass. The process is sometimes called "boning."

Burnishing the belly makes the bow smooth and shiny. If the purist determines to use no finish except grease, it is a good plan to burnish the grease into the bow once a day for several days. Even then, the bow will still require regular greasing afterward for best insurance against moisture.

A good burnisher is some sort of smooth bottle. A round olive bottle works well and is easy to find in any supermarket.

I have pulled a fancy trick or two by heavily burnishing the back of a bow. The most extreme example was a piece of hickory that was very fine-grained in the outer rings. I cut a few foot-long slats of the outside of this wood. They snapped quickly on the back from a moderate bend. I took another such slat and burnished it hard with the round shaft of a screwdriver. This piece could be bent until it took a serious set, and the wood did not break. It is my experience that if such a test slat can take a serious set without breaking, the wood will work with an unbacked bow.

I burnished the back of the hickory bow heavily with the screw driver on three successive days. For the fourth burnishing, I used glass. The back of the bow never broke or splintered.

This and other tests have convinced me that heavy burnishing of an unbacked bow's back makes the outer fibers more resilient and less brittle. It is a marginal advantage. It will not keep the bow from breaking if construction technique is poor, or if the wood is badly strained (as in a bow that is too short or narrow). I once encountered a piece of wood that had no solid summer growth in the outer layers. In other words, the back of this bow was wood mush. It broke and heavy burnishing did not prevent it.

But repeated burnishing of backs is a good plan, particularly if the outer ring is a bit on the thin side.

POWER TOOLS

Power tools are wonderful if you wish to greatly reduce the time and effort of bowmaking. They remove wood quickly and easily. They can also remove skin and fingers quickly and easily. Always carefully follow the manufacturer's directions. And always wear eye protection.

Band Saw

What experienced bowyer does not remember the first time he used a band saw? It was as if the clouds parted overhead, a ray of sunshine beamed down beneficently, a chorus of angels filled the air with soothing music, and a brilliant revelation passed through the bowyer's thick skull: "Wow! This is FAST!!"

True, many aboriginal purists scorn the idea of a "primitive" bow made with a band saw. But band saws were making thousands of wooden bows when the air crackled with radio waves, when cars filled the highways, when airplanes soared through the blue, when electricity cooled the beer and heated the coffee, and when no one had yet thought of using fiberglass in a bow. The wooden bow is not the sole property of aborigines. So move over and make room for me and my band saw.

Why such swooning over a band saw? Because the band saw can do in 10 minutes what it takes three hours to accomplish with an axe, drawknife, and spokeshave.

But, as I have told a number of beginners, "You have to be a coward with a band saw." Because you can wreck a bow in two seconds with a band saw.

You can't get a bowmaking bandsaw for $100 at the hardware store. Bowmaking destroys a small hobby band saw. The wimpy little motor will burn up, usually very quickly. At the very least, you need a bandsaw with a 10-inch opening and a half-horsepower motor. A 14-inch saw with a three-quarter horse motor costs more but is well worth it in the long run if you plan on making many bows, especially bows from quarter logs or super-tough wood like Osage. Sitting on a stand, the saw will be about five feet tall. The band saw is not for

This old band saw has a 10 inch opening, a half-horsepower motor, and is a veteran at making wooden bows.

everyone. It's tough to squeeze one into a one-bedroom apartment, and it throws sawdust all over the place when you use it. But if you have a place to put one and you have the wood, boy, can you make bows.

The blade on a good band saw rests on bearings above and below the cutting table. The band saw can be adjusted so the bearings spin as soon as wood is pushed against the blade. This is a well-tuned band saw, and it's what you want. It will be easier to use and makes straighter cuts than a poorly tuned machine.

The upper guide is usually adjustable. It can be raised for large pieces of wood, and lowered for smaller pieces. The best plan is to have the guide as low as possible while still leaving room for the wood.

There is a limit to the size of wood you can cut with a bandsaw. I try to avoid cutting through anything thicker than four inches. Cutting through big pieces of wood requires a big saw with a powerful motor. One of the largest bowmaking band saws I have heard of is owned by Jim Hamm. This ancient monster was

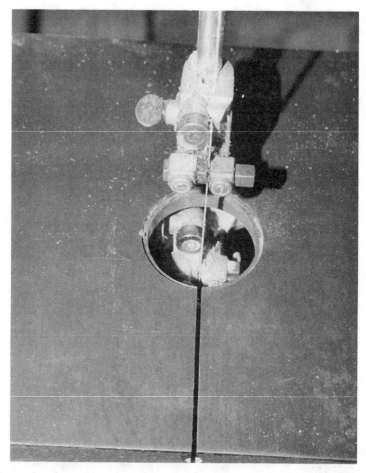

A properly tuned bandsaw will be adjusted so the bearing above and below the table each begin spinning as wood is pushed against the saw blade.

patented in 1910, is made of cast iron, has 22-inch wheels, uses a one-inch blade, and has a three horsepower motor. Hamm says this beast will cut through 12 inches of seasoned Osage.

When working a bandsaw hard with larger wood, it is a good plan to oil the bearings frequently. It's a poor plan, however, when cutting handle splices. You don't want oil landing on the gluing surfaces of the splice.

Opinions vary on the best blade for the bowmaking bandsaw. I prefer a blade 3/8ths of an inch from front to back. When this blade deflects, it will tend to deflect backward. A deeper blade, such as half-inch, is more likely to deflect sideways.

The newer, and sharper, the blade, the better it cuts. An older blade cuts more smoothly if waxed. Just start the motor and run the blade through a piece of wax.

If you try to put too large a piece of wood through your saw, the motor will probably lug, or slow down, in protest. Either pull the wood back slightly to let the motor regain rpm, or shut the motor off to cool it down.

If the motor lugs frequently, you may be straining the saw with a large piece of wood. If so, don't try to make a long continuous cut. Make a series of shorter cuts by frequently running the blade off the side of the wood, and resume sawing by starting a new cut on the pencil line.

The safest procedure is to always draw pencil lines where you plan to cut, and stay just outside the lines. As you gain more experience, you can cut right on the lines.

If you try to pull the wood backward and off the blade, you will probably pull the blade out of its guides. You could also pull the blade off the flywheels inside the saw. Don't pull the wood backward if you can avoid it. If you have to, better shut the motor off first.

The wood must rest solidly on the table. If you raise the front end of the wood off the table, there is a danger the wood will twist to the right or left. If it does, it will probably pull the blade off the wheels, or break the blade. The same thing can happen when you cut wood at an angle when you don't have a firm grip on the stave.

The band saw can cut a curve, such as a narrow handle section. However, it is difficult to cut a curve when there are several inches of wood on the outside of the cut. Cut closer to your pencil line with a series of passes, so there is only about a half-inch outside the pencil line. Then it will be much easier to cut a curve. A 3/8-inch blade cuts curves more easily than a half-inch blade.

A bandsaw can be used like a rasp by holding the bow against the flat of the blade and slowly pushing the wood forward, allowing the teeth to remove small shavings. New, very coarse blades, four or even two teeth per inch, work best for this.

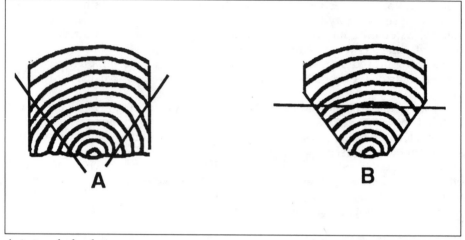

A strategy for band saws.

If you make bows with a band saw, there is one rule that is carved in stone: Never, ever, attempt to cut the bow limb thickness with one pass. If cut from a log, the stave is almost guaranteed to be asymmetrical. There will be dips, high spots, and low spots on one side of the limb that do not exist on the other side. If you attempt to cut such a limb to its thickness with one pass, the blade will be OK on the side you can see, but it can cut the limb too thin on the side you can't see.

Even if the stave is symmetrical, the blade can twist near the bottom guide, cutting the limb too thin.

The answer to this problem is to hold the wood at an angle, and make a series of cuts. This is a variation on the wood reducing strategy discussed earlier.

Figure A shows how to hold the wood at an angle so the cuts are close to the pencil line on the sides of the stave, but the wood is left deep in the center. Most of this deep section can be removed with a series of band saw cuts, as shown in Figure B. Don't try to cut too closely, since the blade could deflect and cut the stave too thinly.

A well-tuned bandsaw can be used to remove fine shavings from a stave. Simply hold the wood against the flat side of the blade, allowing the teeth to chew off tiny bits. But it is best to use slow-working tools to take the stave completely down to the desired thickness.

Belt Sander

Most belt sanders are so large it takes two hands to hold one. A couple of companies make smaller belt sanders which can be held in one hand.

I have done a considerable amount of wood removal using a smaller belt sander with 36 and 50-grit belts. After about 50 bows, the motor burned up. With a price tag of $65, the belt sander cost me $1.30 per bow. I considered that a good investment and bought another one.

Belt sanders, like all power tools, can quickly remove more wood than you wish. Be sure to keep the bow moving across the belt, so as not to gouge the wood.

Jointer and Planer

A power jointer is a large piece of equipment that only a serious woodworker will own. It is handy, however, for creating flat surfaces. This can be useful if a stave is to be backed with hickory or bamboo. Smaller hand-held planers can also be used this way.

Circular Saw

A circular saw can be used for some bowmaking jobs, as long as it is used carefully.

Avoid the temptation to force a circular saw deep into the side of a large log or stave. If you attempt it, the blade can snag and send the saw flying backward at about 300 miles an hour. Circular saws are really meant to cut soft pine, which is like warm butter compared to a tough piece of hickory or Osage.

The best procedure with a circular saw is to make repeated shallow passes, gradually deepening the cut. Do not attempt to cut completely through a thick stave or log. Instead, use a sledge hammer and wedges to split the wood along your cut. If the grain is at least moderately straight, the split will follow the cut. Sometimes it is necessary to make cuts on both sides of a thick piece. If you hammer the wedges into the cut on one side, you can expect the split will seek out the cut on the opposite side.

If you do very much of this work, check your circular saw blade frequently as this procedure creates large amount of heat and friction, and the blade can develop cracks. If you see cracks in the blade, discard it and get a new one.

Moisture Meter, Wood Dryer

For someone making bows from white woods (hickory, elm, ash, birch, hackberry, and oak), a wood dryer is almost a must.

A drying box of the type used in making glass laminated bows is probably best. The box does not have to be fancy or elaborate. Most hardware stores sell plastic or porcelain light bulb sockets, plus wire and plug components. You can use them to make your own lamps. A couple using 40 or 60-watt bulbs should be enough to raise the temperature inside the dryer to 80 or 90 degrees. And that's plenty hot. Nine or 10 percent is the moisture content target for wooden bows. Such a dryer can reduce moisture content from 14 to 9 percent in 48 hours.

Once the wood reaches 9 percent, you can run the dryer a few hours a day and keep the wood at 9 percent, no matter how high the humidity rises. It is my experience that once a good water-resistant finish is put on a bow, the moisture content will stay at 9 percent through a variety of weather conditions. Keeping the bow waxed will also help.

The white woods must be treated differently than Osage and yew. Osage and yew are rot-resistant and seldom take on more moisture once they reach 9 percent. White woods can decay quickly if left outside a few weeks. The only reliable plan for avoiding decay is to cut a live tree yourself. Split the wood immediately and you can immediately debark hickory, elm, ash, birch, hackberry, and oak. I have handled scores of such logs in this manner without a serious problem of checking in the outer rings. (Osage, black locust, and sassafras are trees which can check badly if the bark is removed too soon.)

It is also safest to bring freshly cut wood indoors. Right into your house is probably the best place. Don't leave these woods outside or in a dank, musty shed. They can decay there.

When we look at all these factors in combination, we see the white woods are ideal candidates for rapid drying. Cut the wood long and checking on the ends will not be a problem. If you can't cut the wood long, varnish the ends heavily. Split the log in half, and STOP. Don't split it into quarters unless the log was over a foot in diameter. Do not split it into narrow staves. If you do, you are increasing the odds of the wood warping. Get the bark off and do it now. The wood cannot dry quickly with the bark left on.

Bring sopping green white wood into your house and in two weeks the moisture content will fall to about 15 percent. Then give the half-log an hour in the dryer. If this does not create excessive checking on the ends, leave it in the dryer 48 hours. Now you can rough out the bow. After another 48 hours in the dryer, the roughed-out bow can be tillered.

Letting wood season several years may have some benefit with Osage and yew, but with white woods it is a 100 percent waste of time. White wood can be stored several years, but it is not necessary.

Do not subject the wood to high temperatures for weeks at a time. If you do, the moisture content can fall to 4 or 5 percent and the bow will break.

A moisture meter cost $100 or more. Most serious bowmakers buy one, as they are extremely useful. They are not necessities, however. If you follow the above instructions, it's practically money in the bank the wood will be at 9 percent.

The very first bend on the tillering board is a reliable indicator of moisture content. Bend the bow a few inches on the board and look at the tiller. After a minute or so, take the bow off the board. Look to see if it gained any string follow. If this initial slight bend made the bow follow the string, the wood is still too wet. If the limbs return to their original position, the wood is dry enough to continue.

STONE AND ABORIGINAL TOOLS

If you have any experience in bow-making and flintknapping, you have probably picked up a flint or chert flake and discovered it makes a good scraper. No matter how hard or tough the wood, the sharp flake will peel shavings off with authority. And the tough rock will stay quite sharp while doing it.

Thus is revealed the potential for making a bow with stone tools. But does anyone really expect to make a bow with nothing but a stone flake for a scraper?

Making a bow requires a tool capable of fast and serious wood removal. A flake cannot do this, but a stone-bladed adze or axe can.

A dry, seasoned piece of wood can be scraped successfully with a stone flake. But if you try chopping a piece of dry wood with a stone adze or axe, you may find the tool can only knock little dents in the wood.

It is a different story, however, if the wood is green. A stone adze or axe can quickly chew through green wood. The simplest method would be to rough out green wood close to final dimensions, let the wood dry thoroughly, and finish the tillering with stone scrapers.

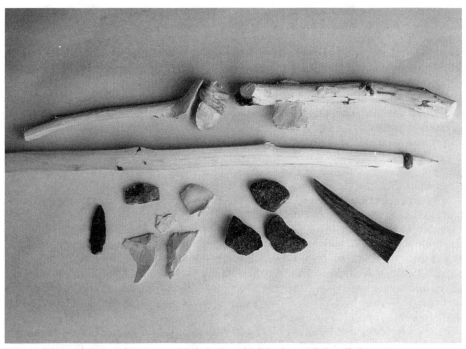

(Top to bottom, left to right) A stone-bladed adze which broke, a celt-handled stone axe, a backward bow made with stone tools, a bifaced knife blade, stone scrapers, coarse abrading rocks, and an antler wedge.

There are two basic types of stone woodworking blades. One is made of greenstone or other hard rock. Using a second, harder rock, the greenstone edge is pecked (hit repeatedly, breaking loose small chips) until it begins to take the shape of a blade. Then it is ground to a sharp edge on a piece of sandstone, a process taking about six to eight hours.

The second type is a large piece of flint, chert, or chalcedony knapped to the blade shape. The cutting edge is fluted, similar to an arrowhead.

A combination of these types was produced in Neolithic Denmark. Flint pieces were knapped in to the shape of a blade, then ground to a smooth and sharp cutting edge.

If working green wood is the first trick to using stone tools, then the second trick is to use heavy stone tools to rough out the bow. One pound can be considered a fair minimum and three pounds would not be too heavy.

To illustrate this advantage, consider a bow I made with a small knapped stone blade set into a wooden handle. Its total weight was about 9 ounces. With it, I made a 72-inch 45-pound bow that took an agonizing 30 hours to finish.

By comparison, Tim Baker made a 66-inch 45-pound bow with two stone hand axes weighing 1.5 and 2.5 pounds. The bow was finished in about six hours. Using the same axes, Baker chopped down the tree and cut free the top end of the stave in 7 minutes. Baker said the hand axes are so crude no self-respecting Neanderthal would have wanted to be seen with one. Regardless, they were still very effective.

My stone axe was hafted with what is called the celt method. The axe blade was wider than the back edge, and the rock was set into a hole carved into a wooden handle. The handle was cut just below a V in the branch, so the pressure of the blade would not split the handle at the hole. I had tried to haft a stone blade onto an adze handle but my skill was not up to the task. I made two adzes and each broke quickly. The celt-style handle was within my capability.

The advantage of a heavy stone blade was apparently well-understood by the ancients. I own a grooved axe artifact that weighs 1.4 pounds.

Working green wood with a stone axe leave a rough, "furry" surface. When the wood was dry, much of this furry surface was removed with the stone axe. After that came the tedious job of smoothing the back completely.

For a number of years I had been on the constant lookout for some coarse rock that could be used to grind off wood. I eventually found a few near Sudbury, Ontario. They appear to be some type of granite, but that's only a guess since the area was loaded with granite. Using these rocks, I smoothed up the surface of the bow's back. The bow would have been difficult to finish without these rocks. Another technique that worked fairly well was taking a stone bifaced blade and using it to rough up the wood by sawing back and forth across the surface. This roughed-up surface could be flattened with relative ease using large flake scrapers.

Primitive tools used by others have included bone cut and ground to a sharp edge, antler and wooden wedges for splitting the stave, and shark skin for sanding the bow.

SOME PERSONAL TOOL PREFERENCES

Tim Baker
Primary types of bows: White wood and lumber.
Reducing backs to one ring: Spokeshave, scraper, file.
Working around knots on back: Goose-neck scraper, knife.
Shaping bow and rough tillering: Band saw.
Final tillering: Spokeshave, Japanese rasp, scraper.

Paul Comstock
Primary types of bows: White wood self bows.
Reducing backs to one ring: Spokeshave, rasp, file and scraper.
Working around knots on back: Rasp and file.
Shaping bow and rough tillering: Band saw, or circular saw, or axe, or draw knife; belt sander, spokeshave, rasp.
Final tillering: Rasp and scraper.

Jim Hamm
Primary types of bows: Osage self bows.
Reducing backs to one ring: Dull draw knife with slightly curved blade.
Working around knots on back: Pocket knife.
Shaping bow and rough tillering: Bandsaw and coarse rasp.
Final tillering: Fine rasp and cabinet scraper.

Al Herrin
Primary types of bows: Osage self bows.
Reducing backs to one ring: Draw knife and rasp.
Working around knots on back: Rasp and scraper.
Shaping bow and rough tillering: Draw knife, axe, rasp.
Final tillering: Rasp, Stanley Surform.

Jay Massey
Primary types of bows: Sinew-backed Osage.
Reducing backs to one ring: Draw knife, Bowscraper, blade from spokeshave.
Working around knots on back: Scraper or blade from spokeshave.
Shaping bow and rough tillering: Draw knife, rasp.
Final tillering: Knife or spokeshave blade as scrapers.

John Strunk
Primary types of bows: Yew longbow.
Reducing backs to one ring: Draw knife, knife scraper.
Working around knots on back: Scraper.
Shaping bow and rough tillering: Draw knife and spokeshave on straight grained wood; rasp, file and Bowscraper on irregular grain.
Final tillering: Bowscraper or knife scraper, 50-grit sandpaper.

Dean Torges
Primary types of bows: Selfwood flatbows.
Reducing backs to one ring: Draw knife, spokeshake, flat and goose-necked scrapers.
Working around knots on back: Goose-necked scraper and a small sharp gouge with a medium sweep (a curved woodworking chisel).
Shaping bow and rough tillering: Draw knife, spokeshave, toothing plane.
Final tillering: Nicholson No. 49 cabinet maker's rasp, half-round second cut file and cabinet scraper.

✧ ✧ ✧

There are a thousand or more ways to make a wooden bow. There are many different ways you can shoot a wooden bow. What counts is what works. And if it works, the opinions of others mean nothing. This is perhaps the greatest glory of wooden bows. Manufacturers of modern archery tackle often ram their own values and concepts down the throats of their customers, making them easier to swallow with slick, four-color advertising. Like a helpless herd, the customers are compelled to follow.

If you make wooden bows, it's a different story. You are the boss. You are in charge. You will select your own destiny. And you alone will deserve 100 percent of the credit for that hard-hitting bow, the clean accurate shooting, and the game you bring home. If you wish, you can defiantly tell the rest of the world where to put its unidirectional fiberglass, its Allen patent, and its anodized aluminum.

Let your selection of tools be an expression of your own preferences, your own needs, and your own personality.

BOWS OF THE WORLD

Tim Baker

Some day you may examine a very old bow, one made long before living memory. Because it was made from the surface of a tree, its back and face will be irregular. You notice how its maker followed the sweep of the grain here, thickened wood under a knot there. You nod your head at each decision he made, the same decision you would have made. You smile wryly, aware that you're in the mind of this man from another time. Against reason you project a "well done" to him, finding it hard to believe you can't go somewhere and talk to this fellow bowmaker. But unimaginative reality prevents this.

People have been making bows for over ten thousand years. But recorded history began only five thousand years ago, about the time agriculture largely replaced hunting/gathering. With the spread of agriculture the bow provided less and less of man's food. In historical times the bow's chief use was in war, and military uniformity discouraged diversity of design. It may well be that by the time we could record its many faces, the Golden Age of archery design had already passed.

This may seem a romantic notion — we all know that technical design increases in complexity and efficiency over time. But consider the ancient Holmegaard and Meare Heath bows for example. These Stone Age designs showed engineering effectiveness not exceeded until engineers with degrees bore down on the subject earlier this century. And considering the scarcity of samples, these rare bog-preserved specimens surely represent just a dot of ancient competence and diversity.

In the recent past, where aboriginal archery existed outside homogenizing military influence, we saw a sample of the genius and diversity the bow world once held. Both for practical reasons, and from simple human curiosity, it would be beneficial to know how the various bow designs of the world performed, both the lost designs of archery prehistory, and those that followed. It would be valuable to move across time and sit beside ancient brother bowyers and look into their minds as they work; to see why they made their bows the way they did; to apply these lessons to our present efforts.

At first it would seem pointless to hope to understand all the distant and diverse designs since the beginning of archery, but in fact this is far easier than it first seems.

> The principal design ingredients are: Straight-stave; deflex tip; set-back; reflex; recurve; contact-recurve; deflex; bow length; mass placement; the range of front-view shapes; the range of tiller profiles; the different cross-sections; percentage of non-bending central section; safety or performance-enhancing backings; Perry-type working inner limbs; brace height; draw length.

There are only about twenty significant design ingredients, and any bow we might imagine will be some mix of only a few of them. Once the effects of these different design ingredients are understood, the performance of any bow can be dependably anticipated.

Any real or imagined bow can then be drawn on paper, or visualized suspended in mid-air, and as in an animated movie, it can be shortened, lengthened, recurved to different degrees, and so on. Each incarnation can be appraised for energy storage, inertia, cast, stack, hand shock, strain, set, etc. Such "ink or air bows" let us quickly understand how any possible bow design would perform, whether from pre-history or the future.

The following 25 bows are selected from across the full span of archery history. They cover the entire range of reasonable bow designs and incorporate all the design ingredients listed.

Bow design classifications, such as double curve, self, etc., are sometimes contradictory, and often unrelated to function. It seems more reasonable to classify the various bow types by side-view profile, the feature which determines performance more than any other.

THE STRAIGHT-STAVE BOW
Holmegaard, Meare Heath, Sudbury, American Flatbow, South American, African, English Longbow

These bows are considered together because they were all variations on a theme: straight-stave, unbacked bows, about man-tall, which stored and released energy with moderate efficiency, permitted full draws, had low stack, were easy to make, were safe, durable, and accurate. Designed thousands of miles and years apart, they represented similar responses to similar needs. These bows represent the full range of variability in this design type, still, in a broad sense they are "the same bow." But knowing how their differences affected construction, use, performance, and durability will help when designing our own similar bows.

Holmegaard Bow

The Holmegaard is the oldest artifact definitely identified as a bow. It arose from a pre-agricultural, pre-warfare culture. Its maker was a member of a band which gathered and hunted for a living without benefit of writing, pottery, cloth, smelted metal, the wheel, or settled communities. It was likely just an average bow of that time and place, but is superior to the average wooden bow of the present.

The original 9,000-plus year-old artifact, for the first time, has recently been both examined and replicated by experienced bowyers: Flemming Alrune of

Callahan's replica, almost 62" long, precisely faithful to the original in width, but two or three millimeters thinner. It pulls about 57 lb at 28". The thicker original would have likely equaled this weight at about 26". (Photo by Linda Abbey)

Denmark and Errett Callahan of Virginia. Neither sees any reason to believe the Holmegaard was made "backward" (flat back facing the inside of the tree) as per early published reports. Both Alrune's and Callahan's replications have been tillered conventionally (crowned tree-surface as back).

Callahan reports that the crowned surface of the artifact was the unworked outside of a small diameter tree. For bow-physics reasons given below, this is strong evidence for a conventional design. When the Holmegaard was discovered in 1943, the bow most familiar to Europeans was the English longbow. Callahan speculates that the English bow's flat back and round belly caused early writers to misinterpret the Holmegaard design. With Callahan's unworked-crown report in hand, Comstock agrees there is no functional reason

Callahan's replica at 24" of draw. The tiller looks wrong, seeming too round-in-the-handle. But this is proper tiller for a bow with narrowed outer limbs. The more extreme the bend in a bow's mid and outer limbs the more straight-line tip-to-tip bow length shortens at full draw, increasing string angle, therefore, stack. This tiller shape diminishes this effect.

to believe the Holmegaard was made backward. Comstock also raises this point: the mid-outer limb was crowned, back and belly; if made backward, the concentrated tension load would be carried by violated fibers on a crowned back, a formula for failure.

At 62" this bow seems short. But gravesites of the time place this length comfortably in the range of adult male heights, making the Holmegaard bow about man-high. It would, therefore, have been drawn about 25". Based on the draw weight of Callahan's replica, the original likely drew just over 50 lbs.

The outer one-half of the Holmegaard's limbs had been narrowed, similar to but less severe than the Andaman Islands bow, discussed later. One reporter theorized this narrowing might be due to decay. But, as Callahan notes, the narrowed portion retains its full thickness — decay would not have been so selective. This outer-limb narrowing appeared on other same-style Mesolithic bows as well. Another reporter believed the limb's mid-limb shoulder once secured a sinew-cable backing (see pg. 110, Vol. 1). But Alrune reports no cable wear. Replicas show a cable was not needed to insure adequate draw-weight or safety. And a cable would surely have been attached closer to the nock. This would have prevented an outer limb of these dimensions from breaking, especially given Comstock's point concerning the outer-limb's crowned and violated fibers.

Bows with narrowed outer limbs require more time and skill to tiller, but their reduced mass yields greater cast and lower hand shock. Narrower than normal outer limbs would be tillered to bend less than inner limbs. This results in a somewhat lowered full-draw string angle. Lower string angle means less stack, therefore higher early draw weight, therefore higher energy storage, therefore greater cast, with resulting increased accuracy and penetration.

Alrune/Callahan's stiffer outer limb tiller was not induced consciously. It resulted from being faithful to the artifact's thickness dimensions. This stiffer outer limb tiller makes sense. While doing outer limb mass lowering experimenting I found exactly the same tiller shape necessary if outer limbs were

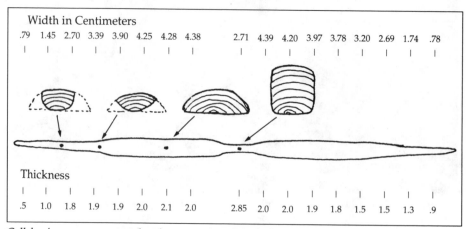

Callahan's measurements, taken from a casting of the Holmegaard artifact. Measurements occur every 10 cm.

considerably narrowed. Because we're dealing with fossil bows, portions of this and following sections are necessarily conjecture. Based on known principles, laboriously thought out and debated, but still conjecture. And because our brains are carbon, not silicon based, mistakes will be made. But even if ten percent wrong we're ninety percent ahead of where we were.

If inner limbs are wider (therefore thinner) and rectangular enough to endure such extra bending, they will take no more set than a conventional design. If perfectly rectangular in section, inner limbs can be made ever wider. But the Holmegaard section was plano-convex. The degree of crown limits the effective width to about that seen in the artifact.

There are sound bow-physics reasons to believe the Holmegaard's crowned side, the outside of a tree, was the bow's back. Wood is weaker in compression than tension; if such a limb is used crowned-side to belly, that belly surrenders easily, requiring more wood per draw weight. As a result, limb mass per draw weight will be high, and the narrow belly will take extreme set. If used crowned-side to back, more belly wood is available to resist compression. Bending resistance is now much greater, and the wide, flat belly takes little set. This is an especially credible design in elm with its high relative tension strength.

A simple experiment will make sense of the above: split a small diameter limb in half, reducing each to about the thickness of a normal bow limb. Bend one half-limb over your knee, crowned side out; bend the other flat side out. Notice

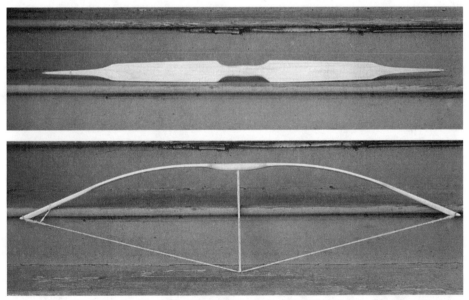

Lessons from a 9,000 year-old teacher. If tillered normally, this 52", 25" draw bow, would stack more severely. Its narrow, stiff, outer limbs occupy a smaller percentage of limb length than the Holmegaard in order to leave sufficient working wood on this 10" shorter bow. Two and one-half inch, perfectly rectangular-section limbs take only 1 3/8" of just-unbraced set. Very light tips and a plump F-D curve produce an unusually fast, pleasant bow for its length, affording stealth and maneuverability advantages of a shorter bow without undue sacrifice in performance.

the limb is *much* harder to bend crowned side out, and takes *much* more set crowned side in, and has more mass per strength.

The Holmegaard was preserved by a random act of nature. It was therefore likely a typical bow of its time. Its sophisticated design implies a long period of development — several thousand years seems reasonable. For the Holmegaard people bowmaking was an ancient art, older than their oldest memories, as natural and eternal as the forests around them.

Meare Heath Bow

The Holmegaard language would have had no word for "work", as such. Hunting-gathering was more like shopping. But by Meare Heath times, agriculture was almost an ancient occupation; Britain was no longer a place of leisure. Yet the Meare Heath bow, like the Holmegaard, was a work of high craft.

Narrower, deep-limbed designs existed alongside, and far outnumbered, the Meare Heath. A clue to why is found when replicating both with simple hand tools: due to its expansive flat surfaces, the Meare Heath design requires about triple the time and effort. But like the Holmegaard, this bow was made by a master bowyer/engineer, who had good reason to invest such labor.

This bow had unusually wide and long limbs. Such a low-strain design safely permitted low-set, high draw weight, and/or low string follow, and/or long draw length, despite somewhat violated rings and fibers on its back (described by Comstock, page 93, Vol. II).

This bow's wide tips are a puzzle. Their higher mass reduced cast and increased handshock. Slight whip-ended tiller would reduce hand shock, and slightly reduce tip mass. Whip-ending causes a bow to shorten in straight-line tip-to-tip length during the draw, raising string angles, increasing stack. This effect is severe on short bows, but not on longbows. Still, such wide tips on such a long bow were inefficient — unless shooting very heavy arrows.

Light arrows need light, fast-moving limbs. Heavy arrows leave the bow more slowly. Which means limb tips move more slowly also, therefore tip mass

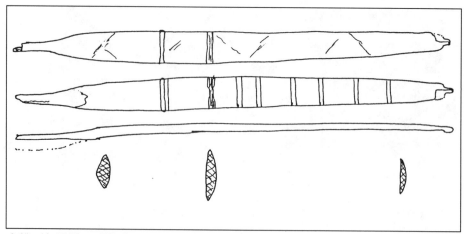

2.6" wide 74" long if limbs are of equal length.

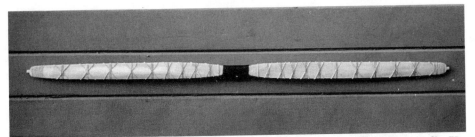

A 68" by 2 3/8" rock maple "Meare Heath" by bowyer Jon Muench. Fairly flat back and belly, 70 lb at 28", 1 7/8" set. Geometric rawhide or leather wrappings found on the original have no obvious function and may have been purely decorative. But on historic bows, "decorations" are almost always functional. Jeff Schmidt feels there is some chance the wrappings served to protect the shooter in the event of failure. If this was the case such use may have been the first timid steps in the evolution of true backed bows.

is not so large a problem. At normal draw lengths the 74" Meare Heath was too long for best efficiency. But the extra inertia of longer limbs was not so big a problem when shooting heavy arrows. Slower, high-mass arrows took a higher percentage of a bow's stored energy with them, permitting greater penetration. The Meare Heath makes best sense if it was used with heavy arrows, which in turn makes best sense if they were used against larger, slower-moving targets.

A Meare Heath-length bow is most efficient when drawn about 31", about right for a 76" tall archer. Clark reports average adult male heights at that time and place as 67", with 72" at the high end. Imperfectly decrowned, with back fibers somewhat violated, and given a draw weight of about 60 lb, durability factors suggest a draw of about 28", appropriate for a tall man of the time. Comstock feels that given its width, length and material, a draw length of 30" would have been safe, and that the Meare Heath was owned by an unusually tall archer. Jon Muench's rock maple replica, though six-inches shorter, safely draws 28", but its back is one flat growth ring.

Upon learning of the Meare Heath Paul Comstock immediately understood its design implications. "Overbuilt" bows, described in his book *The Bent Stick,*

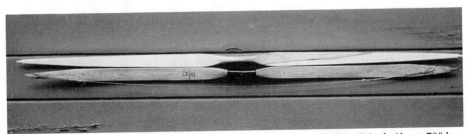

Two "Meare Heaths." Pristine backs let these replicas be shorter than the original. Above: 70" by 2", 53 lb at 28", made by Slovenian bowyer Matjaz Tomse. Designed for targets and hunting. The early width taper of Matjaz' limbs is permitted by its 50 lb weight. Being a semi pyramid, semi arc-of-a-circle tiller is appropriate. Below: 67" by 2", 65 lb at 28", made by Paul Comstock. Designed for hunting. Comstock's limbs taper later — this bow is shorter, and of higher draw weight, so more outer-limb wood is needed for energy storage. Elliptical tiller is called for here.

are adapted from this Neolithic design. As a result we presently see reincarnations of this distant bow in the hands of countless modern archers. Designed for nimble, moderate-sized game, and shooting medium-weight arrows, these modern Meare Heaths are usually a bit shorter, a bit narrower, and narrower-tipped.

For lowest set and highest safety it's important that a particular bow's tiller profile be appropriate to its front-view shape. This is just as important as even tillering, and for the same reason: it spreads the load, storing the energy where the limb is best able to accept it.

Tillering has always been the heart of bowmaking. It seems unlikely that after thousands of tillering years anyone could greatly improve established tillering techniques, nevertheless this was recently done by Jim Hamm. His system, described in "Tillering", Vol. l, delivers a bow to exact intended weight, with no overstraining of limbs. This is an important gift to archery, but modesty has kept Jim from fully proclaiming the system's merits. This is too valuable a technique to wither due to good manners. Here it is again in skeleton form:

- Evenly floor tiller the stave until it bends enough to string safely.
- Once strung, bring to perfect tiller before drawing at all.
- Then begin drawing and releasing the bow, each time a bit farther. If limbs move out of tiller, correct before proceeding.
- If limbs stay in tiller draw to full design weight; this may take only a few inches of draw, say 10".
- Remove wood and pull to full draw weight again, now possibly reaching 15". Adjust tiller if needed.
- Continue removing wood, checking tiller, and pulling to full draw weight each time. Remove less and less wood as full draw length approaches.

Pulling to full weight at each stage of tiller insures the bow will arrive at the exact desired weight once draw length is reached, and without overstraining the limbs.

Sudbury Bow

Made in the mid 1600s, the Sudbury is the most well known and one of the oldest aboriginal bows of the Eastern woodlands. This bow can be seen as a Meare Heath somewhat fine-tuned over the millennia. Even if aboriginal archery had not been replaced by firearms, another six thousand years might have passed without further improvement in straight-stave bow design. The Sudbury-type bow, given labor cost/effectiveness realities of aboriginal life, might be the finest straight-stave bow ever designed. There is much more to it than first meets the eye (see page 65, Vol. II for drawings).

Its 67" length was efficient for normal draw lengths. Its narrow tips increased cast and diminished hand shock. Its wide, near-rectangular limbs stored more energy with less fiber strain. Deeper, narrower, near-handle portions of the limb were virtually non-working. Therefore "shorter" moving portion of the limbs had the *low mass of a much shorter bow*. But at 67" it also had the *low stack of a long-bow*, therefore storing the energy of a longbow. If near-rectangular in section, and sufficiently wide to withstand longbow energy storage, this design would be highly efficient, draw smoothly, and release with virtually shockless comfort.

It is not possible to know the Sudbury's, or any untested bow's, precise draw

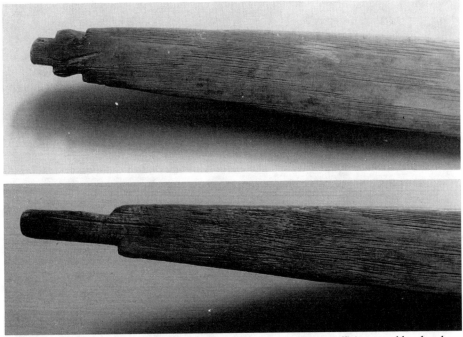

Sudbury's fairly narrow tips, compared to Meare Heath, contribute to efficiency and low hand shock. (courtesy Peabody Museum, Harvard University)

weight. Wood strength per thickness varies considerably even between different staves from the same tree. In addition, a mere 5% difference in thickness alters draw weight by about 15%. But based on replications, its near two-inch limbs, given average-hickory performance, would have fastest-per-pound cast at about 50 pounds.

Heavier draw weight would require stronger, more elastic wood, or wider or longer limbs. Longer limbs would lower efficiency. At about 2 1/8" in width this design would equal 60 lb. For even higher weight, using "white wood", its narrow, graceful near-grip would be replaced by the wide, slightly working near-grip of "The Perfect Bow", page 93, Vol. 1. But 50 lbs. was about the optimum weight for hunting deer and small game. Which is likely the reason the Sudbury's maker engineered this bow the way he did.

The excessive set in the original Sudbury artifact was not likely put there by its first owner. Bowmaking friends from occasionally high-humidity Sudbury country report that hickory bows kept "in the warm, dry lodge" when not in use, or during wet weather, retain low-set and high-cast. Those strung for long periods under humid conditions take sets comparable to the Sudbury artifact.

The Sudbury bow had a moderately thick grip. When using this design, let front-to-back grip thickness be as low as safety and taste will allow. Low risers permit lower brace heights. And each added inch of brace height strains the limbs as if drawn more than two additional inches (at 28" of draw, limb tips

Sudbury replica by California bowyer Paul Rodgers: Hickory, 47 lb at 28", 67 1/8" by 1 5/8", slightly narrower than the original. Just-unbraced set is 1 1/4". Slight kinks in the tree's surface disrupt the lines of these perfectly tillered limbs.

Slovenian Bowyer Matjaz Tomse with a Sudbury replica which has been "STRETCHED" for low stack and stability while target shooting: hickory, 72" by 1 1/2", 55 lb at 28". Note its low string follow, due to longer, less-strained limbs, and its perfect tiller.

have only moved about 14" from their unbraced position). I favor a 5 1/2" brace height, measured from the back. This is low by modern standards, but typical of aboriginal archery. Several wood bowhunting friends have long argued against such low bracing, noting that fletchings scratch against the bow, alerting prey. We grown men of the Space Age worried for years over this problem until it was solved for us by a Stone Age New Guinea boy. About eight-years old, this subject of a child-development documentary was filmed stalking game with his very low-strung bow and long-fletched arrow. The un-nocked arrow was held in place by his bow hand, feathers clear of the bow. When ready for his shot, eyes fixed on the target, the boy simply advanced the string, slipped it silently into the arrow nock, drew the arrow, and fired.

American Flatbow

American flatbows were the clipper ships of archery. Yankee practicality and ingenuity applied to an ancient, artful realm. No nonsense, no frills. And like the clippers, these bows outperformed more traditional designs.

As the name indicates, this design had at least a fairly rectangular cross-section, which induced more uniform strain across the limb's width, which permitted wider, thinner, therefore less strained limbs, which permitted shorter, lower-set limbs. Shorter, low-inertia limbs returned faster, and low set limbs stored more energy. Less strained limbs were obviously also safer.

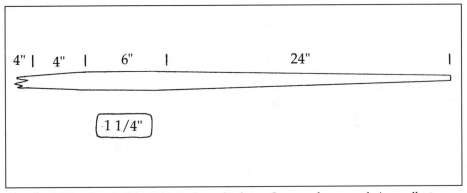

A typical flatbow design of the 1930s, to be made of yew, Osage, or lemonwood. An excellent design for these woods, but about 30% too narrow for the "white woods."

Archery magazines articles and books of the 1930's reported this design as new, or superior, unaware that virtually identical designs had been made by various American Indian tribes, prehistoric Europeans when they were "Indians," and likely many other cultures through time.

The essentially pyramid front-view shape of the following ash lumber bow would accept near arc of a circle tiller. But at its design length of 72" such tiller would yield a long, fully-working limb, moving more mass than needed. Instead, this bow was tillered somewhat like a Sudbury, with its short-bow/long-bow performance advantages. The wider, slightly-bending near-grip areas work just enough to lower overall set, which stands at just 1". The

My current favorite. From a flat-ringed section of 2" by 6" ash lumber, worked down to one growth ring; 72" by 2" at the widest point, 6" handle section. The center of the bow is the center of the grip, so either limb can be on top. Patches of the old cambium layer are left as camo/decoration.

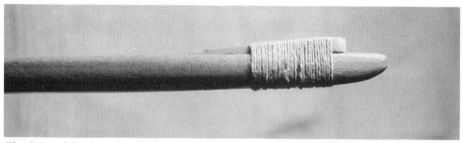

The above ash bow's nocks. Tiny wood wedges make convenient temporary nocks while tillering. And fine "permanent" nocks too — just sand the areas of string contact. If changes of temperature or humidity raise your bow's weight, or if you're a bit tired, just move your nocks out a little. If one limbs goes slightly out of tiller in the field, adjust one nock to true it.

principle working portions of the limbs are narrow and light; the pointed tips are exceptionally light. This is the best designed *long*, straight-stave bow I've ever made. Smooth draw, silky release, excellent cast, and highly accurate. A true pyramid design is slightly more efficient, and at a shorter bow length, usually an advantage when hunting. But shorter bows are progressively less stable and accurate.

The pyramid bow is the most efficient flatbow design, and likely the most efficient straight-stave design possible (see Bows from Boards, Vol. II), for three reasons: 1) most of its mass resides near the grip, reducing mass at the tip where mass costs most dearly, 2) its almost uniform grip-to-tip limb thickness requires near arc of a circle tillering, lowering full draw string angle, 3) lower string angles permits slightly shorter bow limbs, since they will stack the same as longer limbs of normal tiller. And shorter limbs, storing the same energy as longer limbs, obviously return faster.

South American Bow

In *Bows and Arrows,* Saxton Pope reported on what seems to have been a fairly representative South American bow. He concluded the section with, "Considering the excellence of the wood, this bow speaks of a lack of intelligence on the part of the maker." Pope, a product of his times, had an exceptionally bad case of the "English Disease," consistently failing to judge non-English bows in the context of their own use-environment...

A retired bow of the Bari' tribe, shown at normal brace height. Made of extremely dense palm, this 78" bow, is 1 3/16" wide, by 5/8" thick at the grip. It weighs 33 oz now, and more at its rainforest moisture content. About 50 lb at 25", the usual Bari' draw-length limit (being braced only 1" high, working draw length is 24". Braced at 6", our bows' working draw length is about 21"). This bow has zero set. Its double-length string is typical — a built-in spare. Made of bromelia fiber, this five-ply string is a hair under 1/4" diameter.

Rolando Achirabu, 3 1/2, his father Andres Achirabu, and Manuel Lizarralde. Achirabu is headman-by-consensus of the Bari' tribe. Despite missionary-induced Western first names, and occasional Western garb, the bow continues to provide the Bari' with almost all their animal protein. Achirabu is one of the Bari's most accomplished hunters. And personally, I wouldn't want to be mistaken for a monkey by little Rolando.

You're shooting in a jungle, so in order to find your arrows you make them *long*. In the near-saturated humidity of the rainforest your bow's moisture content will be extremely high. To avoid excessive string follow you make your bow *long*, and you brace it *low* — your easy-to-find, four-foot and longer arrows have no trouble whatever paradoxing around limbs often braced as low as one inch. This low bracing stores more energy due to the additional six inches or so of true draw length. You're working iron-hard wood with simple hand tools, sometimes of stone or bone, so you make the bow *narrow*, the most labor-saving design. You're shooting monkeys, almost straight overhead, therefore your arrow will not "drop" as with horizontal flight. As a result speed isn't as important, so you make your arrows *heavy*, both for penetration, and to reduce the handshock such a long, low-strung bow would have with light arrows. The bow gods see what you have done and nod their heads in approval.

Anthropologist Manuel Lizarralde has spent many years in association with the Bari' of Venezuela's rainforest. The Bari' hunt monkeys and large birds in the tree canopy at distances from twenty to forty yards. Peccaries are sometimes taken on the ground, at distances of around ten yards.

Manuel is an experienced archer and bowyer. On his most recent visit to the Bari' he gritted his teeth and took along a fiberglass bow, knowing what the rainforest would soon do to his temperate-climate woodbows. A backdoor but sincere testimonial to the traditional South American design.

African Bow

The bows of Africa cover an extreme range of lengths and draw weights but are generally round or oval in cross-section. The wide, flat bows of tribes along the Zambezi River are one of the few exceptions. A round-section bow of reasonable weight has to be narrow: if wide, a round section obviously becomes too thick. This is not acceptable because draw weight rises exponentially with thickness. Unless made from low bend-strength wood like yew or juniper, a wide, round-section bow is far too heavy to pull.

Round sections, being narrow and deep, are highly strained. If of normal length and draw length, wood in such bows must have exceptionally high breaking strength, and such strong wood is usually hard to work.

Narrow, round or oval designs are the easiest to fashion with simple tools — a similar problem and solution faced by South American bowyers. Africa's generally lower humidity permits higher brace heights and shorter bow lengths relative to archer height. And horizontal shooting favors lighter arrows.

Crowned cross-sections are generally not efficient because the central, thickest portions carries most of the load, making the limb functionally narrower than its measured width. But very strong, very elastic wood can be very narrow. The thinner "dead-weight" side wood acts to stabilized the otherwise thicker than it is wide limb.

The Bushman's bow is a typical round-section African "D" bow scaled down for effortless transport and unobtrusive use. Short straight-stave bows store little energy, but they *dry fire* as fast or faster than full-size bows. Which means they can shoot very light arrows with big-bow speed. If equipped with killing-sized tips, such light arrows literally bounce off of game. The bushman's micro-tipped

A photo taken by Arthur Young in 1926 of an African archer and his obviously heavy bow. This bow was made by a master. Compare its tiller with the described ideal Medieval English longbow, to follow (courtesy Pope and Young Club Museum).

arrows, however, have no trouble penetrating to the foreshaft with its lethal dose of poison.

Ben Walker, who lived with the Bushmen for a time, says they also use their bows as harps, placing a bow tip in their mouth against the cheek, tapping on the string with an arrow, controlling pitch by widening or narrowing the mouth, as with a jew's harp.

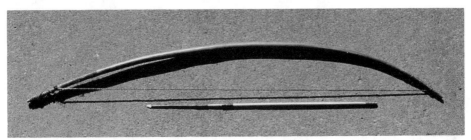

A Bushman bow from southwestern Africa, supplied by Canadian bowyer Ben Walker who lived with the Bushmen. Round in section, 37" long, and made from a small, tapered branch. Ben reports a local dearth of stone for toolmaking, one reason Bushman bows were traditionally small. Possibly for the same reason, Bushmen bows are often somewhat asymmetrical, lightly tillered branch bows (pg. 82, Vol. l), with most wood removal at the base end. Arrows are unfletched and have metal foreshafts.

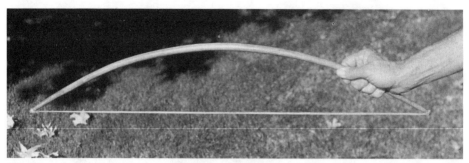

The Pigmy bow is similar to that of the Bushman in length and cross-section. One more example of the near-universal D-bow, round-section African design.

When using wood which is strong and elastic enough to tolerate narrow widths the African D-bow's circular section is a reasonable design. A related design was seen in early western North American bows, and in the medieval English longbow.

English Longbow

"The" English longbow did not exist; there have been many English longbow designs. Refined, lower-weight, shorter, narrower, stiff-handled, high-arched-belly versions shared the name with primitive, wrist-thick armor-piercers of the Middle Ages. Even those retrieved from the wreck of the 450 year-old *Mary Rose* show differences in back and belly sections. But common to all versions is at least a somewhat rounded belly and a limb section almost as deep as wide.

Why was this narrow, deep, rounded, English section popular for centuries? Weren't crowned backs and bellies inefficient? All bow cultures were design-savvy, over time fine-tuning their bows precisely to their needs. It's just left to us to discover the underlying logic. Here are a few tentative suggestions:

- Crowned bellies are less likely to break, behaving as a pressure relief valve — better to take a bit more set than to break under fire.
- Yew bows employ the rounded tree surface as back; if made flat-bellied, the now narrower back crown becomes the weak link.
- A square-section beam tries to reduce in thickness when bent, forcing its sides to bow out. This creates stress concentrations at the corners. Such a beam is likely safer, and at least no worse off, if these corners are rounded. This is not as large a problem for wide, thin limbs, so minimal rounding is needed. Rounding corners on narrow, deep limbs makes them look somewhat crowned.
- Bows with rounded belly corners (slightly crowned bellies) are faster to make, an advantage when hundreds of war bows are needed quickly.

The medieval warbow belly was not as arched as lower-weight, sporting bows of the 1700's and 1800's. These less-strained bows could endure a high arch, but a lower arch would have taken less set, or could have been shorter for greater cast. But for target shooting the low stack and stability of a "too-long" bow bought higher scores.

But why were the medieval warbows up to eighty-inches long? Imagine

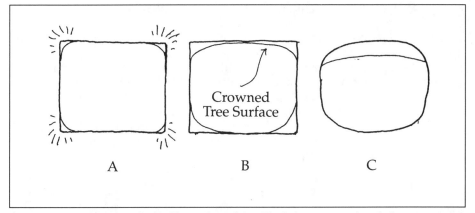

Bend a square-section length of rubber and watch its sides bulge out, creating obvious stress concentrations at the corners — A. This gives the maker of narrow, deep-limbed bows license to save time and work by rounding corners — B, which yields C, a typical Mary Rose cross-section.

you're going to war and need several thousand one-hundred-pound bows. If made 1 1/2" wide of yew and man-tall, such bows would take a large set, or break. But lengthened to eighty inches at the same draw weight this bow became completely safe. Limbs could have been widened instead, like the Meare Heath, but stave and labor costs would rise.

Properly designed, same-length limbs made of yew are thicker per pound of draw weight than any other bow wood. This is an advantage when tillering: minor wood removal during or after tillering obviously has more effect on a thin limb than a thick limb. For the same reason very thin limbs, whether due to low draw weight or wide/thin design, are more difficult to tiller and are more likely to go out of tiller in the future. For this reason, you may have noticed that unless made proportionately narrower for their weight, kids' bow are more difficult to tiller accurately.

Regardless of the wood type used, bow tip diameter tends to be fairly constant from bow to bow. Bows made of low bend-resistant wood, such a yew, therefore end up having thicker near-grip cross-sections compared to near-tip cross-sections. Given same diameter tip sections, greater mass difference therefore exists between tip and near-grip sections with yew than other woods. This results in less handshock and higher cast.

Longbows made of Osage have a reputation for handshock. But if Osage tips are reduced in diameter to the same tip/near-grip ratios found in yew longbows, they will shoot equally sweetly. This applies to all heavy woods. Osage is the worst offender if left wide-tipped because it is the heaviest native bow wood.

For a similar reason, heavy-weight bows have less handshock and more speed than might be expected. In paintings of the time, English warbows were often depicted with fairly circular tiller. Such profiles cause handshock in our mortal-weight bows but are not a proportionally larger problem in very heavy bows. This is true because massive medieval longbows had tips little if any larger than light bows. Therefore extreme mass differences existed between grip and tip sections.

There is a lesson here for mid-weight bowmakers: reduce tip and near-tip diameters to the same grip/tip ratios found on the old English longbow. Hand-shock will evaporate, and arrow speed will rise. Such tips may be very narrow, sometimes too narrow for conventional nocks. Or at least our conventional nocks. Several "less advanced" peoples figured all this out ages ago, tapering tips to virtual points, and using various wrap-on nocks.

One of the reasons ash, elm, hickory, maple, etc. of proper width frequently outshoot Osage and yew is that near-tip diameters are often equal, giving the lighter white woods a near-tip mass advantage.

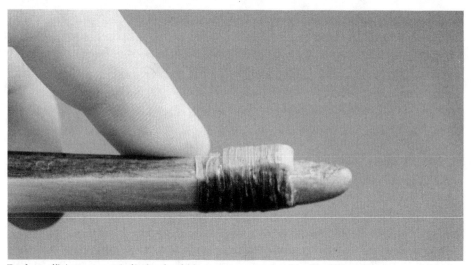

For best efficiency near-tip limbs should be as narrow as possible. The lighter the draw weight of the bow, or the heavier the wood, the narrower the nock and near-tip should be. Longer bows benefit more than shorter bows. If tips become too narrow for side or pin nocks, one solution is a folded and tied-on strip of rawhide, a simple, light back nock.

The old English warbows were usually depicted bending more in and near the tips than later, shorter versions. Whip tillering does shorten bow length during the draw, increasing gross string angle and stack. But on 80" long bows at near-normal draw lengths string angles remain low. On such long bows semi-whip tillering is an advantage because: 1) thinner, narrower wood has less mass, 2) thinner wood can bend farther than thicker wood without taking a set, so the thinner, somewhat whipped portion of the limbs take no undue set. This mild whip tillering benefits the whole bow because the more a limb is able to safely bend in one place, the less it needs to bend elsewhere, which means it would take less set everywhere. On fairly parallel-sided bows tillered so that each portion of the limb is strained to a safe capacity, whip tillering automatically results. The Neolithic-style bow on the cover is a good example.

The low degree of set seen on *Mary Rose* bows shows that despite high draw weight, they were not over-strained. This can be seen in *Mary Rose* replicas

Perfect tiller for long, heavy longbows. Simon Stanley shooting a hickory-backed, English yew bow by Roy King, bowyer to the Mary Rose Trust; 75" long, 150 lb. at 30". This bow casts 925-grain arrows 208 fps.

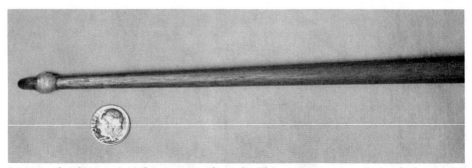

Leverage, therefore, strain, is lowest nearer the nocks. This most important area in which to lower mass, luckily, is also the safest part of the limb. Given unflawed wood and good tiller, even very narrow outer limbs never break near their tips. This see-what-you-can-get-away-with example is 3/16" at the nock and only 3/8" six-inches from the nock.

made by English bowyer Roy King. Tillered up to 150 lb weights, his bows show little set or chrysaling even at this unusually high weight. Roy puts the majority of *Mary Rose* bows at 100 lbs, with as many at 80 lb as 120 lb, and with bows above 120 lb reserved for exceptional archers.

Yew is the only wood which will make a same cross-section, high-weight English longbow. Yew has low bend resistance, so it must be thicker per draw weight. But yew's high elasticity allows it to be thicker without excessive set. All other bow woods which are elastic and compression-strong enough to equal a yew bow's draw weight at equal limb width and weight will have thinner limbs. Too thin for comfortable gripping, unless a riser is added.

✧ ✧ ✧

As we have seen, straight-stave bows store and release similar amounts of energy per pound, and with similar limb strain. The designs that follow behave differently on both counts.

DEFLEX-TIP BOW

It's easy to make a good bow given good materials. But try making a feed-your-tribe weapon from very brittle, very weak wood, such as willow. And add to this the problem of very low moisture content due to desert or near-desert humidities. Indians of the dry, wood-poor Southwest faced this problem. The deflexed tips found on many of the bows of the region may have been their solution.

Deflexed tips lowered the amount of energy stored at a given draw weight, so efficiency was low. A 60 lb deflex-tip bow may only have had the cast of a 45 lb straight-stave bow. But that's enough, and the bow could then be fired without breaking. This was possible because deflex-tipped limbs were under no strain while braced, so that when drawn their entire store of energy was available to the arrow. No energy was left behind in the limbs, as in normal bend-to-brace bows.

Mojave Indians, of the dry Southwest, with typical deflexed-tip bows. Low moisture content, as much as weak, brittle local wood, justifies this low-strain design. Other low-humidity bow cultures also employed deflexed tips, ancient Egyptian wood bows being the most prominent example.

As much as any other, this bow demonstrates the precision with which cultures molded bow designs to their particular needs.

These deflex-tip bows are a good lesson in reverse. If this design is inefficient, designs with opposite qualities will be correspondingly efficient. Asiatic composite bows are the extreme opposite design: recurved, and due to reflexed limbs, highly strained when braced. And opposite-quality materials are needed, horn and sinew being the most elastic. These two designs, and their respective materials, represent the two ends of the bow design/materials spectrum. When designing a bow it's good to ask where your intended design and materials rest on that spectrum. A decisive answer will let you know if you're asking too much or little of your design or materials.

SETBACK BOW

The version most familiar to us is the Plains setback bow. The pre-tillered limbs of this bow were straight, but projected from the grip at a forward angle. Bows shot from horseback tended to be short, and short bows, due to their high

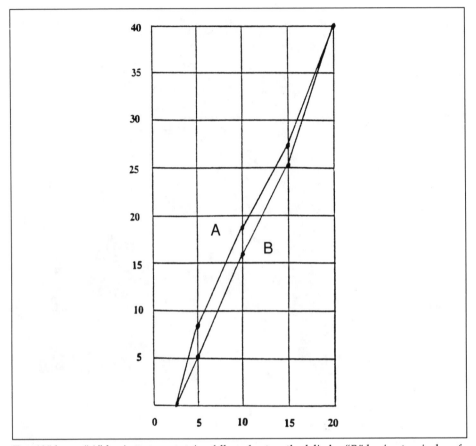

Two 48" bows, "A" having zero net string follow, due to setback limbs, "B" having two inches of string follow. This degree of setback raises cast to that of about a 7 lb heavier bow. Setback is more effective on short-draw bows where a given distance of setback equals a higher percentage of total limb travel.

string angles and/or short draw lengths, stored little energy, therefore they had very low cast per pound when shooting hunting-weight arrows. Setback bows overcame some of this disadvantage: setback limbs must be bent farther when braced, as a result early draw weight was higher, which stored more total energy.

Setback limb tips traveled farther, both when braced and at full draw, than straight-stave counterparts. They were therefore more strained, so modifications were made to safely accept this extra strain. The solution was wider/thinner limbs, or use of more elastic wood or other materials. More effective yet would be to slightly lengthen the limb. Short bows should be made as long as possible, yet still satisfy their design requirements. Very short bows were, and are, almost unbelievably slower than man-tall bows.

The setback bow was as efficient as its reflexed or non-contact recurve

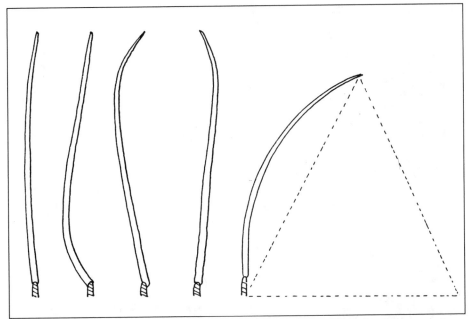

Five same-weight, same-length, same-draw bows, each limb taking a different path from grip to tip. At full draw, the grip, limb-tip, arrow-nock triangle will be identical, assuming identical tiller profile (circular tiller lowers string angle, whip-ended tiller raises it). Assuming the unbraced tips of all five rest at the same point relative to the grip, all limbs will have taken equal energy to brace. Early-draw weight will therefor be equal for all. With equal full-draw string angles and equal early-draw weight all five bows store equal energy.

cousins. But setback was easier to create: steam the grip, bend it over your knee, and it was done.

This design's tips approach the string at greater angles than other designs. But near-tip string angle does not determine stack, as I once reported. Stack due to string angle depends only on the gross angle between grip, tip, and arrow nock.

The setback design is ancient. Longer, non-horseback relatives were depicted in Mesolithic cave-paintings of Caballos, Spain, Neolithic Saharan Ti-n-Tazarift depictions, and others. In *Bows and Arrows,* Pope described a 57.5" juniper setback "cliff dweller" bow. Found in Arizona, this bow "possibly is over one thousand years old."

And this design is modern. For over a century bows made from spliced billets have been common. To offset string follow, such limbs were often set forward one or two inches before gluing.

Short versions of this design can benefit from sinew-backing. Sinew reduces set, and increases safety in these more-strained limbs. Sinew's high mass is not so damaging on short bows, where inertia is less important. As with all bows, string angle will be lower if limbs are made to bend more near the handle than at mid-limb or near-tip. This is even more valuable for higher-stacking short bows. And the Plains setback bow was often seen tillered just this way. Such

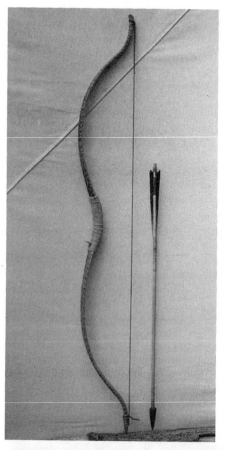

Setback, recurved "Cupid" design by bowyer Dave Kissinger; 48" Osage, sinew-backed, 65 lb. at 22". Unlike more narrow-limbed Plains designs, this bow holds a 2 1/2" unbraced reflex. This is allowed by wider, rectangular limbs: 2" near the grip, 1 1/2" at mid-limb. Non-contact recurves prevent the string leaving its nocks if overdrawn. For the same purpose Dave sometimes makes hook nocks of molded sinew and hide glue.

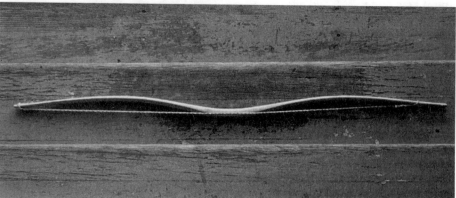

Hickory, 46" by 1 5/8". Made with 4" of setback, then tillered to 80 lb. at 17" (to see if it would blow). Re-tillered to 55 lb at 23", it holds a slight setback, and is fairly efficient for its length and draw length. Eighty pounds seems impossibly strong, but at low draw lengths limbs will withstand tremendous weight. Still, hickory is one of the few wood which can take such abuse.

Sioux sinew-backed hickory, displaying a typical profile of its type. Its unusually low brace height makes more total stored energy available to the arrow, and permits both a longer gross draw and net draw (courtesy Fenn Gallery).

tillering increases strain on near-grip portions of the limb, so sinew is especially helpful here. For sinew, labor, and mass savings, sinew need not extend out to the limb tips.

Many Plains bows were bent forward at the center so severely their tips would have initially rested up to 10" forward of the grip. Similar test bows break when braced and drawn. These limbs were apparently heat-bent back again at inner mid limb, creating a more tolerable tip position. But why advance the tips just to bring them back again? A possible explanation is that this geometry permitted higher-weight limbs by forcing a longer bow's portion of wood into a short bow, for example, if a straight, 48" stave was steamed into a wavy 44" long bow it would handle the weight of a 48" bow. A bit more actually, because it had the string-angle/stack/lower energy storage of a 44" bow. This conjectured longer-bow benefit will make more sense to longbow shooters if put this way: two same width, same draw-length bows, one 61.5" long, the other 66" long. Which can be safely tillered to a higher weight?

Wider limbs also would have permitted higher weight, but steam bending was much easier than working a wider hickory stave with simple hand tools.

REFLEXED BOW

Ishi's bows generally held a sinew-backing induced reflex. Unlike straight, setback limbs, reflexed limbs were curved their entire length. As with setback limbs and non-contact recurves, reflexing was one way to cause unbraced limb tips to rest more forward of the grip than otherwise. Having traveled farther to reach brace height, early draw weight was higher, permitting higher total energy storage.

Natural-occurring reflex was *slightly* safer and more efficient than steamed-in reflex because steam bending weakened the wood. A straight stave clamped in

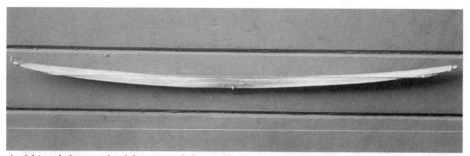

An Ishi-style bow made of the materials he used before contact: sinew-backed mountain juniper; 47" by 2", 46 lb at 25"; 1 1/2" just-unbraced reflex. Juniper seems to be the most sinew-compatible bow wood, taking and holding the largest reflex. Sinew has lower stretch-strength than any wood, and juniper has the lowest bend-strength of any highly-elastic wood I've tested.

Bowyer James Murphy inspecting the rare perfectly balanced natural reflex in this hickory stave. Tillering reflexed staves can be tricky: early weight is so much higher than normal the beginning bowyer believes the bow is headed for too high a final weight and makes the bow too light.

reflexed position while drying was given an apparently permanent reflex, but the bow lost much of it once drawn.

A backing-induced reflex was, and is, the safest and most permanent. Sinew, flax, wood, bamboo, or other animal or vegetable fibers were used.

RECURVED BOW (non-contact)

Non-contact recurves store the same amount of energy as setback and reflexed designs — assuming the unbraced tips rest in the same place relative to the grip. Limb strain is identical, too. A non-contact recurve is thickened so as

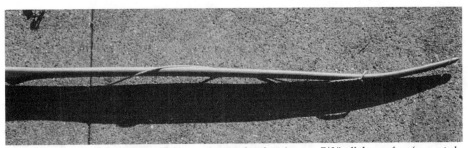

With unbraced back against a wall this persimmon bow's grip rests 7/8" off the surface (corrected for nock length), a net 7/8" reflex. A straight-stave version would have taken about 1 1/2" set. Therefore, its tips now travel 2 3/8" farther at brace than a straight-stave cousin. This bow has an identical early draw-weight advantage as reflexed or setback bows having the same against-the-wall measurements.

not to bend, therefore has slightly more mass than the other two tip-forward designs.

Because of their normally slightly higher near-tip mass, non-contact recurve bows often shoot no faster, and sometimes even slower, than straight stave versions. Short bows don't suffer as much cast loss because tip mass is less important. The pictured bow's recurves are too long and shallow, reducing working limb length, and creating a too long, too heavy non-bending area. Shorter, steeper curves would increase working-limb length and reduce near-tip mass.

REFLEXED RECURVE BOW (non-contact)

If an unbraced bow has, say, two inches of reflex and a two-inch non-contact recurve, it will store identical energy as bows having four-inch setbacks or four-inch reflexes, everything else being equal. In all three cases each bow's limbs travel equal distances to brace and full draw, and as a result do equal work. And in each case full-draw string angle is identical. This assumes all three are tillered the same — circular, normal, whip-ended, etc.

So why bother doing both? Why not just reflex the limbs four inches and quit? Here are a few possible reasons: 1) this is a beautiful design, 2) cultural inertia: this shape, often seen along the North Pacific coast, is reminiscent of Asiatic composites, from which it may be descended, 3) the string angle of short, long-draw bows can exceed ninety-degrees at full draw; strings can actually pull off of their nocks. Recurving solves this problem by lowering near-tip string angle.

Northern Pacific Coast bows were often reflexed, recurved, and of very short length. Which means they were terribly overstrained if of normal design and materials. If design requirements prevented lengthening limbs, one or both of two remedies could be used: wider/thinner limbs, or more elastic materials. Usually the makers of these bows chose both: several-inch wide limbs and sinew-backing.

These Pacific bows were possibly the most highly refined wood-based bows ever made. Exquisitely engineered, crafted, and decorated, they were, however, specialty bows designed for very close-range hunting, typically from blinds. Steve Allely routinely takes game this way, the latest with a 40", 40 lb Shasta replica, released just 12 feet from the deer.

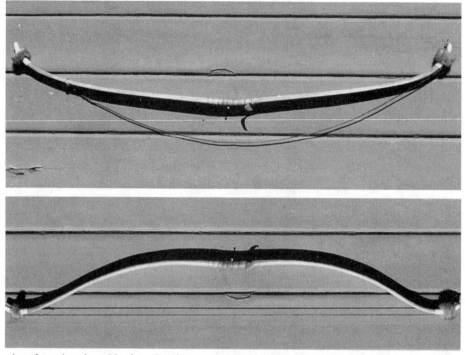

A modern sinew/yew Northern Pacific coast bow by Afief Espindola. Even if far overdrawn the string will not pull off of these curved ends.

Recurves and sinew-maintained reflex helped overcome severe stack common to short, straight-stave bows. It did so by raising early draw weight since weight cannot rise as abruptly during the last inches of draw if starting from a higher early and mid point. Despite lower energy storage per pound of draw weight, moderately light arrows permitted fairly high speed and smaller "bird point" tips permitted adequate penetration. This bow was perfectly suited for its purpose. But it would compare poorly with a longbow for target shooting or hunting at conventional distances.

In length, draw, energy storage, and accuracy, it was related to Plains bows. Plains bowyers did not usually have access to the soft, easy to work yew and juniper available to Western bowyers. If you ever replicate a wide Western design using hickory or Osage you will appreciate the Plains design. These narrower, stiffer, less flexible limbs were not as easily reflexed by drying sinew, and recurving was rare. Set-back limbs made best sense there.

Unlike earlier cycles of interest in natural archery, the present wave was largely sparked by appreciation of American Indian bows and arrows. Longerbow Woodland archery ended centuries before Western states archery. Vastly more artifacts and knowledge exists of horse culture, brushy terrain adapted, and blind-hunting bow designs. These bows were the light modern naturalmaterials archery moved toward, but for the most part this was a misguiding light.

Glenn St. Charles with a recurved, reflexed Wintu bow, restored by Dr. Charles Grayson. With paternal exasperation, Glenn continually and correctly admonishes us for thinking we're inventing anything new. Virtually every possible bow type and sub-type was invented long ago, usually by Stone Age people. Developed over time, each is finely tuned to its use-environment and indicates a grasp of common-sense engineering.

Short bows are... adorable! And for some reason they seem to shoot very fast, especially with their normally shorter, lighter arrows. Bowmaking friends often call to report on their latest little demon bow that, "just spits the arrows."

Several months ago three short-bow devotees drove up from central California with an assortment of recently made 38" to 48" Plains and Pacific Coast type bows. Reverently taken from the car, various protective sleeves and cases were delicately removed. They were beautiful. And perfectly sinewed, tillered and decorated.

There was also a rude longbow in the back seat, made of a broadleaf maple branch, a moderately light, brittle wood. One of the three had scraped the bow out one afternoon just for practice. Sixty-seven inches long, it was knotty and inelegant, but well tillered. I brought it along to test with the others. This evoked good-natured but derisive banter.

Of course this wretched bent stick, with its long, smooth draw, humiliated its elegant little brothers — in both speed and accuracy. In wood-based bows of the 50 lb range, 42" bows for example, well made and sinew-backed, shoot hunting-

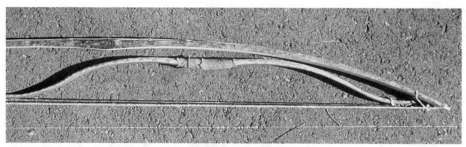

At 20" of draw the 40" sinew-backed Osage bow weighs 50 lb and casts a 500 grain arrow 131 fps. It's crude 67" plum branch all-wood cousin weights 50 lb at 27.5" and casts the same arrow 152 fps. And with far greater accuracy.

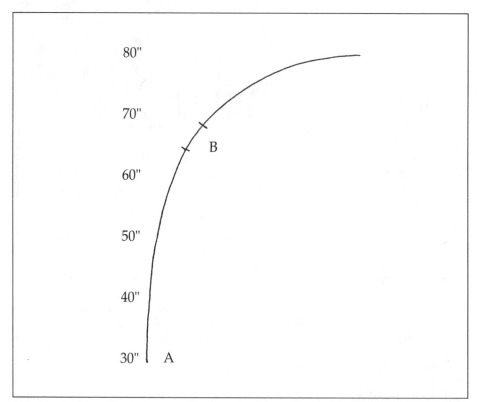

This drawing is meant only to put an idea into visual form. Line "A" illustrates the energy storing advantages of lower-stack string angles, and longer draws. Energy storage rises abruptly as bow length rises to 50", rises moderately from 50" to 60", somewhat from 60" to 70", and slightly from 70" to 80". Disadvantages of greater limb mass, and string mass, cancel these already diminishing benefits in the mid to late 60s, as seen at area "B". "B" is an area, not a dot, because many variables determine the exact point of trade-off: tiller shape, front-view shape/mass, degree of deflex or reflex, arrow weight, and so on. For high reflex or recurve composite bows, curve A's ceiling drops to about 60", and area "B" hovers at about 50".

weight arrows as much as 20 pounds of equivalent draw weight slower than near-man tall bows. Short bows will shoot lighter arrows at reasonable speed, but light arrows leave the bow with less of the bow's stored energy than heavy arrows, so penetration is poor.

The short wood-based bow is a specialty bow, appropriately used only in specialty situations, as when taking buffalo from horseback or as with Steve Allely's very successful close range blind-hunting efforts.

RECURVE/RETROGRADE TIP BOW (contact)

Contact recurves and retrograde tips seem to have originated during mid-stages in the evolution of the composite bow, which means they may have existed for just over one-fourth of bow history.

Possibly the earliest documented recurve was depicted on a sword sheath discovered in a 7th-8th century B.C. Scythian gravesite. Recurves on the Scythian composite occupied a small percentage of limb length, thereby accounting for a small percentage of stored energy. Scythian bows measured between 30" and 40"

Fifty-two inch sinew-backed juniper, contact recurve bow by Joe Dabill. Juniper/sinew is a very elastic combination, permitting long draws from fairly short bows without taking serious set. Even at moderate widths this combination easily handles the extra strain imposed by contact recurves. Mid-draw liftoff gives this full-draw shorter bow the low stack/high cast of longer bows.

long; the recurve may have first arisen to prevent the string from pulling off the nocks, its performance benefits being realized later.

The recurve's late arrival was due to several possible reasons. Contact-recurve bows are "short bows" early in the draw, becoming "longer bows" after string lift off. Being hard to pull early in the draw and not that much harder late in the draw yield more energy storage. But this additional energy must be stored somewhere. Recurved limbs are more strained, and therefore take more set. That, with the usual extra mass of a recurve, can actually lead to sub straight-bow arrow speed.

Efficient recurved bows are shorter limbed than normal. Shorter limbs have even less material available for storing energy, so are even more strained. Only the most elastic materials can hold up under the load. This means sinew on wood, or sinew and horn, if high-weight and full-draw are desired. Short sinew/wood, deep-contact recurves will only hold up to short-draws. Weight and draw length can be raised somewhat with wider, rectangular limbs.

If big enough to matter, recurves tend to be unstable. Efficient recurves are technically complex, require high levels of skill, and take considerably longer to make than simple bows. It made sense to put off inventing them as long as possible.

If both highly reflexed and highly recurved, limb strain becomes too high for full-draw wood-based bows. In its extreme form, horn and sinew are the materials of choice.

A bow holding 3" of either setback or reflex will perform almost as well as the pictured contact recurve. If the recurve is too wide or thick (too massive) a 3" setback or reflexed bow might even outshoot it. Contact recurves must occupy a large percentage of limb length to account for much additional energy storage. Worth noting is that the lower a given recurve is braced, the deeper string contact is made, which raises the effective percentage of recurve.

The most efficient wood/sinew retrograde-tip bow I've seen was made by John McPherson. John and I were comparing bows at an aboriginal technology

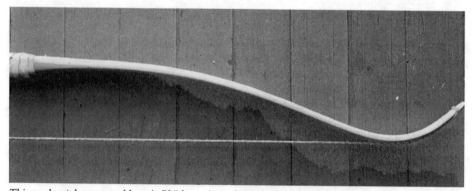

This moderately recurved bow is 52" long, its unbraced nocks resting 3" forward of the grip. When braced, the distance from point of string contact to string nock is 4", about 15% of limb length, a fairly small percentage. This bow shoots at about the speed of a 20% heavier straight-stave version, but most of this increased performance derives from its 3" forward nocks.

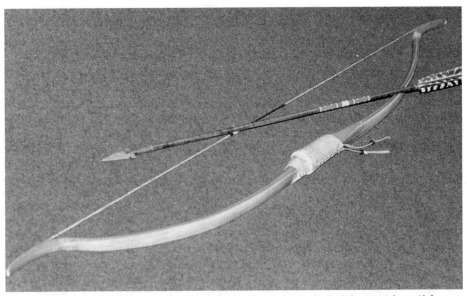

A static recurve made by bowyer Gary Davis of Michigan. Sinew-backed Osage. A beautiful design, and efficient for its length.

meet a few years ago. I brought my most efficient bow to date, a sinew/yew, contact recurve. It was perfectly sinewed, perfectly tillered, and shone like a new penny. John's favorite bow at the time was a roughly-tillered, roughly-sinewed, black locust bow made under "survival" conditions. Both our bows were about the same length, draw length, and weight, and had about the same depth of recurve, or retrograde in his case. But my bow had less limb set and his bow had a gross sinew-wrapped splint on one limb that groaned at full draw. So of course I challenged him to a flight shoot, and so of course his bow slaughtered mine.

This seemed impossible at the time, but now makes perfect sense: the distance from string-contact point to string nock equaled about 27% of his bow's limb length. Although both our tips were set equally forward, my recurve occupied only about 13% of limb length. His bow was "shorter" than mine before string lift off, therefore harder to pull early in the draw. His bow simply stored more energy.

DEFLEX-RECURVE

A deflex/working-recurve yields the fattest F-D curve, smoothest draw, and highest arrow speed of any full-draw, wood-only bow. This design seems to have been invented by Roger Willcox in the 1930's. Robert Elmer regarded Willcox very highly, allotting considerable ink to his innovations, bowmaking skill, and designs, especially the "Duoflex." Elmer's Willcox-made Duoflex measured 62" long, 1 1/8" near the grip, tapering to 1/2" at the tip, 37 lb at 28". From F-D numbers given by Elmer, the illustrated curve can be drawn.

No other wood-only design I know of yields such a composite-like F-D curve. It does so for several clever but subtle reasons. Probably more than any other, a

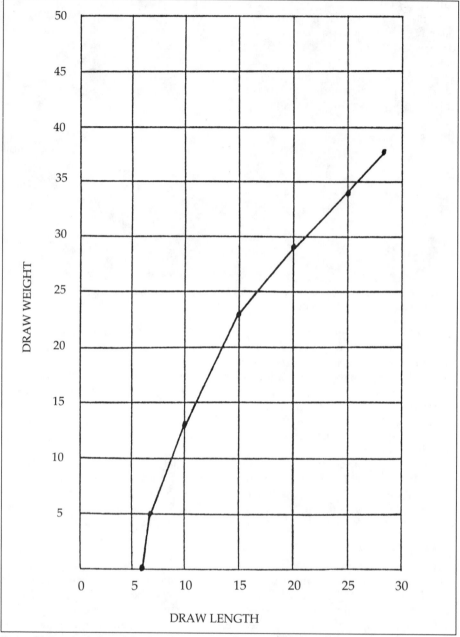

Due to high early-draw weight, late-draw weight rises at only one pound per inch. Apart from high arrow speed, a curve of this shape means a more consistent trajectory from shot to shot because slight differences in draw length and cleanness of release do not affect energy storage as much as on a higher-stacking bow.

full understanding of this design will aid in understanding other bow designs.

Deflexed limbs normally cause low early draw weight; a 50 lb bow, having a near brace-height deflex of five inches will only weigh about 12 lb at 15" of draw. But a 150 lb, equally deflexed version would weight 36 lbs, having the fat early F-D curve of a highly reflexed composite.

Assume this deflexed 150 lb bow is about 40" long. Then picture attaching 10" working recurves to each end. Early weight will still be high, the bow will still think it's heading for 150 lb, but as the draw progresses the ever-lifting string creates an ever-longer, greater-leverage limb. But this in itself would not tame this bow to 50 lbs at full draw.

Before lift-off begins, portions of the limb near the string contact point "think they are the end of the bow." This "end" portion, like all of the pre-recurve limb, is tillered to require hard pulling—for abrupt weight rise. But as lift-off proceeds, this "end of the bow" becomes the middle of the bow. Feeling increased leverage, it begins to bend also. From early lift-off onward the inner limb does not bend very much more; it has already done its job of causing high initial draw weight. During mid and late phases of draw most additional bending and energy storage takes place in the recurve and near-recurve portion of the limb. These areas are tillered to slowly straighten out as lift-off progresses.

Elmer's Duoflex gained one-pound per inch during the last foot of draw. Like all contact recurves this bow became *effectively* longer as lift-off proceeded. But in the Duoflex there was also an *actual* lengthening as the recurve straightened out. This bow rose gently in weight partly due to the greater leverage of its greater length, and its resulting longer-bow string angle.

Working portions of this limb could be shorter per limb width than non-working recurves because these recurves unwound to become part of the working limb. If shorter, they wielded less inertia than non-working recurved limbs.

At only 62" in length the Duoflex already had considerable inertia advantage over most full-draw bows. It had more still because of its long, barely working center section. Similar to the Sudbury in this regard it was, so to speak, a short,

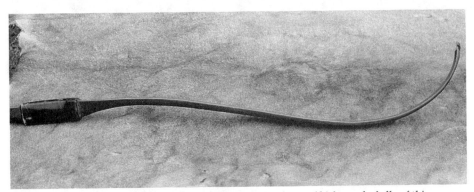

Willcox Duoflexes were made of Osage backed with a thin layer of hickory; the belly of this particular bow is bias-ringed. A "primitive" Duoflex could be made without backing. But stave selection and tillering skill would be more critical. Incidentally, this bow rests on the skin of the lion that Arthur Young killed in Africa in 1926. (courtesy Pope and Young Club Museum).

low-inertia bow on a longer, low-string-angle body. Working recurves could be more severe, and could occupy a larger percentage of limb length without being unstable because they "disappeared" as they opened up during the draw.

Unlike a braced limb, the near and after-string-contact working-recurve portion of the limb was under no strain until string lift-off. None of its ability to store energy had been used up before lift-off, so there was no "brace-energy" remaining in the recurve itself after firing. Since a substantial portion of total stored energy resided in the straightened-out, fully-drawn recurve, this later portion of the draw was more efficient than on straight bows. That efficiency manifested itself in the form of narrower, less massive limb width — since no brace energy was stored, less total energy was stored, so less "bow" was needed.

But why was this design deflexed? Wouldn't all the above still be true if inner limbs were straight or reflexed?

Being less elastic, wood could not store as much energy as horn\sinew. But this design stored near composite amounts of energy, so something had to be done differently: being deflexed, inner limbs were strained very little at brace, and due to their short total travel, very little more even at full draw. Low travel permitted simple wood to store both more total energy and more available-to-the-arrow energy, for two reasons: 1) a certain 1/2" thick stave would break at 50 lb if drawn 28", but if 2" thick it will pull to several hundred pounds when bent just a few inches. It can store more total energy for the simple reason there is more wood available for storing energy, 2) since limbs are barely strained at brace, like the deflex-tip desert bows, almost all stored energy is available to the arrow.

One reason this design, in wood, could almost equal the F-D curve of a horn\sinew composite without overstraining its limbs was that energy was stored over more square inches of limb surface. For that reason (apart from

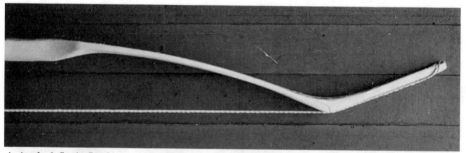

A simple deflex/reflex bow, not as efficient as the Duoflex, but very quick and easy to make. About 62" long, about 2 3/4" wide near the grip. Limbs are just over one-quarter-inch thick wood slats of uniform-thickness. Their pyramid shape produces automatic tiller. Limb slats are set to about 3" of deflex, then a matching riser is glued in place. The siyah is simply butted to the limb, another piece of wood glued to the back as reinforcement, overlapping the splice. A hickory veneer, linen, or sinew backing is then added. Raw linen is the easiest. Nocks rest just forward of the grip when unstrung; retrograde tips occupy 25% of limb length; limbs are deflexed to require three-inches of bend to brace; siyah angle causes lift-off at about fourteen inches of draw. All these figures can be adjusted to swell or shrink the F-D curve, as required by the elasticity of limb materials.

string-angle reasons) it was not likely this design could be shortened to composite bow lengths. But widening would permit some shortening. A pyramid Duoflex would permit less deflex, therefore even higher early draw weight, and a slightly shorter design.

Elmer's Duoflex drew just 37 lb, but was only 1 1/8" at its widest. Keeping every other aspect the same, each additional 1/8" in width would raise draw weight by 4.1 lb: At 1 1/2", weight would rise to 50 lb; a 2" limb would draw 65 lb.

Anyone who intends making a wooden Duoflex might want to read this paragraph again after covering "The Perry Principle," under "A New Design", to follow. Perry inner-limb energy storage should permit better performance by allowing shorter and/or narrower, lower-inertia limbs, and likely less deflexed limbs; an initial excessive deflex would be created during handle splicing by pointing, not bending the limbs in the deflex direction, then, with the splice cured, back and belly would be *pulled* into desired lesser deflex, as per Perry principle. The recurves would be pulled, not steamed, into position for the same reason.

A shortened, less deflexed, pyramid-shaped, Perry-principle Duoflex, its tiller appropriately modified, would out-perform many sinew/horn composite bows.

THE COMPOSITE BOWS

This design has already been covered by Dr. Grayson in Vol. l, and Jeff Schmidt elsewhere in this volume. Instead of traveling such well-covered ground it might be more useful to imagine how the composite might have evolved had firearms not entered the scene.

To a small extent this evolution had already begun; the Turkish flight bow, for example, was perfected for sport. There are many practical, efficient, traditional composite designs, but unfortunately the Turkish flight bow is the only design familiar to most of us. It does cast arrows up to one-half mile... but arrows the size and weight of knitting needles, invisible to the eye in flight, requiring a packed lunch to find... Almost any other composite design is more suited to every-day use.

Although Mongolian and Korean composites have been made continuously to current times, they show no major design changes. But this is not surprising; in composite bow history even one thousand years is not a long time between major design improvements.

The route to a superior composite bow is obvious: reduce outer limb mass and raise early draw weight. Here is one of many possible approaches to a "next generation" composite: outer limbs do not bend, so they can be made of low mass-to-stiffness woods, such as spruce. Only the actual bending portions of the limb need be covered with high-mass horn and sinew, allowing sufficient feathering for safety. The Turkish flight bow makers had already started in this direction.

Increased reflex will raise early draw weight. A wider, therefore, thinner near-grip limb will accept, but more importantly will *hold*, greater reflex because wide, thin limbs take less set than narrow, thick limbs. Early draw weight is determined by a limb's *true* reflex, the amount evident *immediately* after being unbraced. Just-unbraced horn/sinew limbs creep forward into greater and

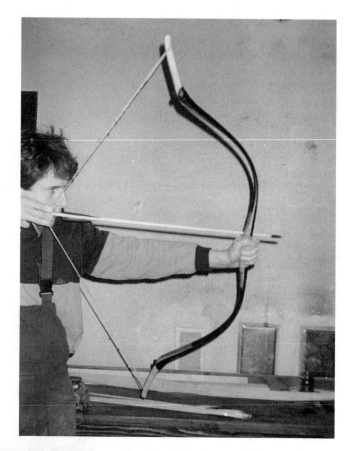

Bowyer Matyaz Tomse testing his latest composite. At about 52" in length materials are not strained to the brink as on shorter flight bows. This is a more rugged, durable, dependable bow, and less temperamental to make and shoot. With true siyahs and unstrung tip-touching reflex for high energy storage, this is a sensible design for real-life hunting and target shooting.

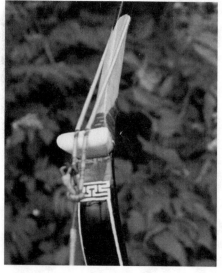

Outer limb of Manchu/Chinese replica by Wayne Alex of Alaska. Polar opposite to the flight bow: at 67" in length, drawing 35" or more, this bow stores enormous energy. But such mass and length cannot react quickly, casting moderate-weight arrows no faster than a good wood bow of equal draw length. It was designed for massive spear-like arrows, which are capable of carrying the bulk of its stored energy with them. You could ruin a rhino's day with this bow.

greater reflex over minutes, hours, and days; but these reluctant profiles are irrelevant. Wider limbs do have more mass, but this small increase occurs near the grip, where travel is short and slow. This small rise in inertia can be more than offset by lighter outer limbs, and higher energy storage due to greater just-unbraced reflex.

Early draw weight can also be raised by increasing the percentage of limb length devoted to recurve. This can't be done on conventional composites without the string lifting off too early or limbs becoming unstable. But this is not true of working recurves. As with the Duoflex, working recurves "disappear" as they're drawn. And like the Duoflex, the actually longer, straightened-out limb reduces late draw weight buildup — another way of saying the bow can have higher early draw weight. Uncurling recurves increase limb length at full draw, lowering full draw string angle. String angle can also be lowered by increasing the length of a bow's non-working center section, increasing bow length but not increasing moving limb mass.

It seems traditional composite bellies had already take some advantage of the Perry Principle. Since sinew stretches so much farther than horn compresses, bellies should likely always be pulled backwards into high belly surface tension

Dave Kissinger with a sinew-backed, horn/wood hybrid. Only the most heavily strained near-grip portions of the belly have been reinforced with horn. This feature safely allows higher-energy-storing designs than sinew/wood alone. Because heavier-than-wood horn is confined to the inner limb, outer limb mass is kept to a minimum. Horn leftovers are often long enough for this purpose, especially on limbs which bend chiefly near the handle.

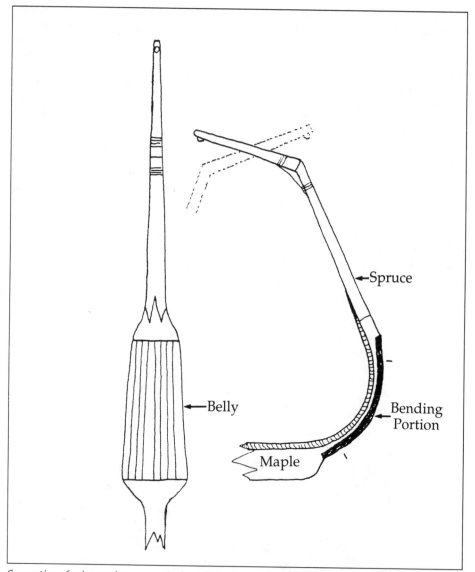

Suggestions for improving composite bow performance: Straight limbs are spliced into about 30-degree setback. Near-grip limbs are 2" or more wide, depending on draw weight, and perfectly rectangular in section. For convenience and economy, horn can be narrow strips. Working areas of the horn are about 4" long, then follow the core's thickening slope for 2" at each end. The working core is about 3/32" sugar maple; it's back is flat. Outer limbs of lighter, stiffer wood, such as spruce, may be spliced-in. Sinew, core, and horn are equal thickness, making about a 9/32" thick working limb. At the nock end, sinew continues past the working portion of the limb for two or three inches, then feathers out over two or three more inches. At the grip end, middle sinew travels across the grip, edge sinew wraps around onto the belly. Before sinewing, the bow is drawn beyond tip-touching reflex.

before sinewing. This lowers belly strain during the draw and makes the sinew do its fair share of energy storage.

Possibly pyramid or short Andaman Island-type limbs could have been the next step in composite bow evolution. Wider, thinner limbs are less strained, take less set, and would permit greater reflex.

If you're considering working up your own composite design it might be helpful to make same-size 5 lb or 10 lb prototypes from limber slats of wood. These very flexible limbs will withstand the big-reflex to full draw range of motion, letting you view the effect of siyah length, siyah angle, lift-off point, string angles, and so on. Its whisper of a F-D curve will reliably show the efficiency of your design.

If you find you have no interest in composite bows, do not feel left out. The simplest wooden bow is archery at its purest. More than any other design, it's what archery is about. It was invented and used for the noble purpose of feeding family and band. The composite was invented and used chiefly for killing people. When all factors are weighed, a well-made wooden bow is a superior hunting weapon, and composite bowmen often prefer them for this purpose.

FLIGHT BOWS

It's terrific fun seeing the near supernatural, gravity-defying flight of an arrow. And the faster and longer the arrow travels the more fun it is. This is the root incentive for flight shooting.

Some argue that world-class, several-hundred-yard flight shooting has no practical value, but neither does dessert, and many performance features in the family station wagon had their origins in Indy race cars.

There are two general types of flight shooting. One involves "normal" bows, shooting "normal" arrows — the type of gear that could reasonably be used for hunting. The other type could be called "exotic." Generally short-limbed, and designed to shoot "arrows" of unusually small length and diameter, typically in the range of 150 grains, but occasionally as low as 50 grains.

The fastest per pound, sweetest shooting "hunting" flight bow I've tested was made by Dan Perry. Narrow pyramid-shaped, extremely narrow-tipped, and well reflexed, Dan simply applied the lessons learned by trial and error while competing at "primitive" flight shoots.

Fast flight bows have two qualities: low limb inertia and fat force-draw curves. Short, low mass limbs reduce inertia. High early draw weight and non-stacking late-draw weight yields fat F-D curves. Severe reflexing and, to some extent, contact recurves insure high early draw weight.

The strongest, most elastic materials are needed for "exotic" flight bows — horn and sinew. But the bowyer's knowledge and skill is as essential. As evidence of this, consider the number of half-mile-shooting composite bows built in the last hundred years. They can be counted on the clenched fist of a three-toed sloth.

A 100-lb flight bow will shoot a very light arrow only slightly faster, and sometimes slower, than a same-design 50-lb flight bow. This paradoxical effect was reported by puzzled writers of past archery literature, but the exact cause remained a mystery. The following may explain this phenomenon:

Imagine dry-firing three same-design, equally efficient 50 lb. flight bows. Upon release, string speed obviously will be the same for all. Now imagine

Harry Drake, shown with Turkish-style flight bow and wooden core. Since 1945, he holds the world distance record of 541 yards with an all-wood bow, a 69# yew recurve shooting 140 grain arrows.

gluing two of these bows together side-by-side, forming a 100 lb. bow (in a sense a 100 lb. bow *is* two 50 lb. bows glued together). This new 100 lb. bow will obviously *dry-fire* at the same speed as when it was two 50 lb. bows. Now imagine shooting *one-grain* arrows from these 50 and 100 lb. bows. Firing such low weight arrows is virtually the same as dry-firing, and will not slow either bow enough to notice. *These 100 lb. and 50 lb. bows will fire this very light arrow at effectively the same speed.* But as arrow weight rises cast will naturally begin to slow. One thousand grain arrows will slow both 50 and 100 lb. bows considerably. But because the 100 lb. version stores twice as much energy it will be slowed less.

In practice, higher weight flight bows shooting very light arrows sometimes cast arrows slower than lighter bows. A bow that is too heavy for the shooter cannot be released with perfect control. Release technique is critical in flight shooting. World-class flight shooters, using the same bow, arrow, and draw length, achieve up to ten percent higher arrow speed than most target or hunting archers.

Natural-material flight bows can likely be made to cast farther than Turkish flight bows. The route will be similar to that suggested for improving traditional composite performance, described earlier. Flight designs should remain short, and with short mid-sections. Longer mid-sections lengthen the bow, lowering string angle without raising moving limb mass, but string mass does increase. And even a few grains of string mass increase is costly when shooting near mass-less arrows.

ESKIMO BOW

Due to their cold climate, Eskimos did not have choice bow wood, and even if they had, wood would have become brash at very cold temperatures. Backing a bow was their answer.

Animal glue is frustratingly difficult to use in cold air, jelling almost instantly. This may have been the incentive for cable-backing. Cable backs, depending on their diameter and degree of stress, take over much of the wood back's tension load, the normal area of failure. Aboriginal cable-backed bows appear in all design profiles: straight, retrograde tips, reflexed, deflexed and so on.

Jeff Schmidt drawing his Siberian Chukchi Eskimo replica. With the patience and tenacity of a hermitic saint, Jeff has uncovered thousands of pages of "new" composite bow information from the libraries of the world, especially the Eastern world. For example, the Chukchis glued a thin layer of sinew to the bow's back before installing its cable. Jeff's 67" replica of yellow birch weighs 65 lb, with considerable plus-or-minus depending on choice of cable tension.

There is no net advantage to cables over glued-on backings. Draw weight can be adjusted up or down, but double nocks, or adjustable nocks can do the same. However, the cable-backed bow does remind us of this: no matter how wretched the situation, somehow there's a way to put a good bow together. If more evidence of this is needed look at the antler-cable bow.

Antler is not very elastic, especially in tension. But it has very high bend resistance, so it can yield decent draw weight even when made thin enough for proper bending, assuming it is made tension-safe by sinew-backing.

My first contact with antler bows involved the segmented-limb variety. Three split antler segments were splinted together with sinew cordage, then backed with a sinew cable. Knowing that antler was fairly brittle, it seemed likely these bows stored energy largely by hinging, the sinew cable stretching more than the antler bent. Canadian bowyer Don Gardner, who makes these three-segment bows, reports this is only partly true.

Danish Bowyer Flemming Alrune with his caribou antler/whale-sinew cable bow replica. Forty-pounds at 21" of draw, 33" long. Sinew from the beluga whale. Based on circa.100 year-old bows from the Thule district.

Sinew/antler bow by Don Gardner. Three long segments of split caribou antler are splinted and sinew-wrapped. The back cable contains 70 feet of braided sinew.

As an example of this principle in the extreme, imagine a bow belly made of three inch-long segments of wood, antler, horn, or bone. When resting belly-up on a flat surface this rig would look like a normal bow, except for hair-line transverse crack along its belly. Each segment could be tongue-and-grooved where they butt together. Sinew-backed, this "necklace" bow can then be coiled into a small bundle when not in use. When laid flat again, segments snugly butted together, then braced, it will look and shoot like a normal bow. Dr. Grayson recently explained that the 29" Eskimo bow pictured on page 151 of Vol. II is made of six butted segments, which do hinge appreciably.

Any material that will bend and return can somehow be contrived into a bow. In a bind an ungainly but deadly weapon can be made of paneling, lawn furniture, bundled golf club shafts, or sinew-backed dominos. We could easily free ourselves from any B-movie captive scene. Just have the bad guys turn away for, say, twenty minutes, and our hero will convert a bush, or flooring, or mop handle into a credible bow, strung with twisted mattress stuffing, or such.

I once suggested to Jim Hamm that we have a bowmaking contest using the most implausible materials imaginable.

After some thought, Jim blurted, "How about the best bow from a crustacean?"

We both laughed for a few seconds, but then there was dead silence as we thought it through.

You know, shrimp shell is kind of horn-like...

ANDAMAN ISLAND BOW

The outer half of the Holmegaard's limbs were narrowed somewhat. Andaman Island bow tips were even narrower, but for just under 1/3 of limb length. In contrast, inner limbs were wider, and had flat lenticular (lens-shaped) cross-sections to permit such width.

Such wide, flat limbs take about three times more effort to make than an African, South American, or English type longbow. After making several similar bows, even though roughed out with power tools, I'm not eager to make more... and the originals were made with an adze and boar's tooth! The unique side-view profile of these bows — one limb reflexed, the other not — seem inefficient. But tips were narrowed for mass reduction, and limbs were wide and thin for safety, so smart engineering was at work here. An almost identical "S" design was also seen in India and in Southern Africa. The reason for such asymmetrical tiller no doubt makes perfect sense, but not yet to us.

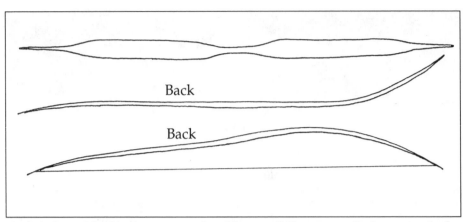

North Andaman Island bow staves were selected from small-diameter trees having a natural reflex in what would be the mid upper limb only. The stave was decrowned, back and belly, creating a wide, flat lenticular — therefore very flexible — finished limb. South Andaman Island limbs were straighter. Longman reported a similar design in the New Hebrides.

The Holmegaard/Andaman principle taken to its logical extreme: red oak board bow; fifty-one pounds at 28". Perfectly rectangular in section, 66" long, 3 1/2" wide at its widest. Limbs are 5/16" wide at the nocks, reaching 1/2" in width 6" from the nocks. Limbs are 11/32" thick at their widest working point, slowly increasing in thickness as they narrow, reaching 1/2" about 7" from the nock, Despite its needle-like tips, this thickness induces "Holmegaard tiller." Due to extremely wide, thin, flat inner limbs, string follow is negligible, despite virtually non working outer limbs. This is a good theory-testing bow, but a lot of work to make.

Like Callahan's Holmegaard replica, the pictured red oak "needle-tip" bow bends mainly in its inner limb. Resulting low string angles contribute to an unusually smooth draw. This design is efficient, shooting about as fast as a 15% heavier weight bow, and with less stack for accuracy. And, as you might imagine, such insignificant outer limb mass yields a shockless release.

JAPANESE

At first glance this design is difficult to justify. It requires more time, effort and skill to make than a simple wood bow, and is more ungainly than a conventional wood or composite bow. And by normal reckoning its too-long limbs should impart slow cast.

Despite its roughly one-inch limb width the tips of a well made Japanese bow can rest more than one-foot forward of its grip when unstrung. The bamboo in these bows was heat-tempered. Even with such long limbs, an untempered belly would surrender much of this reflex.

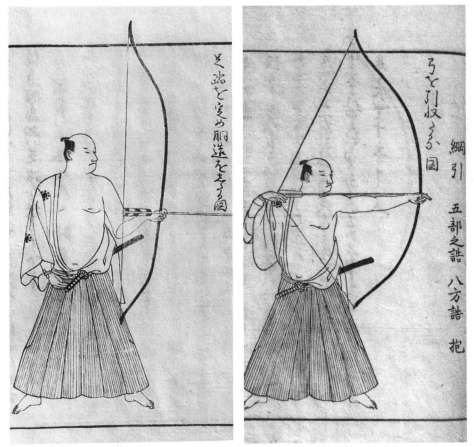

The Japanese bow, braced and drawn. See page 129, Vol. ll. for cross-sections and details of construction. (courtesy Grayson Collection)

But this design, as much as any other, illustrates a law of archery:

Every established bow type is excellent; this will become clear once the design and its use environment are understood.

The Japanese bow is drawn about 36"! Suddenly these "too-long" limbs become efficient. In addition, if shaped by forced-reflex laminate construction, this design might have some of the efficiency-raising features of the Perry reflex.

Its length overcomes short-draw, high-stack, low-cast limitations of other wood-based horse bows. To function on horseback it is a short bow below grip, a long bow above grip. E. G. Heath theorized that the kneeling position of shooting, practiced by early Japanese warriors, initially led to its one-third/two-third grip placement.

Its recurves do not make significant string contact, but do contribute to its several inches of unbraced net reflex. Contact recurves must occupy a substantial percentage of limb length to have worthwhile effect. Such recurves would be unstable on this bow's long, narrow top limb. As is, the design is stable, durable, and untemperamental. Apparently very much so, for it has not changed since the Middle Ages.

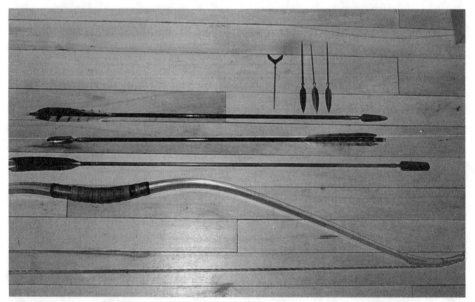

Sixty-five pound replica of a several-hundred year old design from India, by Yumi of Canada. Like the Japanese bow, its back and belly are tempered bamboo (maple core); it is long — 70" — and holds a just-unbraced reflex — 3" in this case. Limbs are only 1" wide. Its setback grip and fairly stiff outer limbs resemble Plains Indian bows. These long, low-mass, reflexed limbs, yield a sweet draw, soft release, stable aim, and high arrow speed.

THE LAMINATED BOW

Before its forty-year coma, induced by the fiberglass virus, American wood-based archery was alive with experiment and invention. The laminated bow was one result.

Very thin laminates will freely bend to any reasonable bow shape. Clamp several glue-surfaced laminates together, to the correct thickness and taper, and bingo, a finished bow of any desired side-view profile. This was economical of wood and time. And as with fiberglass today, a fellow could make a dependable, efficient bow without true bowmaking skills.

A theoretical advantage of this design is that back, core, and belly layers can be selected respectively for excellence in tension, low mass, and compression. In practice, however, same-design laminated and whole-wood bows were reported to perform near equally.

This is gladdening news to a woodbow purist. A bow is derived by natural birth from a tree, not an unnatural creature of unrelated parts. A bow is more than surface form. A Midwest friend has long argued that fiberglass bows can properly be termed "traditional" as long as they are traditional in *form.* The spirit, the special character and imperfection, the beating heart of living wood — none of this matters. For him, form is everything. The fact that fiberglass is about as traditional as the Atomic bomb carries no weight. Recently, while visiting the Bay Area, he asked if I knew a woman friend he could meet while here. I told him I'd have a fiberglass companion laminated up for him. But even when assured she would be of traditional form he seemed to lose interest.

Laminated wood bows of the past may have performed no better than same-profile conventional bows, but there is a way to make them do so: glue central laminates into extreme, exaggerated reflex. Once the glue is set, pull the emerging bow into less extreme reflex before gluing the next back and belly laminates in place, and so on. Final, outer laminates are glued in place to form final intended side-view profile. The progressively more-reflexed interior laminates will be forced to work harder than normally-loafing inner layers. These limbs store more energy, permitting either lower-set limbs, or narrower, lower-mass limbs, or a mix of both.

A NEW DESIGN — THE PERRY REFLEX

This design raises wood bow performance more than any single design element development since the beginning of archery, more than recurving, sinew-backing, or natural, heat-bent, or set-back reflexing. Judging by the enthusiasm of those who have tried it so far, it may become a standard design.

Bowmakers have known for ages that reflexing increases bow performance. But wood bows break, or take a large set, if reflexed very far. Here is a way to safely maintain significant reflex.

Dan Perry of Utah makes bows of bamboo-backed hickory that are faster than any all-wood bows I've tested. The best of them are semi-pyramid shaped, narrow-tipped, and take only about 1/2" or less set immediately after unbracing. Dan reported that despite pulling these bows into two inches of reflex when applying the bamboo backs, they took no more actual set than same-spec straight bows with the same backing. He also reported the limbs seemed thinner than same-spec un-reflexed versions. If what Dan said was true these more-strained limbs were acting as if they were less strained, contrary to common sense. After much worrisome thought the following explanation emerged:

Dan's hickory bellies and bamboo backs were both *drawn,* not steamed, into reflex, then glued. The hickory belly surface was thereby forced into tension, the

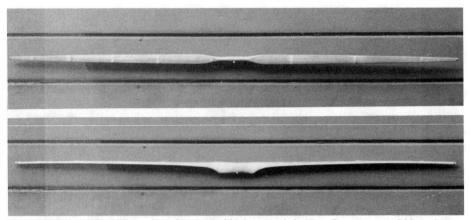

This 58 lb hunting/flight bow of bamboo-backed hickory made by Dan Perry, casts a 500-grain arrow 173 fps, about the speed of a typical 69 lb bow. Its original 2" Perry reflex holds at zero set when first unstrung. Inner-limb energy storage lets these limbs be narrower, thinner, and considerably less massive: 3/8" wide at the nocks, 1" wide 11" from the nocks, 1 3/8" wide near the grip, 3/8" thick at mid-limb.

bamboo back surface into compression, *just the opposite of normal.* Obviously, back and belly surfaces cannot feel normal tension and compression until returned to their straight, pre-reflexed positions.

But considerable effort was needed to bend the finished bow straight again! Where was this energy being stored?

If not in back or belly surfaces, as normally was the case, energy must have been stored inside the limb: as the bow was pulled straight, and beyond, the backing's inner surface tried to shorten, the hickory against it tried to lengthen, *but they were glued to each other and each was therefore forced to resist the efforts of the other.* This resistance increased through the draw. *This design forced the bow to store a good percentage of its energy deep inside the limb* instead of primarily at belly and back surfaces, as with conventional limbs.

This design is easier to understand if you think of it as two bows in one — a bow inside of a bow. The inner bow — the wood on each side of the glue line — begins working early. The outer bow — back and belly surfaces — begins working once straightened out on the way to brace height.

If more energy is stored inside the limb than normally, the limb can obviously be somewhat narrower, or thinner, as Dan noted. If thinner, the limb can bend farther without over-straining — thin wood, after all, can bend farther than thick wood, permitting higher reflex. Greater mass savings result if limbs are made narrower.

Internal energy storage accounts for the low set and high safety of these limbs despite longer limb travel and higher energy storage.

The paradox of this design is that *the farther the back and belly are bent into reflex before being glued together the less back and belly surfaces are strained when drawn.* Just the opposite result when reflex is due to natural, steam-bent, or set-back shape, which forces energy to be stored at back and belly surfaces. Such fixed-reflex bows take much set, or break if reflexed enough to store much additional energy.

To restate: the farther the back and belly are held in reflex before gluing the more they are put into unnatural reversal of tension and compression. The greater this reflex the higher the percentage of total limb travel before limbs are brought straight and back and belly begin to feel normal tension and compression. This results in an ever higher percentage of energy stored inside the limbs, both while being brought straight again, and during the draw. With less energy being stored in surface wood during the draw, less wood thickness or width is needed to reach draw weight at draw length. These thinner or narrower limbs, although bending farther and storing more energy, feel no more surface strain.

There is a limit here of course. A series of test bows, each having progressively more such reflex, are now being tested. We're up to an initial five inches of reflex, which holds almost three inches of reflex when unbraced. This bow draws 48 lb. and shoots a 500-grain arrow 162 fps, about the average speed of a 59 lb. bow. "Pyramid" bows are likely the fastest straight-stave designs. A pyramid version should prove the fastest "Perry reflex" bow. And as with other pyramid designs, should have less stack and less shock.

To get the best of this design it is important not to crudely pull the thicker, belly portion backward before gluing, but to *tiller it backward,* with the same careful attention to proportion as with normal tillering. The bow is then clamped or tied into its reverse-tiller shape and the thinner, bent-into-reflex backing is glued in place.

Because wood is generally stronger in tension than compression, same-wood versions of such bows should have thinner backs than bellies — about one-third to two-thirds. When using stronger-wood backs, drop to one-forth. When applying very strong backing to much weaker wood, drop to as low as one-sixth. Sugar maple on eastern red cedar seems to work best at one-to-four, with one-to-six more appropriate for hickory on red cedar. Doug Walters of South Carolina has successfully made Perry bows, using various combinations of hickory and rock maple for backs, black cherry and red cedar for bellies.

High shear forces are felt at the glue line in this design. Good glue and good gluing techniques are essential here. Use the same standards as when gluing belly to core on Asiatic composites. When using hide glue choose the highest grades, heat all surfaces, size well, bind uniformly, and when done, heat the bow enough to re-liquefy the glue for a moment.

Pulled into 5" of reflex before applying its bamboo backing, this 67" 48 lb hickory bow holds a 2 7/8" reflex. Resulting early-draw weight results in high cast and a speed of 162 fps, but also a surprisingly fluid, low-stack draw.

This bow can be made under near-primitive conditions, so why didn't this extreme version exist before? With such good performance why isn't it a familiar design like the recurve?

The answer may be that the differences between this design and reflexes due to steam bending, splicing, or natural tree shape are not apparent.

Low-reflex versions have occurred in the past. When writing on wood backings Stemmler noted in *Essentials of Archery*, 1953, and Elmer in *Target Archery*, 1946, that applying the backing while in reflex improved cast. But they did not make greater claims than for conventional reflexing. Without understanding that this design paradoxically relieves limb surface stress while seeming to increase it, this design's potential could not be appreciated. Short of this understanding, animal caution would keep such reflexes low: experienced bowyers avert their faces when first bracing and drawing one of these bows, intuitively certain it will blow.

Conventional sinew backing cannot yield much inner-limb energy storage, for two reasons: 1) Sinew has low stretch resistance and is therefore less resistant to tension than wood is to compression. 2) As sinew dries and contracts it pulls wood into reflex, but wood and sinew are glued to each other before this contracting begins, the contracting sinew therefore pulling the wood along with it. As a result, when the limb is drawn little Perry-type interface resistance is created.

Mike Beaven's tillered this elm stave BACKWARD into 9" of reflex, then applied sinew as usual. When dry, tillered, shot, and just unbraced, its reflex maintains at just under 5". To keep the string clear while sinewing the stave was left 4" longer than intended, then reduced to its 62" final length for tillering.

Sinew on low-reflexed wood-based bows has performance-robbing degrees of mass and hysterisis. Reverse-tillering the bow into up to ten inches of reflex before applying sinew at least gives the belly a negative-compression head start, allowing farther limb travel. In addition, when drawn, sinew would be stretched farther, extracting more stored energy per mass.

When braced, these forced-reflex designs look the same as normal longbows. Therefore it would not be fair to, say, spot some unsuspecting soul a mere five pounds of draw weight on a bowspeed wager. Not an unknown occurrence down at the Bowmaker's Bar.

SOME THEORETICAL DESIGNS

Had American Indian archery not encountered gunpowder for a few hundred more years, the Penobscot bow might have turned out to be the first step toward a natural materials "compound." Its small back-bow and cord was likely added to relieve limb stress, or possibly raise early draw weight as with prestressed cable backs.

But this bow can be configured so that as the draw advances its cable winds onto the curving outer limb, lowering the mechanical advantage of the cable. This limb would have greater leverage later in the draw than early in the draw — something of a cam effect.

Which provokes this question: Could very robust F-D curve bows have been made by Neolithic man using only natural materials? Of course a modern compound could be constructed of sinew, horn, wood, bone and linen. But could a simpler design have been made? One more reasonably conceived by pre-technical cultures? Once this thought dawns and one actually sits down with pencil in hand, primitive high F-D designs jostle each other to get onto paper. Here are just a couple:

The first designs running from the pen were simple enhancements of the Penobscot. The barest trace of this ancestry can be seen here: fairly conventional bending limbs are slightly stronger than normal, which added to the cable's resistance causes early draw weight to rise quickly — the first requirement of a superior F-D curve. This bow has a freely hinged siyah, restrained by a sinew cable. Apart from the normal after lift-off advantages of a siyah, during the draw the advancing siyah lowers cable angle, reducing the cable's leverage slowly to zero, further lowering late-draw weight. By adjusting design variables a variety of F-D shapes result, up to and including let-off. Variables are: cable size, cable pre-tension, siyah length and shape, cable attachment position on the siyah, amount of unbraced limb deflex, and brace height.

Because high early draw weight is permitted by later cam action this bow can be highly deflexed. This means only a small portion of the limb's ability to bend is used up bracing the bow, unlike Asiatic composites. This, with the fact that the sinew cable stores a fair percentage of total energy, lets primitive wooden limbs suffice. High-weight or shorter-limbed versions would need wider, rectangular limbs.

The previous bow focused on the Penobscot's cable. This following design focuses on its back bow. In fact, the inner "bow" is thick and non-bending. Hinged siyahs attach at its ends, with siyahs and working back-limbs connected by a strong cord. The back-bow is a thick, "several-hundred-pound" draw-

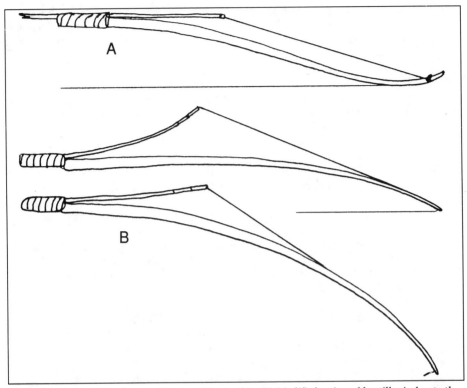

A) The Penobscot Indian bow as illustrated by Laubin. B) Modified so its cable will wind onto the outer limb during the draw.

weight bow, but since limb travel is very short the bow will not be overstrained.

Attaching the cord to the siyah closer or farther from the hinge adjusts the siyah's leverage; this, plus limb strain when braced, and siyah length and shape, determines F-D shape.

Here too, limb lengths and widths must reflect intended draw weight and F-D shape. All but very light-weight versions would be rectangular in section.

The above bows are illustrated by drawings instead of photos because I don't like making "complicated" bows. Testing the parts and principles, to be assured they would work, was enough. Each of us has occasionally tried to explain to a just-doesn't-get-it friend exactly why we love wooden bows. We stammer and sputter on, never satisfied with our explanation, seldom seeing faces light up with comprehension. We fail because language only works when based on shared experience. For us, a bow evokes near-mystical connections with our primordial origins. For those who have this sense, just placing a wood bow in their hands brings understanding. For those who don't, no amount of explaining will do.

Complicated bows are not elemental. They can't transport us back to beginning times. They belong to complicated times. And if beyond the *likely* technical

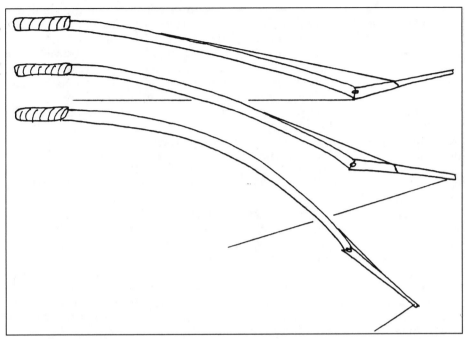

The cable rests at some angle to the limb when braced, creating high early draw weight. But after string lift-off, as the hinged siyah moves more parallel with the limb, the cable angle slowly reduces to zero, the cable, thereby, having ever diminishing leverage against the siyah. Late-draw weight rise is therefore low. The siyah should not quite reach parallel with the limb, easily prevented by a simple stop.

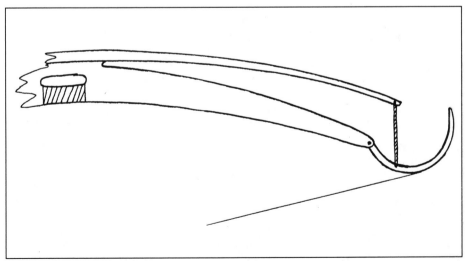

Attaching the cord to the siyah closer or farther from the hinge adjusts the siyah's leverage; this, plus limb strain when braced, and siyah length and shape, determine F-D shape.

competence of a Mesolithic bowyer, in design or construction, the challenge quotient is reduced, the principle objection to the modern compound.

My definition of "abo-legal," my personal self-imposed boundary is this:

The bow is not only made of natural materials, but could have *reasonably* been made by natural, pre-agricultural cultures. For example, sinew-backed recurves and the American composites qualify. The more exotic Asiatic composites, and multi-laminate bows don't, both requiring a complex technical culture.

Someone else might opt for a less severe, "class B" limit: could theoretically have been made 10,000 years ago, "So for all we know it was." Asiatic composites, multi-laminates, and the above "abo-compounds" now qualify. But by this definition gunpowder is legal also. Ten-thousand years ago surface charcoal, sulfur and saltpeter existed. We could have enclosed this mix in a wrapped bamboo barrel, as the Chinese did in the early gunpowder era. But it's not likely this happened.

This is all part of the prime human dilemma: our natures cause us to invent, then we invent ourselves right out of nature. The first bowyer likely noticed dried wood shot faster than green wood. It was good and proper for him to use dried wood. But this impulse for improvement, in all sincerity and innocence, led in time to the present Plasticene Era and the laser sighted compound. Creatures with minds like ours may not remain simply innocent, because we invent ourselves into unhappy circumstances. To preserve our contentment we must be wise innocents, constructing artificial boundaries to the garden lest we stray out of it. A tough job, but that's what adults are for.

KOREAN ARCHERY

Jeff Schmidt

Korea has a very ancient tradition of excellence in archery. The Chinese referred to the people of Korea as

夷

a character comprised of 大 (great)

and 弓 (bow).

This character translates as barbarian but carries with it the implication of Korean prowess with the bow. The pride of this tradition has been carried up to the present time; the Korean palace guard carried bows well into this century, and target archery remains a common recreation today.

Records from the Silla period state that Chinese T'ang emperors attempted to recruit Korean bowyers to learn the secrets of their composite bows capable of shooting 1000 po or 5000 feet. (The old Korean foot is 7/10 of our own. This puts the range at about 1000 yards.) It is unknown whether or not the composite bow spread to Korea from central Asia or was an independent invention. It is clear, however, that Korean ingenuity worked long and hard on the bow, resulting in a design dramatically different from those of neighboring countries and in the end producing a weapon distinctly Korean.

Perhaps the most highly strained of all bows, the Korean composite bow pushed the materials used to their limits. Despite the short length of around 48-50 inches, the bows commonly drew 32 inches, the archer using the thumb lock and an anchor point behind the ear. The reflexed handle and the sharply bent ears or siyahs gave the unstrung bow a nearly circular sweep. Even on heavily used specimens the tips still touched as often as not.

This design differed significantly with respect to other composite bows. The Chinese, Indian, and Middle Eastern bows in general employed limbs with virtually no taper in either width or thickness over the bending portion of the limb. The ridge section and ear remained completely rigid, being thicker than the limb, and underwent almost no bending movement. The Indian type bow, from the Sind region, represented the only one to carry a strong handle reflex, as most composites were nearly straight through the grip. On the other hand, the Korean bow had narrow tapering limbs and bent slightly at the base of the siyah when the bow reached full draw. Most of the bend concentrated in a three or four inch limb section at mid limb, and the ridge section became almost parallel to the arrow at full draw. The narrowness of the limb made this design very sensitive to twisting, and any slight misalignment or mishandling of the bow during the stringing operation could have led to a broken bow (or archer).

Having built over twenty composite bows of most every design from Egyptian angular to Turkish pishrev, I hoped to learn about the limits of composite bow design and so began replicating a Korean bow graciously provided by Dr. Charles Grayson. Because of the unavailability of certain materials, an exact replica of any Asian bow was impossible. Substitutions were made: native mulberry or Osage orange for the Korean wood and Thai water buffalo horn substituted for the horn used by the original Korean bowyer.

Characteristics of the original

Careful study of the original target bow revealed that the horn strips were laid down on a dark bamboo core with the tip of the horn flowing into the handle. The horns had a fine whitish channel or pith near the tip, which was evident next to the bamboo in the handle area. The two horn strips were of slightly mismatched color and texture; one was likely cow or steer horn, the other buffalo. The grain of the cow horn was severely violated, evidenced by the appearance of chevrons or "vees" on the belly, similar to the growth rings of trees and whitish in color. In water buffalo horn, which the other belly strip appeared to be, the homogeneity of the material made them harder to spot. These strips were narrow and flat bellied, with the side next to the wood deeply and unevenly scored. The bamboo was also faintly scored. These grooves did not match up as in certain types of Turkish bows, but served to hold glue and perhaps prevent slippage of the horn as it was wrapped and bound to the core.

A gap of nearly two inches between the ends of the horn strips in the handle was filled with two odd-sized horn scraps loosely fitted together then glued in place. This certainly dispelled the old notion that such spacers in composite bows served as shock absorbers. Where no strain (bending) existed, there was no stress, and the center of the handle did not bend. No doubt this particular bow saw use for years and yet the limb tips still nearly touched when unstrung. Though clearly strained overall to a tremendous degree, the poor fit of these spacers provided testimony to the basic engineering rule above: the handle was meant to be rigid.

The glue joint between the horn and bamboo core was quite close on one limb but rather thick on the other. It seemed likely that this bow was repaired; with one horn strip having been replaced. A marked difference existed in workmanship between the original undamaged limb and the repaired limb. Both horn and bamboo were filed flat on the good limb and merely roughed up prior to gluing. On the poor limb the horn and bamboo were both deeply scored, some cuts being over 1/100 of an inch deep with a drunken meander as they flowed down the limb. Glue and air bubbles were trapped in the grooves, yet the joint clearly held up under use. The average glue joint thickness exceeded 1/100 inch but was everywhere less than 1/50 inch. On the good limb the fit was somewhat better and much more uniform.

All of this investigation revealed an obvious truth: a generous latitude exists in composite bow production. The mystery of the glue and the horn to wood joint often stymies the bowyer who first sets out to build a composite bow. In truth nearly any animal protein glue with low viscosity and fat content will make a fine bow, there is no secret recipe (see Glue, Vol. 1). Composite bows came in varying degrees though, and to produce a durable, highly stressed weapon, the best grade glue was the most desirable. According to the hide glue manufacturers, a wood to wood joint should be no more than a few thousandths of an inch. This may require considerable clamping pressure. On most composite bows, cross-sections showed a thicker glueline, and this Korean bow was no exception. The two materials to be joined should be freshly finished before gluing and heated to aid in the absorption of the glue into the wood pores.

Sinew thickness on this specimen exceeded the horn and core thickness combined. Two separate thick layers were put down to a depth of 3/16 of an inch. Sinew was piled along the side of the bow, and it overlapped the horn by about 1/8 of an inch. Between the bamboo and sinew there was a very thick layer of brown glue, over 1/64 inch thick. When rewetted, this glue had a distinct fishy odor and did not gel up readily when cooled, unlike fish bladder glue or isinglass. It is likely that this glue, used to assemble the bow, was a lower grade fish glue processed with lye. This was evidenced by the fact that the glue had stained the bamboo dark, just as lye used to degrease a bow stains the wood.

The ridge and ear were formed of a single piece of steam-bent mulberry, stained with age where it was exposed to the air. The ear bent very sharply at the end of the ridge and formed a broad spatula-shape tapering to the nock. This was ridged on the belly side, with the ridge straddled by the string loops. This ridge was triangular with a flat back and concave sides. The nock was covered with a green leather nock shoe.

Except for the horn belly, the entire bow was covered with white birch bark laid down with its grain running the length of the bow. Large oval laminated leather pads served as string bridges, covered with green and red burlap. Dark

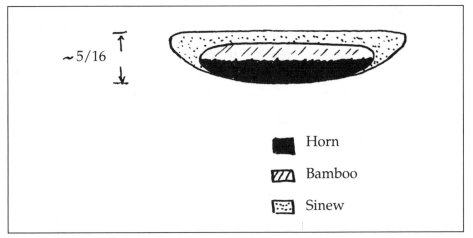

Cross-section at mid-limb.

brown burlap wrap formed the handle which was padded on the belly side with coarse cardboard.

Construction

Lacking mulberry in this part of the country, I turned to fellow composite bowyer John McPherson who provided several beautiful naturally curved sections of Osage orange. This is in the mulberry family but is a bit heavier and more finely grained. It has better color and bends more readily with steam.

Two boards were chopped out and roughed to conform with the ears on the original, and their curve was accentuated by steaming. The parts were about 3/8 of an inch thick, and an hour of steaming followed by bending over forms with ropes and levers resulted in siyahs of just the right curvature.

While these parts dried, a bamboo core 36 inch inches long was cut from a log provided by Tim Baker. Quartered first, the log was cut by machete into shape and filed into a 3/8 inch thick board with a maximum width of 1 1/2 inches. A centerline was drawn, and the strip was tapered to match the limbs of the original. The skinside (outside) of the bamboo was placed against the horn, but the shiny side and dark underlayer were removed down to sound wood. This core was next steamed into a sharp bend at the handle but not as severe a bend as on the original, this in order to follow advice provided by Dr. Grayson in his Volume II article on composite bows. The deep handle curvature was a problem spot on the Korean bow, as it tended to destabilize the weapon. Horn could also become detached at this point. It was thought unwise to copy too closely the original bow in this respect.

Fishtail joints for the siyah ridge and core were next cut about 4 inches long and glued with a high grade of hot hide glue mixed with fish bladder glue. These splices were clamped with ropes and tourniquets to provide sufficient clamping pressure. Next, a reverse riser cut to shape from rock maple was glued down over the curve in the handle on the core's back side. At this step the core was technically complete. A narrow strip of maple 1/4" x 1/8" x 8" was glued down the center of the ridge section, so that this ridge would not have to be built up with sinew.

The horn selected for this project was gemsbok, because of the narrowness of the strips required by such a bow. Water buffalo horn was much thicker and so more waste would have resulted from cutting the strips down to size.

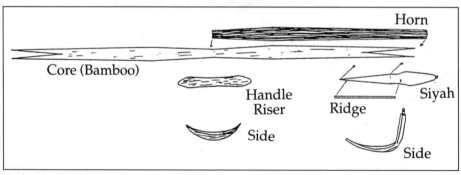

Exploded view of core.

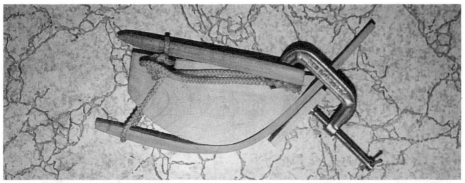

Simple tourniquet for bending the steamed Osage siyahs into final shape.

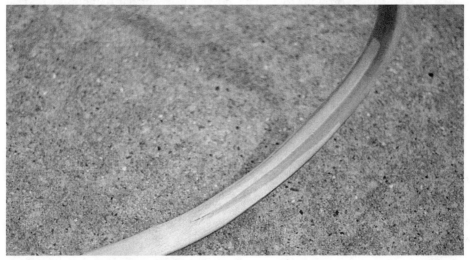

View of the splice of the Osage siyah into the bamboo core. The bamboo was steam bent into shape prior to joining and a narrow ridge glued over the centerline of the splice.

Shape of the siyah is a tapered spatula.

Economic considerations helped select the gemsbok, which was long and narrow and could be quickly cut lengthwise and flattened into strips by clamping and steaming. The flattening process was accomplished slowly with several steamings until two 19 inch strips 3/16 of an inch thick were produced with flat inner surfaces. These were next filed perfectly flat and scored longitudinally but not nearly as severely as on the original bow.

The horn was next joined to the core using a mixture of hide and fish glue. The parts were heated and coated with glue separately then pressed together and spirally bound with rope. At this stage care was taken to avoid any twisting of the limbs. The two inch gap in the center of the bow was filled in with a single carefully cut and curved section of horn clamped in place. The entire assembly was then given two months to dry thoroughly.

Once the core had cured properly, the bamboo was filed into shape. The squared edges were brought to a sharp edge. I learned that bamboo should be scraped carefully to avoid slivers under the fingernails (I can finally laugh about this now). In the original bow, the core was scraped very thin over the entire working limb but was crowned along the centerline of the bow. Average thickness of bamboo should be about 1/8 inch or less and horn thickness about the same. The mulberry or Osage portions of the belly of the siyah were scraped concave and ridged in the center with a curved cabinet scraper. The rest of the limb and ridge were not cut to this thin edge but were left rectangular to keep them more rigid.

At this point the bow was warmed and flexed a bit to check for soundness of all the glue joints. Regluing or even soaking apart and reassembling was preferable to a catastrophic failure such as a siyah stuck in the side of one's head after the bow was completed.

Sinewing a composite bow was much like sinewing any other type of bow. In preparing the sinew, I selected leg and backstrap sinew and hammered the tendons until separate fibers could be teased out. These were sorted according to

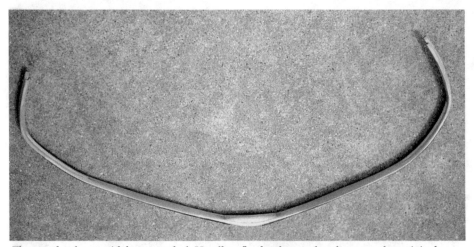

The completed core with horn attached. Handle reflex has been reduced compared to original to make the bow more stable.

The siyah and ridge combination before application of sinew.

their lengths. Very short fibers were used in areas where little or no bending was expected.

The bow was freshly scraped and given a coat of fresh glue. Bundles of glue-soaked fibers were next laid down overlapping one another — first over the handle section and other joints to build up thickness. The author preferred running the bundles through hot hide glue, squeezing out the excess and laying them on the bow, smoothing them down with the fingers. Bundles should be laid down a bit slack over areas of deep concave curvature on the bow, or else they may shrink and lift up later upon drying. Long fibers were laid down over this foundation from one limb end to the other. The bow was then set in a warm dry place to cure for about twelve weeks. After this another layer of sinew was put down over the first and given its twelve weeks to dry. Finally, sinew was laid down deeply on the sides or edges of the limbs, overlapping the horn by about 1/8 of an inch. The back of the bow after being sinewed was no longer crowned, but flat, the edges square. The outer layer of sinew was continuous with no joints.

After perhaps two more months, the sinew was sanded smooth. Sinew bindings over the handle section were added at this time. It seemed advisable to do this after reading Dr. Grayson's Volume II article and learning that Korean archers often had to reinforce their bows in this way.

The exposed Osage siyahs were next scraped smooth and the siyahs cut on the belly side into the concave-sided ridge final shape. The nocks were cut out

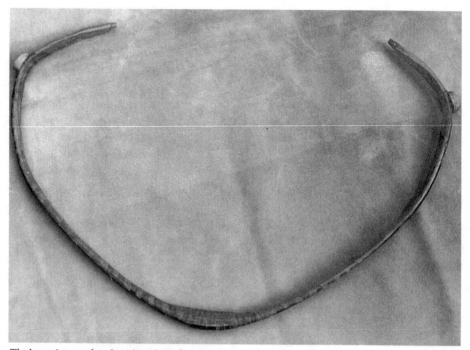

The bow six months after sinewing, showing increase in reflex. The alternating bands are shadows left by the binding of rubber tape wrapped over sinew to hold it in place over concave portions of the bow during curing process.

and sanded, then the horn scraped clean of any old glue or file marks. It was tiller time.

At this point it may be useful to reflect on how the composite bow construction differs from a wooden bow. The most explicit, detailed instructions for making a wooden bow comparable to that just presented for the Korean bow would run like this. Obtain a yew stave. Cut it to 72" x 1 1/4" x 2" deep without violating growth rings too badly on the back. Taper it to 1/2" width at the nocks. All that has been said so far, and all that has been done on the composite bow, over one half years' work and waiting, only gets one to the stage where the bowmaking begins.

To tiller a wooden bow, one removes wood from the belly until the curvature of each limb and the draw weight match the requirements of the bowyer. A composite bow is different. Scraping horn from the belly of the bow is a last resort, and usually has to be tried only if the bow is a near-failure. Horn cannot be put back on if too much is removed. If a wooden bow is overtillered, so what? Toss it aside and start again; a good wooden bow can be made in a few hours or days. Overtillering a composite bow ruins perhaps a hundred hours worth of work and many months of time.

In this case, the author's Korean pattern bow was begun with a core whose limb curvature did not match so tillering would be necessary for the sake of this

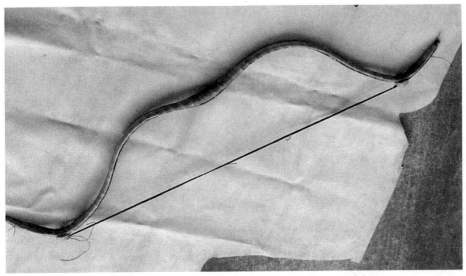

Untillered bow immediately after bracing. Tiller is not off by much.

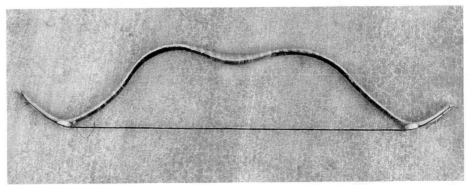

Finished tiller, accomplished by heat and pressure only. Upper limb is at left.

article. However, the tillering job proved trivial because the limbs balanced very well. Examine the pre- and post-tiller photos of the strung bow; they are fairly closely matched. This tiller was achieved by binding the strong limb to a bending form and warming it repeatedly over a single day's period. This enhanced its curvature enough that the two limbs matched afterwards.

The resulting bow had a draw weight of about 55 pounds at 28" draw. The draw length was gradually raised to 32" by drawing the bow many times a day until by small increments the 32" mark was reached. Bringing a bow like this to full draw too quickly could damage the bow; it took a while to equilibrate and settle on to its string.

Nock shoes were made of rawhide soaked in water, then glued tightly to the nock and bound tightly with string to keep from lifting off as the hide shrunk down. Lastly, these were trimmed, sanded, and dyed red.

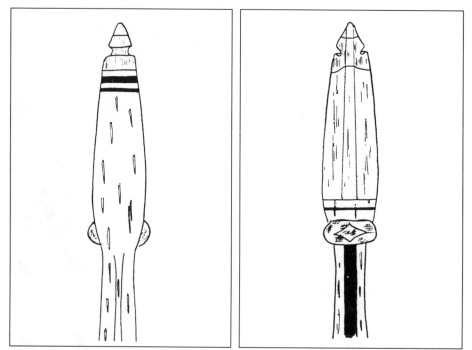

Siyah, back.   *Siyah, belly.*

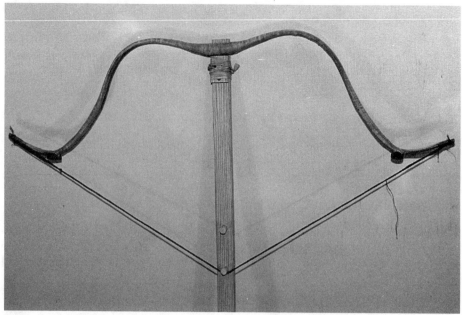

Bow at 2/3 draw. At full draw the limb will be parallel with the arrow.

The Bowstring

The Korean bowstring was made of linen thread. The main body of the string itself consisted of an endless loop skein that had to be long enough to stretch from bridge to bridge on the braced bow. This was made by first measuring the required distance — 34 1/2 inches for a full fistmele brace height of 6 3/4 inches. Linen thread was then wound around two supports this distance apart until the resulting string was reckoned to have a breaking strength of 400 pounds, about an eight to one margin of safety. The very ends of the string were served for about one half inch, and the "middle" near the nocking point was served as well for about 6 inches.

The end loops were tied into the main skein with a pair of modified bowline knots, of a design peculiar to Korean archery. The end loops were made of a similar cord served or twisted over its entire length. The portion that would come into direct contact with the nock was served to prevent abrasion, with the knots themselves barely resting on the bridge or string pad. The string loop straddled the belly ridge of the siyah. String abrasion was further reduced by covering the nock with a soft leather nock shoe as on the original bow. This was glued in place with hide glue and cut to fit.

The unique knot served several purposes. It could be loosened or tightened in order to change the brace height without having to change strings. If a loop showed damage due to abrasion, it could be replaced without replacing the entire string. This particular knot was easy to loosen by pulling on both ends of the loop cord which stick out of the top of the knot. These were normally bound together after the knot was tied.

The string bridge or pad was an essential feature on such a narrow bow. Its purpose was to keep the string from slipping over the shoulder of the bow. This

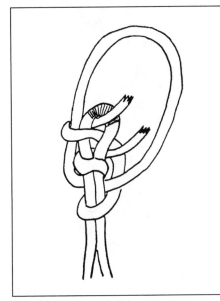

Bowstring loop, exploded.

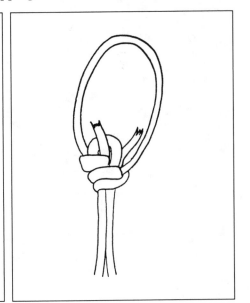

Bowstring loop, tight.

would have almost certainly twisted and broken the weapon. Korean bows were notoriously finicky in regards to twisting, and many were broken when they shed their strings.

The pad on the original was made of laminated leather which resulted in a very stiff but light pad, one that could be made to fit the shoulder of the bow precisely where it was glued in place. Its outer surface was slightly concave, its underside very concave where it rested on the bow's shoulder. The pad was nearly twice as wide as the bow itself at this point of attachment — the site of the bend in the siyah.

In order to tiller the bow, a pair of rough bridges of wood were glued and tied in place. These proved too high to be acceptable as the final bridges and were eventually removed and replaced with laminated leather pads. These pads were held in place with glue only and were covered with red felt and decorated with a green felt diamond in imitation of the original.

Lacking any thick weight leather, copies of the original pads were made by laminating about 10 layers of chrome-tanned leather ovals 1 3/4 inch by 1 inch soaked in hide glue, stacked, and pressed. These were cut to shape and sanded. The width and depth of the bow's shoulder were marked on each, and these portions dug out with a very sharp gouge. They fit extremely well and were glued directly onto the bow with no binding and were later covered with felt after the birch bark was glued in place. The pads made this way were as hard as wood but could be made to fit the bow much more closely.

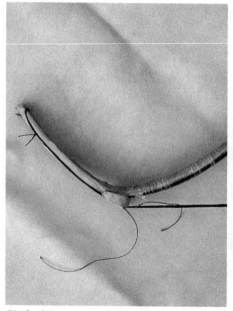

Siyah of strung bow showing placement of leather bridge.

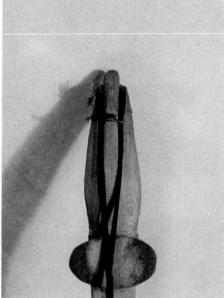

Proper function of the bridge. The string loop straddles the ridge on the belly of the siyah and the knot rests on the bridge.

Decoration

The entire bow was given a waterproof covering. A traditional material for this was willow bark, bound spirally around the bow. The more modern Korean target bows protected the sinew by having birch bark glued directly over it. This was a messy job, but if properly executed was extremely attractive and practical as the bark was virtually waterproof.

On birch, the grain of the bark winds around the tree, not up and down as the wood grain runs. Bark from a long dead and rotted tree was usually in fine condition once all of the outer papery layers had been stripped. At any rate, a tree was supplied for this purpose by a relative, and the bark was removed and peeled into separate layers soon after the tree was cut. It was of sufficient diameter that bark strips long enough to run from grip to each tip were cut. Sound strips with no holes or blemishes 2 inches wide and 22 inches long were cut out and peeled into individual paper-thin layers. The inner surface of each was coated with glue and allowed to dry. Next the unstrung bow was given a coat of hot glue, as were the bark strips which were then bound in place with a long rubber cord. An electric hair dryer was used to heat the bark to reliquify the glue, so that air bubbles and creases could be worked out. This covering extended right up to the nock shoe on the back of the bow and to the string pads on the belly. It covered all sinew but was cut away from the horn which was left exposed along the belly. Once dry (which took months), this bark was oiled or lacquered to further render the bow waterproof.

The handle section also needed to be protected from moisture and dirt from the hand of the archer. The bark itself would get dirty fast, but it is not a good idea to clean a composite bow with water. The belly side of the grip was padded with rough cardboard on the original bow. Homemade paper was easy to prepare with a blender, rag and paper scraps, and a bit of window screen. This was twisted into rope and bound around the handle for a grip. The original bow had a dark brown burlap cover over the paper grip, and this material was easy to find. Another option was to wind the handle with heavy silk cord, and then sew it in place by passing a threaded needle back and forth through the coils. A few black painted bands on the siyah and an inch of fine silk thread windings on each side of the handle finished the bow.

Bindings that reinforce such a highly stressed bow could be made to appear almost entirely decorative, for example, very fine silk thread or braid wound tightly around the limb at the point of greatest curvature. The limb would be coated around its circumference with glue to keep the binding from slipping or unraveling. Some Korean bows had this binding for a few inches on each side of the handle.

Limb Tracking

The Korean bow proved to be a very difficult bow to keep strung. The combination of a sharply angled shoulder and set-back handle made a very unstable bow with respect to twisting. Wide limbs would have helped, but this was perhaps the most narrow limbed composite bow type. When braced and drawn for the first time, the limbs tracked perfectly. When shot into a bale the next day, the bow shed its string and reversed. No damage was done since the joints were wrapped with a spiral binding of sinew. The bow was quickly restrung and checked for alignment. The moral of this story is that alignment must not be good, it must be perfect, or the bow will shed her thread. Wide string bridges would help the problem, but it is best handled by eliminating the cause, imperfect tracking of the string, before drawing the bow.

If a limb on a *narrow* composite bow such as this twists off to the side, it can be corrected by heating the whole bow and tying it to a board, binding down the troublesome limb and overshooting slightly perfect alignment. Leave the bow tied this way for a day or two. If the problem persists, the process must be repeated. This may be necessary every time the bow is strung and prepared for shooting. It is obvious that this Korean design was not meant for war — using such a fickle weapon under adverse conditions would be suicidal. This was a target bow.

Since cast was not a major concern in target shooting, part of the instability problem could be dealt with by bracing the bow a bit higher than normal. Though traditional Korean target competition used a *minimum* of 161 yards, requiring excellent cast, Korean bows were usually seen to have a high brace height in old pictures or photos of actual competitions.

The Arrow

The Korean target arrow was very long and fletched extremely low. The usual length was about 32 1/2 inches with an average diameter of 5/16 inches. It was made of bamboo with thick walls with an inter node spacing of around nine inches.

The nock on a simple target arrow was a self-nock cut into the lower end of the bamboo near a node where the wood was thickest. This was bound with sinew for about one inch, then covered with a very fine layer of parchment glued on and polished smooth. The sides of the nock were about 3/8 of an inch long.

Fletching was three vanes of Korean pheasant about five inches long glued on with no binding at the ends. The nock end of the feather touched the parchment wrap. These fletchings were cut extremely low and tapered to a point or bare quill at the forward end.

The shaft itself was polished considerably and had very little taper. The arrow terminated in a distinctive pile or stop with a square cross-section spike at its center. The front end of the shaft was reinforced with a 1/2 inch wide wrap-around mild steel band hammered tight around the shaft. The entire arrow weighed around forty grams (six hundred grains) but was stiff considering the weight of the bow with which it was used.

Conclusions and well meaning advice

The best reason to build a Korean target bow is because you desire to have one. The bow is beautiful, but like many other things of this nature, it is finicky and difficult to keep in working order. Some of the associated problems can be dealt with by making minor deviations from the tradition design.

To counteract the problem of stability, the string pad can be made wider than normal. A rawhide nock shoe will wear much better than leather since it resists abrasion.

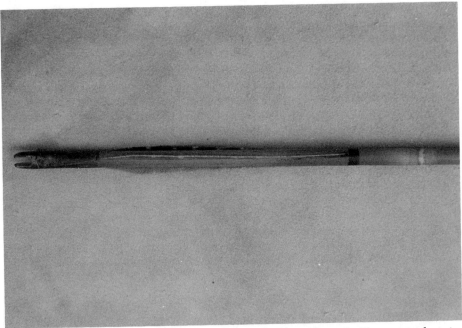

Korean arrow nock and fletching. The nock is sinew-wrapped and covered with green parchment. The fletching is very low-cut and held on by glue alone.

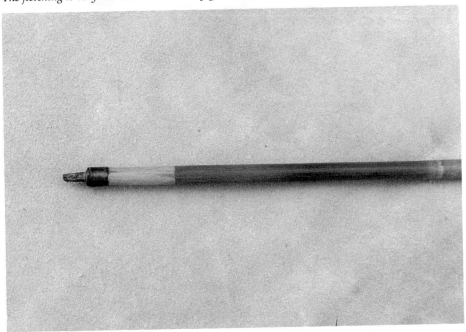

Bamboo arrowshaft with metal target point.

The handle reflex increases twisting problems, lowers brace height, and places undue tension stress on the horn to wood joint. This may be alleviated by slightly reducing handle reflex.

The termination of the horn belly can be bound with a spiral wrap of sinew. This can be hidden under the bark cover and adds to the structural strength of the bow. When strung, any portion of the belly of the bow that is convex could pull away from the core as compressional strains cause that portion to bow outward. Such places occur at the handle and ridge of the bow; binding will eliminate the possibility of the bow popping apart.

A high brace height reduces cast but helps stability by making the bow less likely to shed its string over the knee portion of the limb.

Short siyahs have a lower chance of twisting than do longer ones. This is especially true in the narrow Korean design.

The Korean bow is highly effective, very attractive, and fairly efficient. But the best reasons to build the Korean bow are its appearance and character. Any hope that the design itself holds any secret advantage in the area of cast or accuracy are probably in vain.

The lessons learned here, however, apply to all composite designs, and that alone makes it well worth the time and effort.

PLAINS INDIAN BOWS

Jim Hamm

Few images are so deeply imbedded in the American consciousness as that of a dashing Plains warrior, short bow in hand, thundering across the prairie on his horse. Though the image has a solid foundation in reality, before horses were introduced to North America by the Spanish it was a far different story. The Plains were parched and forbidding to men on foot, with reliable water many days apart. Buffalo lived in incredible numbers but migrated with the seasons, so people whose mobility was limited often couldn't follow, resulting in a classic case of feast or famine. The unlimited buffalo meat was attractive for men who fed their families with the hunt, so forays were made into the heart of the Plains in pre-historic times, but for the most part people lived on the periphery or made only temporary hunting excursions onto the plains.

Bows in those pre-horse days were not in line with our modern impression of a short "plains" bow. In fact, most evidence shows that these early people hunted with various types of longbows! Wooden artifacts only rarely survive from prehistoric times, so intact bows from this period are relatively scarce. Occasionally, however, an unusual set of circumstances preserves a bow from long centuries past, and at least two examples I've been fortunate enough to examine revealed some interesting refinements.

The first was found far out on the Plains buffalo country, in northwest Texas. The Llano Estacado is a vast treeless flatland, whose edges include often spectacular escarpments called the Caprock with springs, shelter, and timber. In the early 1980's, a small rock shelter under the lip of the Caprock was excavated in Blanco Canyon, yielding an ancient skeleton along with an intact bow, stone pipe, arrowshaft smoothers, and stone arrowhead.

I may as well tell you now that I'm less than thrilled when called upon to examine artifacts taken from graves, and invariably decline, although I couldn't resist this bow. But if it was up to me (and of course it wasn't), all of the items would have afterward been reburied with the skeleton, along with some tobacco and cedar.

But the bow is a beauty, and remains one of the most interesting weapons I've ever seen. At 57" long, it just barely belongs in the longbow category, and has almost as much in common with a recurve. With a pronounced set-back at the handle, the natural string follow of the limbs, along with slightly bent tips, gives the bow a graceful gull-wing shape. This alone is unusual enough in a prehistoric weapon but closer study yielded some surprises. The bow has a *round* cross-section. We know now that a rectangular cross-section is best — less prone to breakage and more efficient — and a round cross-section the worst since the forces of tension and compression are concentrated along narrow strips of the back and belly. So it seems remarkable that a highly stressed bow like this would stay in one piece. It speaks well of the bowyer's skill that it not only stayed together, but lasted until the owner's death.

The nocks of this bow are unusual as well, since each tip has two sets! At first glance, it may seem that the bowyer wanted to raise the weight, and so cut the inner set of nocks. And it may have been just that simple, although it must be remembered that a sinew, or perhaps rawhide, string was used on this bow and that such animal fibers are affected by moisture or even changes in relative humidity. The two sets of nocks could be a clever way to allow for string stretch or contraction while keeping the bow braced at the same height, all without having to retie string loops. The inner set of nocks was used in dry weather and the outer set during damp, when the string stretched slightly.

Besides the two sets of nocks, the upper tip of the bow sports an additional enigma. Though broken now, at one time apparently there was a small hole carefully carved at the very tip. Its purpose is pure conjecture, although reminiscent of a hole in the horn nock of an English longbow where the string-keeper is tied. Or some sort of decoration, such as a bundle of feathers, could well have been hung there. Though a mystery to us, it obviously held importance to the bowyer, as he went to considerable trouble to fashion it with stone tools.

This unusual bow holds yet another unique feature. A shallow groove, 1/4" wide and flat on the bottom, runs the entire length of the belly. Its function is unknown, though again the bowyer spent many hours carving it out with stone tools. The closest parallel to it can occasionally be found on late historic Comanche bows, from the 1860's and 70's, where the pith of a small Osage tree was removed, yielding a rounded groove on the belly side. I'm almost certain, first of all, that the prehistoric bow is not made from Osage, although it is so old the wood has become difficult to identify. And this bow's groove does not result from some natural feature, such as a pith, being removed, but was laboriously and carefully carved into the wood. As far as I'm aware, this is the only Native American bow grooved in precisely this way (though some Makah bows from the West Coast sport a groove in the central ridge of a double-fluted belly). The groove's function remains a mystery.

Where did this bow come from? Probably not from the heart of the Plains, where it was found, but more likely far to the west. A case for a western origin comes from Pueblo bows, which were often round in cross-section. Anasazi bows, too, from northwestern New Mexico sometimes had a round cross-section. Slim evidence, perhaps, for the origin of the Plains find, but bear in mind that since prehistoric times the Pueblo Indians have journeyed out onto the Plains to secure a winter's supply of buffalo meat and hides. I have often found broken Pueblo pottery and obsidian (whose nearest source is the Jemez Mountains in northcentral New Mexico) in the sandhills of the Llano Estacado. In historic times, from the early 1700's, Comanchero traders from New Mexico regularly travelled to and set up semi-permanent camps along the eastern edge

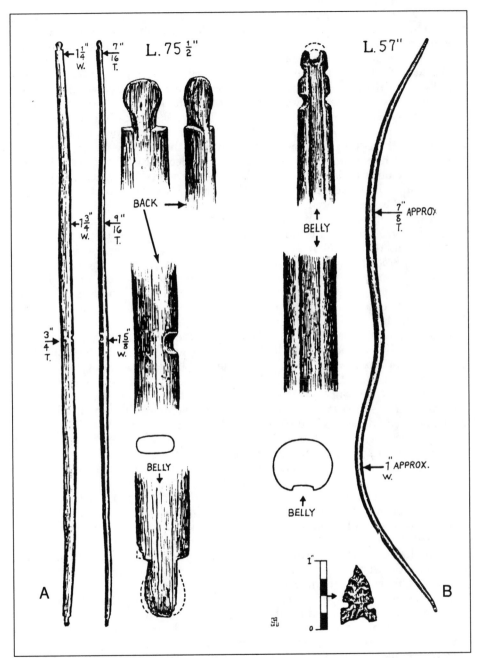

A) Prehistoric bow found leaning against the wall of a cave in Central Texas. (courtesy Mahan collection) B) Prehistoric bow from a rockshelter burial on the High Plains of Texas. Flint point was found with bow. (courtesy Owens collection).

of the Caprock where the ancient bow was buried. Modern Pueblo songs still refer to buffalo hunts and trading out on the Plains. So there were certainly periodic migrations from the west, and it was probably one of these journeys which left the hunter and his bow behind.

The second Plains prehistoric bow may be even more spectacular in its own way than the first, for this one is truly the Meare Heath of North America. A giant of a bow just over 75" long and 1 3/4" wide, it is apparently made from hickory, now covered with tiny age checks. This bow is exceedingly "overbuilt", to borrow a phrase from Paul Comstock. As you would expect from a bow of this design, it has no string follow, though with the massive tips, 1 1/4" wide, the resulting handshock must have made it unpleasant to shoot. Although not optimum by our standards today, the bow clearly served its owner well because the grip area is darkened and smoothed from long years of service. It was designed not to break and it didn't.

Apart from its size, this bow is unique for another reason — an arrow shelf. The finger-sized notch is the only cut-out arrow shelf I've seen on an Indian bow, though I don't think it was put there for the usual reason: consistent arrow placement. Since the bow is 1 5/8" wide at the grip, I believe the wide handle was notched to reduce the archer's paradox and improve arrow flight. Though the bowyer may not have understood modern scientific principles of ballistic dynamics, he clearly had a vast practical knowledge and knew how to improve his arrow flight.

This bow was found in Central Texas, on the eastern edge of the Plains, around the turn of the century. Remarkably, it was found leaning against the wall of a deep cave, which accounts for the slight deterioration of the lower tip while in contact with the ground. One has to wonder why a man would lean his bow against a cave wall and walk away, never to return. Only the most pressing circumstances — or perhaps death — could have enticed the owner to leave his prime means of defense and obtaining food.

It is interesting that both of these ancient bows came to the Plains from outside areas, west and east respectively. But with the acquisition of horses, beginning in the 1500's, Native Americans were finally free to possess the Plains and call them home. No longer were they limited by what they could carry on their backs. No longer could buffalo migrate out of reach. A mounted man could travel further in one day than he could in ten on foot. And he could kill enough food in a day to last his family a year. With the wonderful windfall of the horse, the people began cleverly adapting their ancient weapons to mounted use. War club handles grew longer. Ten to twelve foot lances, copied from the Spanish, replaced short jabbing spears. And, most importantly, the bows were shortened to facilitate their use from the back of a running horse.

Today, some who shoot targets or hunt on foot denegrate short bows as inaccurate and inconsistent, and for their style of shooting what they say rings true. But the short Plains bow cannot fairly be separated from the horse, indeed they must be considered as a single weapon. Native Americans found, as the Persians, Mongols, and Scythians had discovered in Asia long before, that horses and short bows were an almost unbeatable combination. Archery historians may well remember that Howard Hill once killed a buffalo from the back of a running horse with a longbow and a longbow would have served the Plains tribes just as well purely for hunting purposes. But the mounted Indians were fighters and gloried in warfare, just as the Asiatic horsemen before them, and their bows were shortened primarily for military purposes. Few army officers or travellers on the Plains in the early part of the last century failed to express amazement at the riding and shooting ability of the Indians.

Of the Comanches in Texas, W.B. Parker wrote in 1854, "In the saddle from boyhood to old age, he acquires such skill as to realize the appearance of the famed Centaur of mythology. Throwing himself entirely on one side of his horse, he will discharge his arrows with the utmost rapidity from beneath the animal's neck, whilst at full speed, shielding his person by the animal's body, and regaining his seat with no effort except the muscles of the leg."

In 1843, General H.P. Bee also wrote of the Comanches, "On one occasion I accompanied some of the braves on a buffalo hunt, and noticed the skill and dexterity with which they sent the quivering arrow in the sides of the ponderous animals. Their aim was very accurate — rarely failing with the first arrow..."

On the subject of hunting prowess, few would doubt the skill of a Cree described by Rev. John MacDougall in 1862, who, from the back of a running horse, killed sixteen buffalo with seventeen arrows.

George Catlin, in the chronicles of his travels across the Plains in the 1830's, wrote of Blackfeet warriors, "They are almost literally always on their horse's backs, and they wield these weapons (bow and lance) with desperate effect upon the open plains; where they kill their game while at full speed, and contend in like manner in battles with their enemy."

As many of the first explorers and settlers found to their sorrow, the short bow was superior to early firearms for a running fight across the open plains. Texas Ranger Noah Smithwick wrote of fighting the Comanches, "Primitive as the Indians' weapons were, they gave them an advantage over the old single-barreled, muzzle-loading rifle in the matter of rapid shooting, an advantage which told heavily in a charge. An Indian could discharge a dozen arrows while a man was loading a gun, and if they could manage to draw our fire at once they had us at their mercy unless we had a safe retreat."

A U.S. Government report of army surgeons from 1865 to 1871 warns, "Dr. Bill, remarking upon the rapidity with which the American Indians discharge their arrows, states that it is exceptional to meet with a single wound; that if one arrow takes effect it is immediately followed by two or more others. The force with which arrows are projected is so great that... an arrow will perforate the larger bones, resembling the effect of a pistol ball."

The short bow's superiority for mounted combat managed to hold the army and settlers at bay for decades. But in the early 1840's, the Colt's revolver revolutionized Plains warfare and signalled the beginning of the end for its tribes. Though the fights and horrors of both sides continued for another forty years, repeating firearms finally held sway over the so-called "primitive" weapons of the Plains Indians.

Most of the bows and arrows used on the Plains were similar in size — bows 35" to 54" and arrows 20" to 26" — so the major differences from tribe to tribe were in raw materials and decoration. I've always found it difficult in most cases to exactly identify an unknown museum specimen as belonging to such and such a tribe, since there are often more differences between individual craftsmen than tribal differences. It is relatively easy, however, to identify the region a bow or arrow originated due to the materials used.

On the northern Plains, sinew-backed bows were common. Sinew-backing was employed, I believe, because the stronger bow woods were scarce or non-existant. Blackfoot, who lived in Montana and southern Canada, employed ash, cedar, chokecherry, and serviceberry for their short, highly-stressed bows, any of which follow the string less and are far more durable when backed with sinew. Occasionally, however, a bowstave from distant places would find its way to the northern Plains. At least two surviving Blackfoot bows in museums are made from Osage orange whose natural range is a thousand miles away. Lt. Col. Dodge mentions the use of Osage orange for bows during the 1870's, "This wood grows in comparatively a limited area of the country, and long journeys are sometimes made to obtain it." I thought I was obsessive about Osage, but the Blackfoot bowyer who made a thousand mile trek through enemy territory to obtain it has to be the undisputed champion of all time (of course, the Osage orange could well have reached the Blackfoot through trade, but somehow I prefer the notion of the thousand mile trek, a romantic failing which I freely admit).

The most beautifully decorated bow I've had the pleasure to examine is Blackfoot. Only 40" long, it appears to be made from yew. A striped prairie garter-snake skin overlays the sinew-backing, and ermine fur wrapped with dyed quillwork adorns each limb. The handle and each tip are wrapped with the fine bark of a wild cherry tree. The overall effect is stunning. This bow and the matching arrows were purchased by a museum in 1897 for $7.00. The curator was not amused when I offered to double the museum's money.

Composite bows, too, were fashioned on the northern Plains and Plateau by Blackfoot, Nez Perce, Snake, and Crow bowyers. They primarily used sheep-horn, though buffalo horn and elk or caribou antler were also employed on occasion.

Based upon museum specimens from the northern Plains and Plateau, the favorite arrow wood appeared to be red osier, a very strong but flexible species of dogwood. Wild rose, too, grew in profusion throughout the region and was readily employed.

Though Osborne Russell wrote in 1835 of an encounter he had with Snake Indians in northwestern Wyoming, "They are well armed with bows and arrows pointed with obsidian", after about 1850 steel arrowheads were used almost exclusively on the northern Plains. Stone and bone points were clearly effective but were time-consuming to make, so the more durable and increasingly avail-able metal replaced them.

The Sioux, or Dakota as they refer to themselves, lived in present day Min-nesota, North and South Dakota, eastern Montana, and eastern Wyoming. In addition to the ash and cedar growing on the Plains, this tribe had access to hardwoods from the forests of Minnesota, and often made their 40" to 48" bows from hickory, white oak, and black walnut. About half of their bows were self bows and about half were sinew-backed, with rawhide occasionally glued over

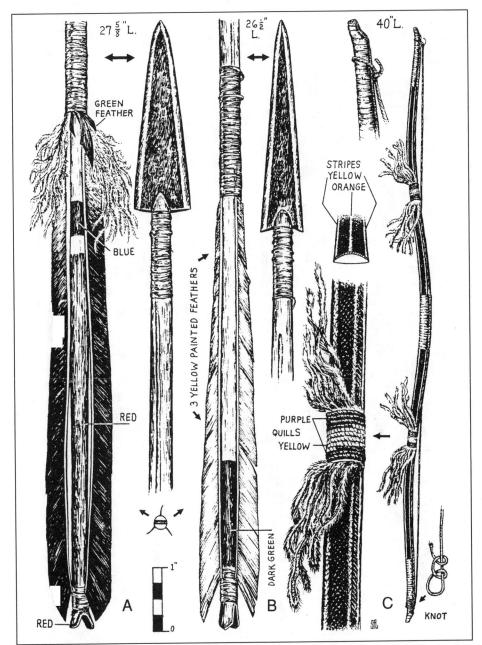

Blackfoot: A) Grooved Red Osier Dogwood shaft, mature golden eagle wing feathers split, no glue, goes with bow "C". (Field Museum) B) Grooved shaft, yellow painted feathers split and glued. (Milwaukee County Museum) C) Sinew-backed bow covered with Western Garter Snake, porcupine quillwork over ermine fringe, tips and grip wrapped with cherry inner bark. (Field Museum)

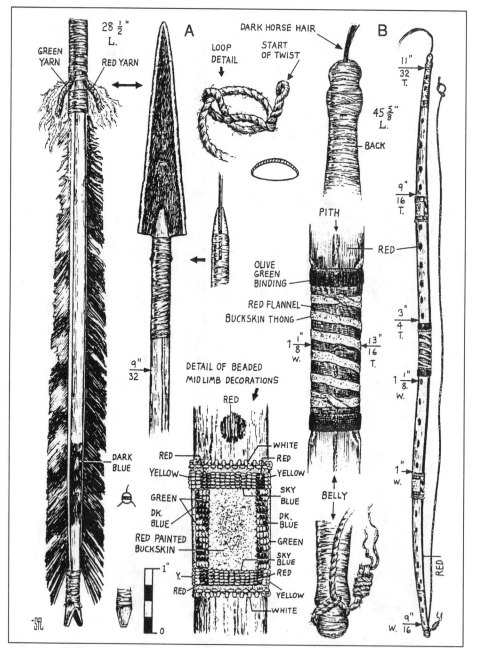

Montana, Blackfoot or Crow: A) Arrow fletched with two hawk feathers and dark feather used as cock feather, blue, red, and green yarn wrapped with front sinew binding, original point tip broken. B) Sinew-backed chokecherry bow with pith visible in belly, belly painted vermilion red, dime-sized vermilion spots on back, beaded panels at mid-limb. (The High Desert Museum)

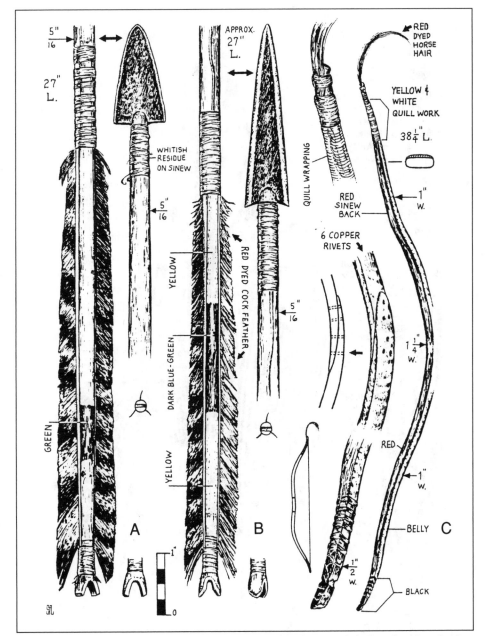

Nez Perce: A) Two turkey wing feathers with turkey tail feather as cock feather, fletching glued, no shaft grooves. B) Two turkey tail feathers and red dyed cock feather, shaft grooved. (arrows from Nez Perce National Historic Park) C) Sinew-backed sheephorn bow, limbs riveted together at grip, deep cross-hatches cut in back of horns for sinew-backing, handle was likely wool stroud cloth with buckskin lash over it. (Horner Museum, Oregon State University)

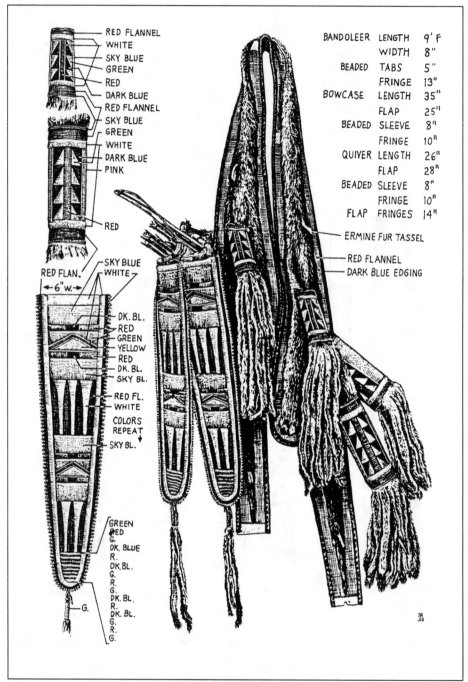

RED FLANNEL
WHITE
SKY BLUE
GREEN
RED
DARK BLUE
RED FLANNEL
SKY BLUE
GREEN
WHITE
DARK BLUE
PINK

RED

RED FLAN.
← 6" w. →

SKY BLUE
WHITE

DK. BL.
RED
GREEN
YELLOW
RED
DK. BL.
SKY BL.

RED FL.
WHITE

COLORS
REPEAT

SKY BL.

GREEN
RED
G.
DK. BLUE
R.
DK. BL.
G.
R.
G.
DK. BL.
R.
DK. BL.
G.
R.
G.

G.

BANDOLEER	LENGTH	9' F
	WIDTH	8"
BEADED	TABS	5"
	FRINGE	13"
BOWCASE	LENGTH	35"
	FLAP	25"
BEADED	SLEEVE	8"
	FRINGE	10"
QUIVER	LENGTH	26"
	FLAP	28"
BEADED	SLEEVE	8"
	FRINGE	10"
FLAP	FRINGES	14"

ERMINE FUR TASSEL

RED FLANNEL
DARK BLUE EDGING

Nez Perce quiver and bowcase. (courtesy Steve Honnen Collection)

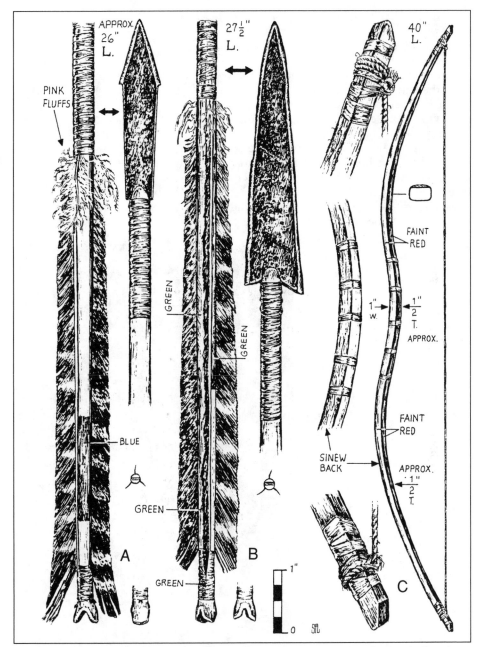

Sioux: A) Mixed turkey wing and tail feathers, split and glued, unusual steel point. (Milwaukee County Museum) B) Eagle and turkey feathers mixed, large iron point, belonged to Chief Crow Eagle of the Two Kettle Sioux. (High Desert Museum, Doris Swayze Bounds Collection) C) Sinew-backed hickory, wrap-on sinew nocks, wood stained red. (Panhandle Plains Historical Museum)

the sinew to help protect it. The backing or even the entire whitewood bow was often painted red. Horsehair, natural white or dyed red, sometimes adorned the upper tip of a bow.

Nocks were either cut directly into the wood or built up from sinew wrapped around the tips. Jim Welch, a modern Sioux bowyer from Minnesota, sometimes dyes the sinew wrapping for the tips of his bows in blueberry juice, yielding a beautiful, natural decoration. Jim advises that his people even made static recurves, complete with belly grooves for the string, as in one oak museum specimen which he examined.

The Dakota also made 36" composite bows, from elk antler, cow horn, or even buffalo ribs. The horn or antler was usually overlapped and spliced at the handle (one bow had the two sections of cow horn belly overlapped and held by three rivets), then heavily backed with sinew. A rib bow was another matter, a section of rib being too short to make half a bow, so the sections of bone must have somehow been held together. One possible way to accomplish this was by

Sioux Jim Welch shooting one of his sinew-backed bows.

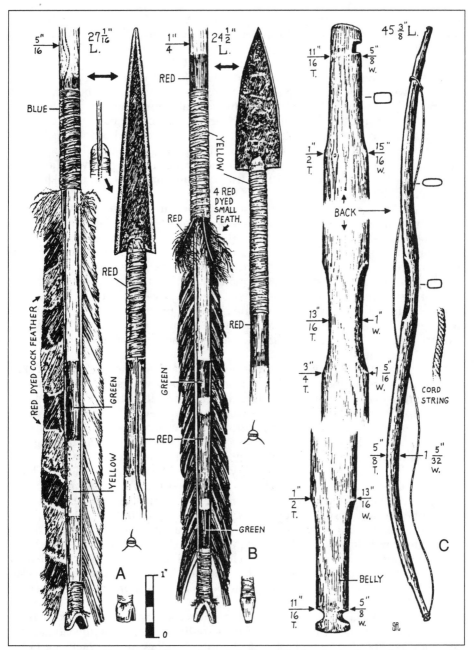

Sioux: A) Hawk and buzzard feathers split and glued, cock feather dyed red, two shaft grooves. B) Buzzard feathers split and glued, no shaft grooves. C) Hickory self bow, handle offset about 1 1/2", bow and arrows all belonged to Chief Crow Eagle and go with quiver and bowcase (next drawing) on the right. (High Desert Museum, Doris Swayze Bounds Collection)

gluing the ribs to a wooden core, then backing the core with sinew, the way most Asiatic composites were made (see Composite Bows, Vol. 2). Sadly, no rib bows have survived to modern times, so we may never know for sure how they were constructed. These prized composite bows, whether antler, horn, or bone were usually heavily decorated with horsehair, dyed cloth, quillwork, or beadwork.

Strings were made from the standard reverse-twisted sinew, but Jim Welch says the Sioux also used long strips of rawhide cut from a snapping turtle's neck as it was not as affected by moisture. The inner bark of the basswood tree was also twisted into strings, Jim states, and though dampness did not affect them, they were made larger because basswood is not as strong as animal fiber. A loop was sometimes plaited into one end of the string, not to go over the nocks directly, but for the other end of the string to pass through forming a slipknot, preferred by the Plains tribes.

Most of the Sioux arrows I've examined were made from Red Osier Dogwood, but Jim reveals that his people also employed phragmites reed with a hardwood foreshaft. On rare occasions they even made shafts from long splinters split from logs of conifers such as pine or fir. These shafts were drilled at the front and fitted with a hardwood foreshaft, much as a reed arrow was made. But the vast majority of arrows were made from shoots such as dogwood, and most of these were grooved (more about these grooves later when we discuss arrow making). Sioux archers shot arrows with a pinch grip of the thumb and forefinger, so most arrows were made with a bulbous or raised nock to aid the grip and release. A few arrows had a length of sinew wrapped below the nock in lieu of a wooden bulb.

After cresting with pipestone red, blue clay, charcoal black, or yellow ochre, Sioux arrows were fletched with hawk, eagle, turkey wings, or goose feathers. They were usually glued down, though if not, the feathers were sometimes wrapped with sinew at the center as well as at each end. The point end of the shaft was usually tapered somewhat before the steel arrowhead was attached.

Modern archeology at the Little Bighorn Battlefield has revealed some surprises. Contrary to popular mythology, the Sioux and Cheyennes who faced Custer and the 7th Cavalry were mostly armed with bows, not rifles as Hollywood would have us believe. After the battle, "thousands" of arrows were noted on the battlefield. Though the Native Americans did possess a hodgepodge of firearms, most of the damage they inflicted resulted from their arrows.

The Cheyennes made 42" to 54" bows from juniper, cedar, and ash, all of which grew in their territory. They often sinew-backed these woods so the bows could be shorter and more durable. Heat bending the bow into a gull-wing shape — reflexed at the handle with the limbs deflexed — was a common practice. The Cheyenne also made composite bows from sheephorn heavily backed with sinew.

Osage orange did not exist in the Cheyenne's country, but they discovered it grew to the south in the homeland of their traditional enemies, the Comanches and Kiowas. About 1836, in eastern Colorado, the Cheyennes attacked a group of Kiowas from western Texas. To protect the women and children quirting their horses toward the sheltered timber of a creek, the outnumbered Kiowa warriors mounted a desperate rearguard defense. One man in particular, riding

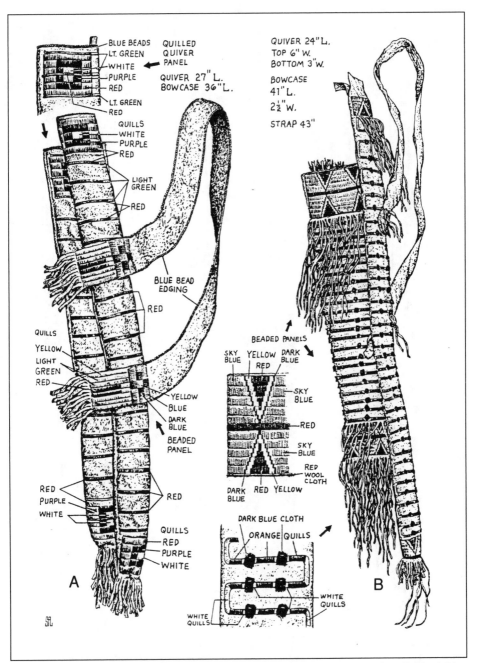

Sioux: A) Quilled buckskin quiver and bowcase. (Field Museum) B) Beaded and quilled buckskin quiver and bowcase, dark blue cloth patches from U.S. Army uniform, belonged to Chief Crow Eagle. (High Desert Museum, Doris Swayze Bounds Collection)

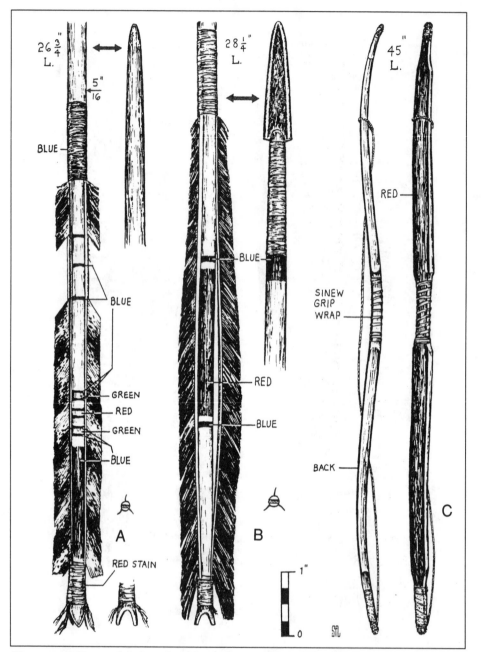

Cheyenne: A) Dogwood shaft, turkey wing feathers stripped and glued, feathers cut out where they lay across bow. (Museum of the Southern Plains) B) Buzzard or eagle feathers split, no glue. (Robert Ranley Collection) C) Sinew-backed hickory, backing stained solid red, narrowed handle and tips. (Smithsonian Institution)

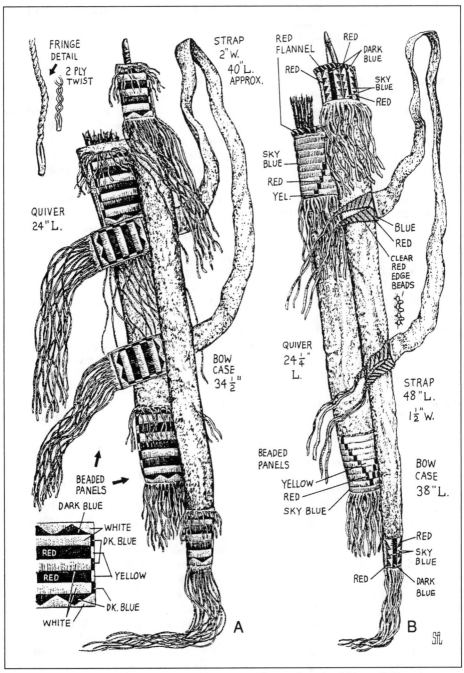

FRINGE DETAIL
2 PLY TWIST

STRAP 2" W. 40" L. APPROX.

QUIVER 24" L.

BOW CASE 34½"

BEADED PANELS

DARK BLUE
WHITE
DK. BLUE
RED
YELLOW
RED
DK. BLUE
WHITE

A

RED FLANNEL
RED
RED
RED
DARK BLUE
SKY BLUE
RED

SKY BLUE
RED
YEL.

BLUE
RED
CLEAR RED EDGE BEADS

QUIVER 24¼" L.

STRAP 48" L. 1½" W.

BOW CASE 38" L.

BEADED PANELS
YELLOW
RED
SKY BLUE

RED
RED
SKY BLUE
DARK BLUE

B

Cheyenne: A) Beaded buckskin quiver and bowcase with two-ply twisted fringe. (Milwaukee County Museum) B) Beaded buckskin quiver and bowcase. (Robert Ranley Collection)

a white horse, charged the Cheyennes time after time to disrupt their attack. Finally, during one of his reckless charges, the Kiowa was shot with an arrow and fell from his horse. Among his captured weapons was a bow made from yellow wood, Osage orange, which the Cheyennes did not recognize. Four years later, in 1840, the Cheyennes and Arapahos made lasting peace with the Comanches and Kiowas, and finally began obtaining Osage orange occasionally in trade.

Preferred arrow woods were red osier, chokecherry, currant, and rose, approximately in that order. Turkey wing feathers were normally used for fletching. In fact, one interpretation of the sign-language term for Cheyennes — one hand indicating striped marks up the other — is in reference to the striped black and white turkey feathers on their arrows. But buzzard, hawk, or any other type of large feather would be employed if turkey was not available.

On the southern Plains, Comanche and Kiowa bowyers invariably used Osage orange. Of the several dozen old bows I've examined either in museums or still belonging to Indian families, every single one is Osage. This wood grew on the eastern edge of their territory so it was readily available. And it was such a strong, durable bow wood that not one of the old bows I've seen was sinew-backed.

Lengths of Comanche bows ranged from a low of about 40 inches, which could have been a child's bow, all the way up to 54 inches. These bows are deceptively simple: rectangular in cross-section, widest at the handle, and a "D" tiller which bends slightly in the handle. But closer inspection shows that the bowyers carefully removed the sapwood and worked down to a single growth ring of heartwood, allowing extra strengthening wood for knots. And the bows were often slightly set-back at the handle, with the tips gently recurved. Comanche bowyers knew their business, for their weapons were simple, durable, and deadly from horseback.

Nocks were usually, but not always, cut only on one side of the upper tip, probably so a string with a slipknot, which they preferred, would be easier to unstring. The lower tip sometimes had a single nock as well, though two were just as common. In most cases, the very end of the upper tip had the added feature of a carved protrusion of wood which served as a base to tie a tuft of horsehair, dyed red, as decoration. There was rarely any other adornment, not even a leather grip, but a couple of exceptional bows were incised on the belly side, then the grooves painted.

Comanches used dogwood almost exclusively for their arrowshafts. It is easy to identify in museum specimens due to the smoothed-over knots left from tiny alternating side branches. Their arrows ranged in length from 20 inches to about 26 inches, with bulbous nocks larger than the shaft, and the point end often tapered down. Arrows were usually painted with simple bands of red, black, or blue, the dark bluish-green coming from laundry bluing, used among the frontier settlers to whiten their wash. Sometimes the sinew wrappings of feathers and points were painted as well.

The fletching of choice was tail feathers from an eagle, hawk, or buzzard, though feathers from almost any bird would be used if nothing else was available. Feathers from any bird but an owl. They were never used for fletching by the Comanches, since owls were thought to be spirits or ghosts. In fact, for this reason owl feathers were virtually never used on the Plains, as modern Sioux,

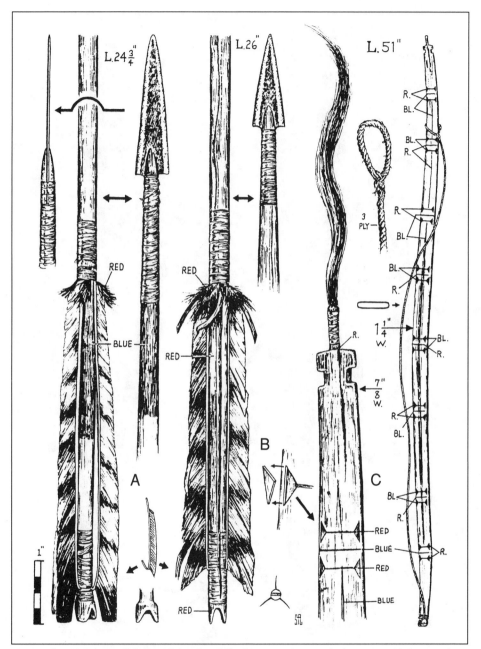

Comanche: A) Dogwood shaft with hawk tail fletching, no glue, no shaft grooves. B) Dogwood shaft with hawk tail feathers, three shaft grooves. (arrows from Panhandle Plains Historical Museum) C) Osage orange bow with rare incised and painted designs on belly. (Fort Worth Museum of Science and History)

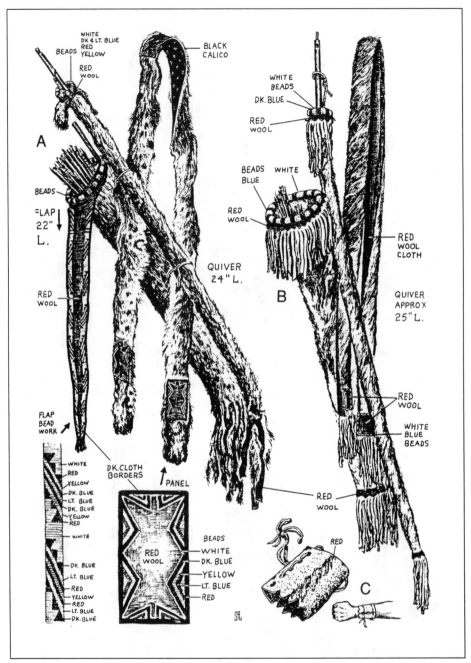

A) Kiowa mountain lion quiver and bowcase. (Milwaukee County Museum) B) Comanche quiver and bowcase of brown and white cowhide with hair left on. (Panhandle Plains Historical Museum) C) Comanche buckskin armguard, stained red. (Smithsonian Institution)

"Man on Cloud", Comanche, circa. 1875. Note horsehair tuft on Osage orange bow and mountain lion quiver. (courtesy Panhandle Plains Historical Museum)

Kiowa, and Comanche informants are quick to point out. Owl feathers were too soft and too easily crushed and distorted in a quiver to make durable fletching anyway.

Comanches were among the first to acquire metal for arrowheads, due to trading with the Spanish Comancheros from the Santa Fe area or raiding down into Old Mexico. From about 1700, they stopped using stone or bone for points and switched to the readily available metal. Modern Comanches smile about the "mean arrows" their great-grandfathers used to make in the old days, which consisted of notched, barbed metal points wrapped with sinew around only one notch. This was so when an enemy tried to extract an arrow, the sinew would turn the arrowhead sideways in the wound and make it impossible to pull out.

Any modern bowyer should be able to duplicate the bows from these Plains tribes without great difficulty, but the arrows are another matter. Matched, well-made arrows built from scratch take time, even more time than bowmaking, but the end result is ample reward — whether they are for display or actual use. I often deer hunt with arrows made for my draw length (28") based on Plains raw

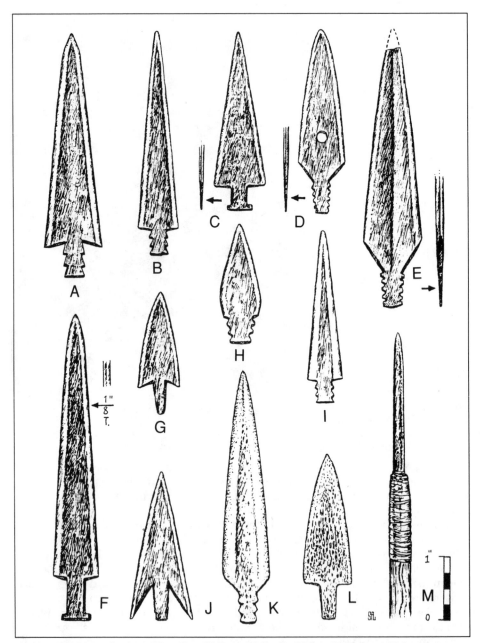

A) Sioux. B) Iron point from Wyoming. C) Excavated at Ft. Union, N. Dakota. D) Iron point from Wyoming. (Stewart Collection) E) Forged iron point, possibly from Custer Battlefield. (Stewart Collection) F) Heavy iron point, Northern Plains. (Wallman Collection) G) Iron point, Wyoming. H) Kiowa. (Grayson Collection) I) Southern Plains. (Petrie Collection) J) Iron point, Wyoming. K) Bone point. L) Sioux bone point. (Miles Collection) M) Hafted iron nail.

materials and fletching techniques. They fly perfectly from a medium weight bow, fifty pounds or so, and have never failed to impress the deer.

The arrow begins with the shaft, and I've often thought that once the shaft is complete, the arrow is three-quarters finished. Cut dogwood shafts in the winter because they split badly if cut in the summer. Be choosy when collecting shafts — take only the straightest available as it will make your life much simpler during the reduction and straightening process. The best shoots, whether dogwood, rose, or viburnum, normally grow in the shade where reaching for the light makes them longer and straighter. Once a quantity are cut (several inches longer than the finished arrow), straighten them as much as possible by hand then tie them into bundles, butt ends together, and let them dry for a couple of weeks. Don't wait too long to reduce them, as totally seasoned dogwood is even denser and harder to work than Osage orange, and will sour you forever on making your own arrows from scratch.

When the shafts have dried somewhat, remove the bark with a knife and select ten at a time to work through the following process. Reduce the shafts in diameter with a small block plane, set fine, or a Surform plane. To ensure that the shafts are of the same diameter throughout their length, and that all of the shafts in a set are the same, drill a hole in a block of wood slightly larger than the desired finished diameter of the shaft. This oversizing allows for wood removed during sanding. Beginning at one end, reduce the wood with the plane, then test it in the hole. Where the wood hasn't been reduced enough it will bind up, leaving marks on the shaft which tell you where to continue removing wood until the entire shaft is the same size. The plane removes high spots and knots, leaving the completed shaft with parallel sides, though it will not be straight. If you wish to leave a raised nock, as was found on most Plains arrows, leave the end of the shaft larger, then shape the nock end with a fine rasp. When ten shafts are reduced, sand them carefully with 220 grit sandpaper only, then straighten them as much as possible, bundle them again and set them aside for a month or so to allow them to dry further.

When they are seasoned, next comes the mystical grooving of the shafts. I say mystical with tongue in cheek, because so much misinformation has been written over the past hundred years about grooving arrows. They were blood grooves, some say, designed to make an animal bleed more freely. Others insist they represented lightning and so were "ceremonial" — the fall-back position when an anthropologist or writer hasn't a clue. Some have theorized that the grooves somehow relieved stresses in the wood and so hypothetically helped keep the shaft straight. This last group was getting warm, but without long practical experience combined with the theories, one cannot hope to solve the riddles of archery.

Being personally short on theories but fairly long on experience, I finally discovered — accidentally — why arrows were grooved in the old days and why arrows made from shoots today should be grooved, as well. For the first decade of arrowmaking, I always put three grooves in arrows for appearances after they were heated and straightened three or four different times, but was in the dark as to why Native Americans went to so much trouble. And then one fine afternoon I grooved a set of arrows as soon as they were sized, then greased and heated them for the tedious straightening process, which normally took several days. The next morning, when I returned to heat and straighten the shafts yet again, I found it wasn't neccessary, that the arrows had miraculously stayed straight and true as never before. I felt like a cartoon character when the giant lightbulb clicked on over my thick head. *The grooves keep the shaft straight if they are heated.* Ridiculously simple, as the most useful discoveries usually are, but here's how it works. Heating wood hardens it, so the ridge on the edges of each groove is exposed to more straightening heat and gets hotter, and harder, than the surrounding wood. These harder ridges, six of them if using three grooves, help prevent the shaft from warping. No wooden arrow stays perfectly straight indefinitely, but arrows made from shoots, if treated with grooves then heated and straightened as described, will be almost maintenance-free and stay remarkably true. This is why 90 percent of all Plains arrows were grooved (and probably half of the West Coast arrows).

Once straight, sand the shafts with 400, then 600 grit sandpaper. Dogwood makes a particularly pretty shaft because its density allows it to take on such a high polish during this sanding. Three hacksaw blades taped together works well for cutting nocks, which can then be shaped or enlarged with a razorblade knife. Be certain to round off string-damaging sharp edges.

Before fletching, paint any cresting on the shaft. You can fashion paint from charcoal or ground earth pigments with hide glue or the juice from a prickly-pear cactus used for a binder. Many old arrows were painted with water colors obtained from traders, and the modern powdered tempra paints are very similar. Water-soluble acrylic paint, available in hobby shops, comes in earth tones, also making it a substitute for natural pigments. Personally, I dislike modern electric colors on arrows handmade from scratch, preferring the old-time colors which lend an authentic look.

By the time you cut, season, reduce, groove, straighten, sand, nock, and paint a shaft, you'll see why at this stage you're already three-quarters finished with the arrow.

Fletching, though not all that time-consuming, is tedious and difficult to get perfect without some practice, but keep in mind that even a less than exact

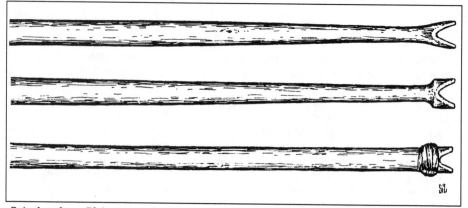

Raised nocks on Plains arrow shafts to aid in a pinch-type release. The bottom shaft is wrapped with a sinew thread.

fletching job will fly surprisingly well out to twenty yards or so. Like a plumber with a leaky faucet, my practice arrows are normally just short of pitiful, with feathers ragged and half missing. But they still fly surprisingly well. The point is not to become discouraged if your first attempts at hand fletching yields less than perfect results, vow to improve in the future while taking comfort that the arrows are still quite functional.

Almost all feathers, wing or tail, can be split along the central groove in the rib with a sharp knife, then the rib scraped or otherwise reduced and made uniform. A small one inch belt sander is ideal for carefully grinding feathers. Turkey wing feathers, which are both excellent fletching and legal to possess, are the one exception to this splitting and grinding technique. Strip these from the small end by squeezing the rib and narrow side of the feather with a thumb and forefinger, then grasp the vanes of the feather on the wide side with the other hand and pull both away and toward the base of the feather. This takes some practice and you will undoubtedly destroy some feathers at first. But a feather can be stripped in less than ten seconds, and it is ready to place on the arrow without any further preparation, which is far easier than splitting and grinding.

Once enough feathers are prepared to fletch the arrow set, trim the vanes with scissors to finished length while leaving the entire spine intact. Most Plains feathers were about six inches long, though I trim mine slightly shorter so they

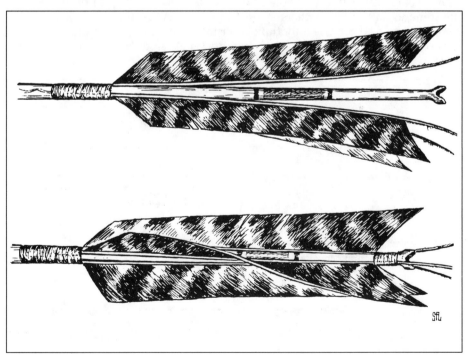

When gluing down feathers, wrap them at each end with sinew as shown, run a bead of glue under the feather, then pull the feather tight using the extra quill at the back of the arrow. When glue is dry, trim off extra quill.

will not touch a bow when hunting. At this stage, don't worry about the height.

If the feathers are to be glued, and sixty to eighty percent of originals were, then secure the front of the feather first. With a finely stripped thread of pre-soaked deer back sinew, take a couple of turns around the arrowshaft where the front of the vanes will lie. This secures one end of the sinew. Lay one of the feathers on the shaft at right angles to the nock for a cock feather, then make a turn or two of the sinew over the feather's spine to secure it. Add the remaining two feathers in the same way, making sure to space the feathers equi-distance apart. Holding the shaft in the crook of a knee and the end of the sinew between the teeth frees the hands when arranging feathers and wrapping the ends. Smoothly wrap the sinew forward over the spines until you get close to the end of the thread. Carefully trim the spine of the feathers at a taper, wrap the ends with the remaining sinew, then pull the tip of the sinew back under the previous wrap. This leading edge of sinew and feathers *must* be smooth and neat, as an arrow shot without a rest, as were all of the originals, will nick the bow hand if there are protrusions or rough places.

Secure the back of the fletching in exactly the same way as the front. Most Plains feathers were laid on straight, though slightly offsetting the backs of the fletching in relation to the front adds a helical twist to the feathers and makes the arrow spin in flight which aids accuracy. When the back of the feathers are being secured, after every couple of wraps of sinew gently pull on the ends of the spine to flatten the feathers against the shaft. When the sinew wrapping is complete and tied off, use a toothpick to run a thin bead of hide glue under the spine of each feather. Or use a small fine-tipped brush to "paint" hot liquid hide

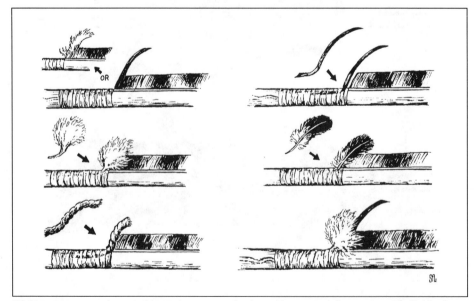

Plains arrows were decorated in various ways, the decorations as much a matter of individual choice as tribal affiliation.

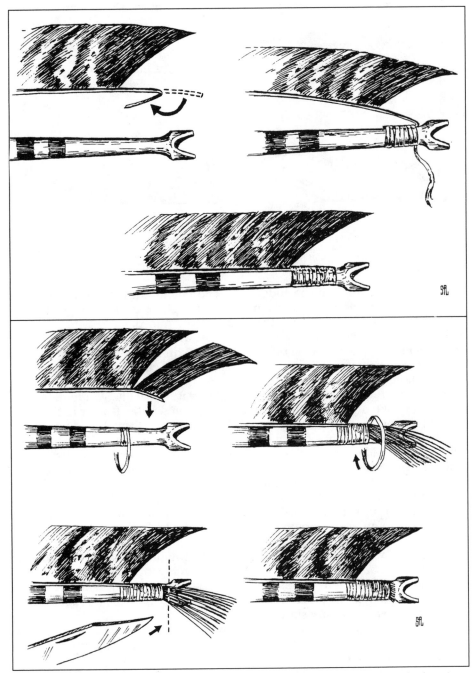

Two methods for locking down the back of the feather so it can't pull loose when the fletching is not to be glued.

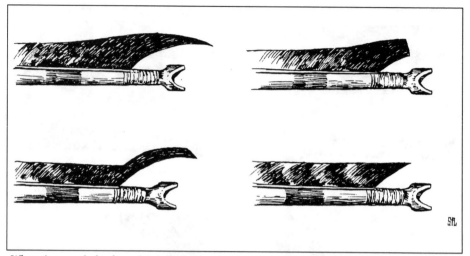

When sinew and glue have dried, the feather can be trimmed to individual tastes.

glue under the quill. You can fudge a bit and employ fletching cement so the feathers won't be affected by moisture. When the glue has dried, the remaining spine of the feather protruding at the back can be trimmed.

Attaching feathers without glue is the most difficult type of fletch. In most cases after some time the spine pulls up and away from the shaft due to contraction and expansion from temperature and humidity changes. Several methods can help keep the fletching in place.

Lock down the back of the feather by folding it over while wrapping it with sinew, as shown in the drawing. By securing one end of the feather in this way, half of the movement problem is solved. You can also cut small grooves around the shaft where the front sinew wrapping lies, which gives the binding a better grip. A dab of hide or pitch glue under the front binding helps keep fletching in place, as well. Soaking feathers in warm water prior to fletching is a good trick, as it allows them to stretch further initially and stay in place better during humidity changes. Ishi often soaked his feathers, but Steve Allely has taken the method a step further and employs a steaming kettle to treat his feathers prior to attaching to an arrow. Some or all of these methods should be used when fletching without glue.

Many original Plains bows and arrows are rough and strictly utilitarian, which is understandable as they were shooting their game from horseback from only a few feet away. But just as often the tackle shows painstaking workmanship and decoration, the pride and skill of the craftsmen taking the weapons far beyond what was necessary simply for survival.

Reproducing a quality Plains bow, arrows, and quiver is not easy. If it were, handmade archery gear would be for sale at the sporting goods store, right next to the tackle boxes and boat cushions. But we all know it takes great measures of time, dedication, and persistence to produce quality natural bows, arrows, and strings. And this is as it should be, for therein lies the joy and challenge.

AFRICAN ARCHERY

David Tukura

The old man sat on the floor of his hut, his gaze intense as his hands demonstrated the action of the story. I was only ten years old, but remember sitting in rapt attention, oblivious to the shimmering heat of the African sun outside.

"The hunters spotted the 'Chief' (name of honour for the leopard) among the long grasses. The first arrow hit him in the thigh. With fire in his eyes he sprang from the bush and rushed towards the hunters, who scattered. The leopard caught Gebi the son of Kaura and both of them crashed into the bush. Gebi's bow and quiver fell into the long grasses. The leopard tore at Gebi's head with his claws, ripping flesh and bringing out blood. Gebi cried, 'Nnle moo!'(Save me!). Daku, Gebi's brother, heard his cry and turned to face the struggling pair. He raised his manga (dagger), shouted a war cry, 'Ayuuuuu hah hah!', and ran to where his brother and the 'Chief' were struggling. Leaping into the air he fell on the leopard, stabbing him again and again. Bele, a cousin of Gebi and Daku, came down from the tree he had climbed and joined in the fight. He grabbed the leopard by the tail and plunged his manga into its side. Blood flowed like the waters of a stream. Round and round they rolled on the ground, wrestling, clawing and stabbing. Finally, the 'Chief' looked dazed as the fire in his eyes died slowly. He fell on his side with low growls and grunts, the sand slowly drinking his blood."

This story, based on a real life event about a hunter who saved his brother from a leopard, is a sample of some of the images with which I grew up. A world of bows and arrows and tales about leopards, Cape Buffalo, wars and the heroic deeds of archers and bowmen. With stories like these you can understand why my interest in archery is so intense.

This bow disease is shared by archers all over the world without regard to race or nationality. The roots of this attachment to the bow stem from deep in our consciousness. Thus, despite the effectiveness of traditional archery tackle in harvesting big game, the fascination of bent stick advocates is not solely based on technical grounds. The value of the bent stick lies in its hidden spirituality and cultural significance. In many ways, the early history of the ascent of man is inseparable from the story of the bow, but the "meaning of the bow" is not easily accessible to people nurtured in industrial societies. Having been born and raised in Africa, I have had the privilege of growing up in a cultural environment where the bow is more than a simple tool. In fact, my culture, history and community identity are tied up the bow. Only those who have made their own bows from wood and have looked far enough back into their own history could understand. Though I won't ignore the practical aspects of the bow, technical details are meaningless without being situated in their historical, cultural and biographical context. My story begins from ancient times, though it is also a story about today.

AFRICAN ARCHERY IN ANCIENT PERSPECTIVE

Though they were different, they stood with the others: Persians, Medes, Assyrians, Parthians, Bactrians, Indians and Arabs. From their dark skins and woolly hair, everyone knew they were the African contingent from Ethiopia. The time was 480-479 B.C. The Persian ruler, Xerxes, was preparing a massive invasion of Europe. He wanted the best fighting men in the world to crush the rebellious Greek city states. The Ethiopians were some of the ancient world's best archers. Herodotus (490-425 B.C.) noted that the Ethiopians wore leopard and lion skins. Their bows, of palm wood, were as much as six feet long, and their arrows were made from cane.

It would surprise many today to learn that in ancient times, Africans were known to all the world's greatest empire builders — Persians, Assyrians, Greeks and Romans. African encounters with peoples of other races and continents were not under the humiliating conditions of slavery. They were not only part of the fighting forces of ancient empire builders, but were themselves empire builders who competed for land, territory and the splendours of conquest. Africans were known to the ancients as "Ethiopians," "Kushites," "Nubians," "Napatans," or "Meroeites," and were familiar faces in the major cities and battlefields of the Mediterranean world.

One of the major kingdoms founded by an African people was the Napatan or Nubian kingdom of Kush. This kingdom became so powerful that it occupied Egypt for almost five hundred years and ruled it as the Twenty-Fifth Dynasty (circa. 750-300 B.C). The rulers of Kush later founded Meroe to the south (circa. 300 B.C.-350 A.D.). The military might of the Nubians was so significant that one of its rulers, Kashta, first ruler of the Napatan kingdom, was able to seize Upper Egypt about 760 B.C. and assume the title of Pharaoh. Taharqa, one of Napata's rulers, was considered a sufficient enough danger to Assyrian control of Palestine and Phoenicia to convince Sennacherib's successor Esarhaddon to invade Egypt. He was defeated by the Nubians in 674 B.C.

What were the tools of these ancient African empire builders? What weapons brought them fame on the battlefields of the ancients? Historical writings and records indicates Africans were able to participate in the power struggles of their times partly because of their mastery of archery.

To the ancients, the identity of the African was so tied up with the bow that in Egyptian writings the bow, called petchet, was the representative weapon of the people of Nubia. Nubia itself was called "Sti" or "Ta-sti" "Stiu," "the land of the bow" or "the land of bowmen." The significance of Nubian archery in Egyptian empire building was commemorated in the making of the model of forty Nubian archers from Asiut in circa. 2000 B.C. In the depiction of the conquests of Pharaoh Rameses II, he is shown charging Nubian archers in his chariot.

Wooden models of forty Nubian archers from Asiut, circa 2000 B.C. (courtesy Egyptian Museum, Cairo)

Among the tribute presented to Rameses from Nubia is a pile of longbows, thus cementing the association of Africans with the bow.

Ancient historians leave us records of African archery as it was perceived by them. According to information provided by Strabo, "The Ethiopians used bows of fire-hardened wood four cubits long (between six and seven feet)." Writing of the Ethiopians, Diodorus gave the information that "Their bows are four cubit long, and when shooting their arrows they use their feet to bend their bows; when their arrows are exhausted they fight with their clubs." Heliodorus, in his 3rd and 4th century romance *Aethiopica*, mentions the conflicts between Oroon-dates, the viceroy of the Persian king and Hydaspes, king of the Ethiopians. Writing about the archery of the Africans in an encounter with the Persians, Heliodorus noted that:

> "So from the battlements, as though on the walls of a citadel, the archers kept up with a continual discharge of well aimed shafts, so dense that the Persians had the sensation of a cloud descending upon them, especially when the Ethiopians made their enemies' eyes their targets and conducted themselves as men not so much fighting a pitched battle as engaged in a trial of marksmanship, So unerring was their aim that those who they pierced with their shafts rushed about wildly in the throngs with the arrows projecting from their eyes like double flutes."

African confidence in their archery abilities was recorded in Herodotus's account of the encounter between an Ethiopian king and spies sent by the

Persian king Cambyses (circa. 530-522). The Ethiopian king said to the spies:

> *"The king of Persia has not sent you with these presents because he puts high value upon being my friend. You have come to get information about my kingdom; therefore, you are liars, and that king of yours is a bad man. Had he any respect for what is right, he would not have coveted any other kingdom than his own, nor made slaves of a people who have done him no wrong. So take him this bow, and tell him that the king of Ethiopia has some advice for him: when the Persians can draw a bow of this size thus easily, then let him raise an army of superior strength and invade the country of the long-lived Ethiopians. Till then thank the gods for not turning the thoughts of the children of Ethiopia to foreign conquest."*

The king of Ethiopia then unstrung the bow and handed it over to the spies.

Quintus of Smyrna wrote of the adventures of Memnon and his African soldiers. The arrival of the Ethiopians brought joy to the besieged Trojans during the Trojan-Greek war. As late as the seventh century A.D., Arab invaders so respected the archery of their African foes that they nick-named them "pupil smiters" since they had the "bad habit" of hitting the pupils of the eyes of their enemies.

The exploits of the African "bent stick" certainly qualifies as an object of interest to serious modern archery students and enthusiasts. Why was an African bow so strong that the Ethiopian king dared the Persians to string it? But more significantly, what did the bow and arrows "mean" to Africans? Why was it so significant to some African communities? The information we have seems to indicate that for Africans, the bow was not just a tool but an extension and indeed an expression of the personality and identity of the archer.

The obstacles to understanding African archery today are historical. In the New World, for instance, people of African descent are hardly associated with the bow in any indigenous sense. This is a direct consequence of the forced migration of the Trans-Atlantic Slave Trade. Millions of African prisoners of war and kidnapped women and children were shipped to the Americas. Bound in chains and manacled, stripped of their language and culture and above all their weapons, no one asked or cared about their ancient skills. In fact, slavery not only denied these Africans a history, it took them out of history and turned them into a mere colour — "Blacks." The history of civilizations like Nubia, Meroe, Axum, Ethiopia, Ghana, Mali, Songhay, and the Hausa City States — civilizations in which archery played significant roles — remained unknown, ignored or in some cases flatly denied. While in ancient times Africans were viewed with honour by other members of the human family, an aftermath of the Trans-Atlantic Slave Trade was the association of Africans with slavery. The more they were associated with slavery, the further the image of the African in the New World drifted away from the bow and arrow — the symbols of all that is original, wild, and free. The image of the enslaved African was only reinforced by the colonial conquests of the late nineteenth and early twentieth centuries. Armed with rifles and Maxim guns, European powers parceled Africa among themselves. From the sands of Nubia to the stone walls of Zimbabwe, Africa became a mere European possession. Like the silent ruins of Napata, the fame of the great bows of the kings of Africa lay ignored by conventional historians.

AFRICAN ARCHERY IN CONTEMPORARY TIMES.

Modern Western interest in African bows and arrows, especially during the early 20th century, was part of an anthropological and sometime scientific curiosity about the weapons of "primitive" peoples. This curiosity was within the context of colonial rule. Armed with repeating rifles, European armies crushed African resistance to European domination from Cape to Cairo. The Anglo-Ashanti War, the Anglo-Zulu War on the battlefields of Ulundi (1879), the Fulani-British encounters between the late 1890s and 1903, and a host of other battles proved, just as it did in North America, that except in some exceptional cases modern firearms were superior to spears, shields, bows and arrows.

Colonial curiosity about primitive weapons lingered for three reasons. First, in their encounters with African groups, the deadliness of African arrows left a lasting impression. Despite the disadvantage African warriors had against their European enemy, whenever their arrows found a target, death was almost inevitable. Second, after colonial conquest, these weapons were still being used with deadly efficiency by Africans in the revolts and riots which reminded Europeans that they were not welcome on the African continent. Third, these weapons remained vital tools for harvesting game animals, a practice which continued to frustrate colonial plans to turn Africa into a huge continental zoo.

Western interest in African archery also came by way of the impression African archers had on Anglo hunters like Saxton Pope, Arthur Young, and Stewart White. In his visit to Kenya in 1925, Pope, using a yew longbow and a flight arrow, was outshot by a Wakoma archer using a heavy hunting arrow. In a second trial Pope used his strongest yew longbow and managed to

Photo of African archer taken by Arthur Young on his 1926 expedition with Saxton Pope (courtesy Pope and Young Museum).

outdistance the Wakoma by a mere ten paces, at which point he was happy to call a halt to the contest. Thus, for modern Westerners, the only information available about African archery is brief notes and reports made by early hunters, anthropologists and scientists.

The archery customs, traditions, and practices of any place are a product of the interplay between environment, technical innovation, historical events, social and political division of labour, community, spirituality, and sheer necessity. Thus, as late as the second half of this century, the Liangulu and Kamba of Kenya harvested elephants as part of their subsistence. The Liangulu killed elephants by the hundreds and their "elephant" bows drew over 100 pounds and could easily drive an arrow through an elephant's hide.

The marksmanship for which the ancients respected Africans has also persisted into recent times. Hardy reports the case of Wambua, a Kamba archer in an archery contest. The range was fifty paces. The arrow was headless, thus less stable, and the target was a five inch diameter circle cut in a tree. The contest was between Wambua and forty other archers. Hardy writes that:

> "If he missed he would never be able to show his face again. He turned to the target, and a hush settled on the crowd. Then he quickly drew and loosed, and the arrow flying through the air, and he was actually walking away, not even bothering to see where it went. There was a tight smack of the arrow striking, that sound that is characteristic, unforgettable in its sense of urgency, and for the thrilling jump it never fails to give the heart. A sudden, ecstatic cheer broke from the crowd. It was not just a hit, it was in the pinhole, the exact centre of the target."

For many Africans, the bow and arrow not only puts food on the table but is the most readily available, efficient and economic means of defense and offense. One fact cannot be mistaken: the bow is alive in Africa. It is a very useful tool which in some areas is yet to be replaced by a viable or sustainable alternative. In the "outback" or "bush" the bow is a harvester of game. In the city, it is a dreaded weapon in the hands of guards and security workers. In the outback, the bow's credibility is sustained by its simplicity and affordability. In the city, it is a "psychological weapon" and derives its modern applications from its ancient reputation.

I will be using the case of the Bassa ethnic group (of which I am a member), of northern Nigeria to illustrate the historical, social, spiritual, and technical dimensions of African archery. I cannot tell you when I first knew about the bow, as it is part of my earliest memories. The Bassa have a reputation for being some of the "meanest" archers in Nigeria's Benue Valley. One of the skills for which they are known is the "back-fire" archery technique. Those who do not understand the technique think the Bassa can shoot backwards without having to look at a target. In reality what happens is this: When the enemy's defence would not yield, the Bassa would organize a mock retreat. This made the enemy think the Bassa were fleeing the scene of battle and would induced them to pursue in disorder. After moving about eighty yards, the Bassa would suddenly stop. The archers turned their bows towards the enemy without fully turning round their torso or trunk. With the head turned backward and the torso bent sideways, the archers would shoot at the rushing and disorganized enemy. The Mongols, I understand, had a similar technique. The other technique was called "agba gba sele" (plucking or shooting the skies). The technique involved shooting into the sky above the heads of their enemies. Aided by gravity, the arrows fell like piercing rain. Being preoccupied with trying to protect themselves from the peril from the skies, the enemy would expose his front and leave it unprotected.

The instrument of Bassa military prowess was their archery. This is proved by the results of Bassa wars of offense and defense. In the 19th century, the Bassa fought two kinds of wars. The first was with neighbours when seeking new lands to expand their dominion. The Bassa did not have much trouble in dealing with adjacent tribes who fought on foot like themselves. Thus, McGregor Laird, a 19th century Scottish traveler in the Benue-Niger region noted that the Bassa were "the dread of their neighbours."

The second type of battles were fought with a new and formidable enemy, the Muslim Fulani who had declared a jihad (holy war) in 1804. As time went on, the jihad became nothing more than a cover for slave raiding. The Fulani were a special enemy because they fought on horseback and sometime wore chain of mail or quilted armour. Their weapons were the sword and lance. In dealing with the Fulani, the Bassa experience proved the versatility and flexibility of the bow for new tactical situations. The Fulani relied on swift surprises, thus allowing them to bring into full use the combined shocking power of horse, lance and man. These tactics were effective for some time and resulted in the loss of some Bassa settlements. Bassas dislodged by Fulani raids crossed the Benue River and founded new settlements. Both oral and written records clearly indicate the Fulani advantage over groups like the Bassa did not last long. The Bassa began to build walled towns, dug deep ditches around their settlements, and moved their villages into dense woodlands and hills, all to counteract the effects of a mounted charge. Combining these natural advantages with well schemed ambushes, the Bassa prevailed in fight after fight, especially in the last years of the 19th century. Bassa resurgence so threatened the Fulani that in 1889, the Emir (Muslim ruler) of Nasarawa went incognito to the Mockler-Ferryman Expedition asking for firearms to help him contain the "pagans." The town of Orokowo (present day Loko), which the Bassa had lost to the Fulani had to be relocated because of Bassa raids and attempts to recapture it. Bassa resistance became so successful that some neighbouring groups flocked to them for protection. Temple notes:

> "The Bassa of Tawari...repelled the attacks of the Fulani and gave refuge to the people of Koton-Karfi, who were less fortunate."

Samuel Crowther and John Christopher Taylor, native African missionaries of the Anglican Church, also noted that the "Bassa ...have opposed Masaba's ambition, and with their poisoned arrows expelled his soldiers from their rocky defences."

By the late 19th century, the Fulani had lost the fighting ardour exhibited in the first fifty-four years of the Jihad (1804-1860). They had taken most of the Hausa States, but had only succeeded in establishing bases in the Middle-Belt, an area peopled predominantly by non-Muslim peoples. In their southward march, they had to make detours around Middle-Belt communities. The horse, which had given the Fulani great advantages, was increasingly leading them into deadly ambushes — a guerrilla warfare tactic the Bassa had perfected to an art. The guns which gave the Fulani another advantage were becoming harder to obtain because the British had lost interest in the business of "slaves for guns" and were moving into the more civil pursuit of trade in raw materials and government.

The ambush tactics of the Bassa may give some clues as to how invention takes place in archery. The deathly silence required when making an ambush led to the development of silencers among the Bassa. An informant told me this: "Our fathers used to tie something on the string to keep it from making noise, that way our enemies would not know where the arrows came from." I did not know the significance of this information until I came to Canada and saw bows with silencers, because silencers fell out of use among the Bassa when the wars ended in the very late 1890's and early 20th century. Their use at a certain time in Bassa history shows how necessity was indeed the mother of invention.

Some of the ambush tactics of the Bassa were quite sophisticated. When the lookout gave the signal of approaching enemies, the gate of the town would be quickly opened! This was to entice the Fulani into believing the residents could be taken off guard — a Fulani raider's dream. Archers would then take positions in elevated but concealed locations. The Fulani would rush into the town, shouting war cries, thinking this was going to be an easy victory. After they were in the town, the gate would be locked. Like Spanish bulls in the arena, the Fulani moved in circles, looking for an escape while the archers picked their targets at leisure. It is no surprise that many Bassa families entered the 20th century with Fulani artifacts — knives, shoes, charms, and swords.

Some of the stories that came from the Bassa-Fulani wars were preserved in family histories. A cousin of mine, the son of one of my many great aunts told me a story that was passed down through their branch of the family. During the wars, his family engaged the Fulani in battle. At one stage of the encounter, one of his great uncles was left to look after the women and children. The other warriors had to engage the enemy elsewhere. While they were away, a Fulani raiding party attacked the women and children since they would fetch a good price at the slave market. This great uncle stood his ground alone in the field and began bringing down the horsemen with his arrows. The harder they charged, the harder he hit them, dropping one Fulani after the other. One horseman however, managed to rush him. The Fulani took off his head with a long sword. As this was happening, other members of the family arrived on the scene. They saw Fulani horses and men either dead or in the final stages of dying. They also saw the headless body of the fallen archer. The other Fulani horsemen took flight, but the warriors pursued and managed to capture one Fulani. The throat of the captured Fulani was cut at the feet of the fallen archer as a mark of honour. To us today, this may seem like a brutal act, but my ancestors lived in an era when freedom was earned — not given. Despite the intense conflicts between Bassa and Fulani, a fact one cannot ignore is the healthy and mutual respect they had for each other. Some Fulani regarded the Bassa as their "cousins" — this is probably a term of respect for an opponent they regarded as worthy. The Bassa respected Fulani horsemanship and kept their long swords as trophies. These swords were obtained in battle and kept as mementos of valour in family shrines. The swords were displayed during the Bassa national dance (Ugunu) and warriors brandished them to impress the women. The Bassa, however, had no respect for Fulani archery. They regarded their bows as "wimp" bows. They thought Fulani bows were too small, stiff-backed and had no "rhythm." In fact a Bassa insult was, "You have a back as stiff as a Fulani's bow!" The small size of Fulani bows was obviously because they rode horses.

People from other ethnic groups also bore witness to the skill of Bassa archers. My father went to a missionary school among the Igala, neighbours of the southern Bassa. He said whenever he told an Igala he was a Bassa, a typical response was: "Ama tofa yio!" — meaning, "They are great archers!" The Bassa and Igala fought in the 1850s in the woodlands of Dekina, Ayingba, Keteshi and Bashikworo. The impression Bassa archers made in 1850 lingered in the collective memory of their former enemies (I have many Igala friends) more than a century later! Even the present day Fulani bear witness to Bassa archery. I was talking to a Fulani elder who went to a government sponsored festival in Sokoto State, the Argungu Festival. That year, archery was one of the shows at the festival. This elder said his regret was that there were no Bassas to show the audience what true archery was. To emphasize his point, he picked up a piece of wood about an inch in length and said, "A Bassa can hit this!"

After the Berlin Conference of 1884-1885, when the European powers divided Africa among themselves, the British intensified their activities on the Benue River. This brought them into conflict with the Bassa. David Carnegie was sent to the Bassa stronghold of Tawari to arrest someone described as a "troublemaker." Carnegie fell into a Bassa ambush, was hit on the thigh by an arrow and was dead in fifteen minutes. This was the excuse the British needed to attack. Tawari was bombarded with artillery shells, then assaulted with repeating rifles. The British were greeted with a shower of arrows. British records note that Tawari was "stubbornly defended," but the bullets of Manchester had the day. Bassa chiefs and warriors fell under the steady hail of bullets and Tawari was razed to the ground. This was sometime in December 1900. In September 1914, the Bassa rose in revolt against the system of local administration the British had imposed upon them. Once again, they fought with their bow and arrows against rifles. The Bassa had most of the casualties in the encounter, and their leaders were either killed or arrested. An interesting thing about the revolt were the fines which followed. The Bassa were asked to rebuild the towns they had destroyed and ordered to pay ".... a fine of bows and arrows...". This was a policy of disarmament. The same policy was applied in the town of Zwere, where the residents can still point to where the victorious British burnt their great bows. The British figured that if the Bassa were dispossessed of their bows and arrows, they would be less restive and less rebellious. The strategy was tactically wise from the standpoint of military psychology. The bow had a way of triggering in the Bassa traits a British explorer described as "...turbulent and wild."

Despite the turn of events at the beginning of this century, Bassa archery is alive today, and the bow has continued to hold its ancient meanings for the Bassa people. As late as May 7, 1986, violence broke out between the Bassa and a neighbouring ethnic group. In the ensuing fracas many people were killed and property was destroyed. The Bassa were blamed for most of the deaths. Before the clashes took place, the police reported that they "...met about 500 people from the Bassa Community with bows, arrows and other weapons" and had to wait for reinforcements.

A tool for Bassa expansion in the 15th century and a weapon against slave raiders in the 18th and 19th centuries, the bow remains an actor in the tribal politics of Africa in the late 20th century. The bent stick has enjoyed a long life.

The reader may well be wondering about the practical purpose for all of these historical details, anecdotes and personal recollections. The answer is simple. When next you hold your bow, it may stir your imagination that you are holding a weapon which has been an actor in the destiny of peoples. In Africa, less than two hundred years ago, the bow played a role in the choices which were to determine the destiny of entire tribes. For some, it was a choice between life and death, freedom and slavery, shame and honour. In the case of the Bassa, the bow stood between them and enslavement and forced conversion to Islam. Today, the Bassa are one of the peoples of northern Nigeria who have preserved a distinctly African culture without the homogenizing influence of Islam. Some northern Nigerian communities have become so Islamized and Arabized that aspects of their pre-1804 language and culture are either lost or forgotten. So I am thankful for the bent stick because my culture is not something I have to look for in the dustbin of history. It is alive and here with me, passed down from my ancestors who, with their wooden bows and arrows, were able to protect themselves from being captured, held in the holds of slave ships, or sold on auction boxes. For me, the bow and arrow symbolizes not only history and culture, but freedom itself.

BASSA ARCHERY

Having situated the bow in the history of a particular African group, we will now the focus on the more technical aspects of archery. Writing about "primitive weapons," Meek stated that "Spears are the par excellence weapons of Africa." This is not only a sweeping generalization, but a misconception which only fits the stereotyped association of the African with the spear. This stereotype was an aftermath of European encounters with the assegai-thrusting Zulus and to a degree the popular use of spears by the hunting guides of the "great white hunters" of the late 19th and early 20th centuries. As Meek himself notes in his survey of Nigeria, "Bows and arrows are, with a few exceptions, found among all the tribes."

From my experience, the variations of archery among different groups are degrees of use, intensity of archery skill, and the ways bows were integrated with other weapons. The story of Bassa archery is therefore the biography of the bow in one ethnic group. It is hoped that the great significance of the bow in the history of this community qualifies their being treated as an example of African archery.

THE BOWS

For all that has been written about Bassa bows, they are remarkably simple, resembling in many ways English longbows. They are made of wood, have no sinew backing and form an elongated oval arc. The Bassa's bow wood is a slender tree which grows besides streams. This tree may be related to the North American locust family, in which case the botanical name may be Robina pseudoacacia. After being cut, the tree is split into staves and the bark removed. The wood is allowed to season for months. Once the hot African sun has dried the stave, the bow is shaped and tillered with a metal headed axe. The bowyer fashions the weapon so that the outside of the tree becomes the bow's back and the cross-section is round or oval. The size of the bow depends on the height of the user, tall and strong persons tend to have bows ranging from five to five and a half feet while smaller persons could have bows ranging from four to five feet. The bowyer shapes the wood until it gracefully tapers towards both ends. The limbs are then bent to create a "D" shape. A bow ready for stringing looks like a large oval shape with a round and robust middle. At the center, or riser, the bowyer may tie strings around the wood or fit in metal rings. These rings are "magical" or decorative. However, they seem to have the functional role of helping the archer find the center of the bow with his hand. Some archers back the riser region of their bows with the skin of the monitor lizard or some other animal's skin.

Though Bassa bows are straight, bowyers in some regions, Ghana, for instance, recurve the wood by heating it while still green. The recurve is tied in place, then the wood left to dry.

When the bow is tillered, the Bassa bowyer places a metal awl or pin in the fire. When the pin is red hot, it is used to burn a hole in the upper limb of the bow, about one and a half inches below the tip of the limb. This procedure is also used among Ghanaian bowyers of the Dagooma, Dagaaba, Isaaba and Frataa groups. This is different from the nocking method used in North America. A groove or hollow about half an inch deep is carved into the very tip of the upper limb. The importance of this groove will be explained below, but first, let us talk about the strings.

Except for children's bows, the Bassa do not use vegetable fibre. The preferred bow string material is the skin of the various members of the antelope (bovidae) family. The Liangulu of Kenya use giraffe sinew. Somali bowyers use sinew from the neck of a giraffe, an antelope or a cow. Richard St. Barbe Barker reported seeing six-foot natives of Equatorial Africa using bows taller than themselves with strings of buffalo hide.

The antelope rawhide which the Bassa use is tough and remains springy through Africa's rainy and dry seasons. The skin is cut in long strips while still fresh. Then, it is twisted until it forms a long tough fibre. The twisted string is knotted at both ends and dried in the sun. When it is dry, it is stretched to produce an even suppleness throughout its entire length. The stringing begins at the lower limb of the bow and is completed with a tight knot. It is passed, from back to belly, through the hole made by the metal awl or pin described earlier, then secured by wrapping around the limb so that it can't slip back through the hole. The knotting of the upper limb is all done below the hole made by the metal pin — never above it. After tying on the string, the bow still remains relaxed and there is little tension in the limbs. This is how the bow is allowed to "rest." When a Bassa wants to go to war or hunt, he does the following. He holds the upper limb of the bow with his left hand (if he is right handed) and

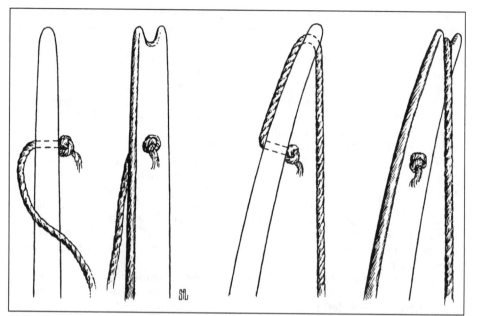

Unique bow stringing method of some African archers.

Arthur Young photos of African men stringing their bows in 1926 (courtesy Pope and Young Museum).

bends the bow by bearing down his weight on it and placing his left knee on the riser to help bend the bow. This is why the bow must be in tune with the user's strength. When the bow bends, the string becomes "lax." The archer then uses his right hand to fit the relaxed string into the groove on the tip of the upper limb, above the hole made by the awl. The string loops over the tip, from back to belly, and the bow immediately become tight and loses its relaxed state. The string becomes very tense like a trap about to be sprung. When you touch the string, it sings like the strings of a very heavy guitar. It is ready for action. The bow is so tight that it cannot be drawn with bare hands.

Nothing gives a Bassa archer more pride than a bow nobody else can string or shoot. The more difficult it is to string, the greater the prestige he has among his peers. This is because his bow is a measure of his strength and masculinity. When the archer wants to relax his bow, he follows the same procedure described above. He bends the bow using his left knee to loosen the string. Then, he removes the string from its grooved crown to relax the bow. This is done whenever the weapon is not in use to reduce the pressure on the bow and to lengthen the life of the limbs and string.

To pull bows so strong, the Bassa use a release mechanism called **manga** and in the verb form **umanga.** This is a very curious device and to my knowledge, the only other groups who use a similar device are the Tiv and Mada of Nigeria. It is interesting to note that all these groups successfully defended their independence from Muslim Fulani invaders. The manga is made out of metal though children improvise theirs using the bark of the raffia palm. The upper part of the manga is an oval shape, which the archer can fit into his palm. The lower part of the devise is a long dagger. The length of the dagger varies and ranges from six to ten inches long and is between two to three inches wide. When the archer wants to shoot, he fits the manga into his hand, places the edge about half an inch below where the arrow's nock fits the bowstring...and then draws. When the draw is being made the string and arrow are pulled towards the archer's chest. The friction and "pain" of the pulling process is borne by the metal, not the archer's fingers.

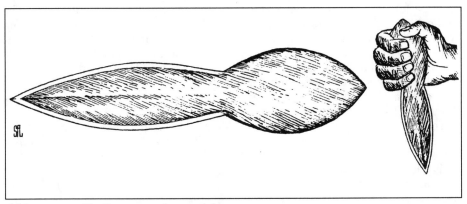

A Manga, a combination arrow release and dagger.

Apart from being a release mechanism, the manga is a weapon in itself, as earlier described in the fight with the leopard. It was used in close combat, such as striking an enemy trying to attack from behind or the side. It was also used to perform a coup de grace on struck down foes. I remember talking to someone whose ancestors were among the defenders of the Bassa stronghold of Tawari. He was told that after his forefathers had successful ambushed a Fulani war party, one of the enemy was still alive, but lying on the ground. One of the warriors used his manga on the fallen enemy. The English equivalent of the word my informant used to describe the act are "slash" and "carve!"

The first time I came into contact with the Mediterranean style was in Canada. I had gone to the archery store and while there was asked to demonstrate a shot. The method I used was the Bassa style. I bent or cupped my four fingers into a kind of bent half-punch. I placed my bent fingers by the string, the way I would do if I was using a manga. I closed the circle around the string with my thumb. The string was now securely nestled between my thumb and cupped fingers-giving my grip a "pinch" style look. The archery dealer "corrected" me and asked me to use the Mediterranean style. I was wondering what I did wrong. I now know I was not doing anything wrong. What happened was a clash of shooting styles. In fact, the Kiowa gentleman in Jim Hamm's *Bows and Arrows of the Native Americans* is shooting "Bassa" style except he has no manga! The Mediterranean style is used in some parts of Africa, for instance, by the Somalis.

THE ARROWS

The arrowheads (called ayn'la) are of metal. They are designed to cut and "hang on" and so come with barbs which could be straight, twisted or curled. The barbs make the arrows hang in the body of the enemy or animal to allow the absorption of poison into the bloodstream (more about poisons later). Different African groups make really diverse arrowheads. Some are moon-shaped, other look like "hearts," while some look like small spear heads. The functions are also diverse. For instance, some arrows could even be described as "mercy arrows." A convex shape arrowhead called "kapyassa" (swallow) is used to speed the death of a wounded animal.

Bassa arrows reflect this diversity since they come in "calibers." The type selected for use on any occasion depends on what the archer wants to do. The first calibre of Bassa arrows is a class referred to as "shalougou." The metal from which the arrowheads are made is twisted to form rings, grooves and ridges. The ringed arrow is then crowned with a sharp spike-like point, the only Bassa arrowhead without a cutting edge. They are about two to two and a half inches long, less than an inch wide, and have barbs about half an inch long. This class of arrows are designed for small game like rats, grass-cutters, and small birds. They are also suitable for young archers because of their lightness.

The second calibre of arrows are the "kalou" class. There are different sub-calibers of arrows in this class and they constitute the "middle-range" of Bassa arrows. They could vary from two and a half to three inches long and about an inch wide. A well sharpened kalou is as good as a small knife. Because of their medium weight, they can be used by archers of different levels of strength. They are also the warrior's favourite arrows because of their diversity, stability and

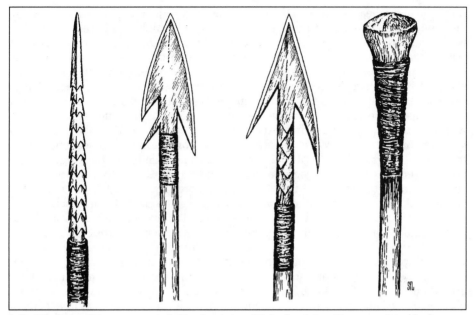

L-R, "Shalougou" (grooves are to hold poison), two "Kalou" points with asymmetrical barbs, "Ukpu kpu" or blunt for small game.

straight-flight. The barbs for this arrowhead are as diverse as its class. In some, the barbs stand like the anterior dorsal spiked fin of the catfish the Bassa call "ukpache." Thus, it is called "aba kpache" (meaning: back of the spiked catfish). In others, the barbs are like the pectoral fin of a fish. Other have major and minor barbs. In all Bassa arrows, the arrowhead ends with a tapering three inch long metal tail or tang. A large part of a Bassa arrow is therefore hidden in the shaft. An arrowhead measuring three inches may actually be six inches long if you include the tang.

The third calibre of Bassa arrowheads is the "ayama" class. These are literally "knives in flight." An arrowhead in this class could range from three to four inches in length. They are about an inch and a quarter wide. The Bassa use these arrows when they want to punish an enemy "with extreme prejudice." They could also be used for large game in the buffalo class. They are generally not popular because of their cumbersome weight.

The fourth calibre of arrowheads are the "headless arrows." These are wooden blunts used to stun birds and rodents. Their name, "ukpu kpu," sounds dull as they are blunt.

Arrowmaking in Bassa is the smith's craft. He cuts out the amount of iron needed for a particular arrowhead and then heats the metal until red hot. The metal is then twisted into various shapes using the hammer, anvil and pinchers.

In Africa, the craft of making arrow shafts can be very complex. Among the Wakamba group of Kenya, the shaft is made from wood. The shaft is enlarged at its end into a bulbous shape into which the arrowhead is inserted. The insertion is "light" and is held together only by a light gum. When the arrow strikes the prey, the arrowhead sinks into the game, the shaft pulls free and is recovered by the hunter. Other African groups use cane shafts of straight rigid grass stems. The woodland terrain of the Bassa is blessed with long tough grasses, one of which is a member of the Elephant Grass family. The stem of this grass has a back as smooth and tough as glass, though it possesses a soft inner core. The splinters are sharp and can inflict severe cuts. The stem of this grass grows to between twenty-seven and thirty-two inches long and thus makes wonderful arrow-shaft material. These grasses are harvested just as the rainy season ends in August so the grass won't be destroyed by bushfires. At this stage, they still contain their sap and so require some drying. When the stem chosen for the arrow is seasoned, it is trimmed. The grass is cut with its ends intact. These ends are the ridges where one stem ends and another begins and are almost as hard as wood. One ridge (the smaller end) is cut to expose the stem's inner core. The metal tail or tang of the arrowhead is then inserted into a piece of wood about one and a half inches long. This wood is sharpened and tapered to serve as the insert which is pushed into the soft inner core of the shaft until only the arrowhead and barbs remain visible. The neck of the arrow (where the arrowshaft hugs the arrowhead) is then tied with a fibre cut out of the pods of the Locust bean tree. This fibre is chosen because it is waterproof and tough. After wrapping about six rounds around the arrow's neck, a knot is made. The fibre is then affixed to the arrow's neck with a glue made of Guinea corn or millet meal, which is almost one hundred percent starch and makes excellent glue. The next step is to create a nock called "bubeku," made by making a "V" shaped indentation in the ridge at the second end of the shaft. The ridge must be deep enough to accommodate the bowstring. The edges of the "V" shaped indentations are then trimmed and smoothed. The fibre from the pod of the Locust bean tree is used again to make about six wraps around the end of the shaft, below the nock, then covered with starchy glue. Surprisingly to some, Bassa arrows have no fletchings! It appears, as S.B. Leakey noted, that the flight of the arrow is guided by the arrowhead itself, the way a rocket's head does. The wing-like and fin-like barbs of the arrowheads (especially in the kalou class) probably act as a stabilizing device. This is possibly why kalous have straight flight qualities. Some African groups fletch their arrows. For example, the Kasai of Zambia use four short feathers as fletchings. Others use the tough leaves of the palm tree for fletching.

When this process is complete, the bowyer looks at his arrow and smiles, for a more interesting part of his craft is yet to come — the dressing of the arrow-heads with poison.

To make good poison (called "mangai"), the bowyer must abstain from sex! In fact, no Bassa archer, bowyer or warrior crafting or making "the things of man-hood" (phrase used by the Bassa with reference to weapons), would go near a woman. The bowyer believes he needs inspiration from his ancestors in order to make the most effective weapons. He therefore has to harness all his spiritual strength. Abstaining from sex is a form of fast, an act of self-denial which will sharpen the spirit and keep all the senses alert. The making of the poison is regarded as a holy act. The weapons are also holy and spiritual and must not be tainted with the "carnal" and "fleshly powers" that the woman possesses. In some older archery books I even saw pictures of women archers! Now, before feminists have me strung up on a meat hook, please understand my plight. I come from a world where there is no confusion between what is "male" and "female." The distinction between the sexes is expressed even in the manner of walking and talking! I have tried to imagine what a Bassa archer would think if he were asked to go shooting with a woman. No one in his right senses would think of such a thing. No, I would not even consider asking a Bassa archer such a question, I would only end up having my sanity questioned. But I have harboured the thought that if I have a daughter, I will teach her how to shoot. Why not? She would be as much Bassa as I am, a descendant of archers. I also think that one of the most beautiful things a man's eyes can behold is a woman with a bow. I am talking heresy here! Back to the subject of poisons...

Every Bassa family has its formula for making the poisons. These recipes are closely guarded. The basic ingredient is a plant called "bukulua," a member of the legume family from which physostigmine is made. This plant has a creeping stem and spongy fruit. What is used are the seeds. The seeds are ground with the dried heads and fangs of vipers, puff-adders, mambas and other venomous snakes. With its thriving rattlesnake population, Texas would be a Bassa poison brewer's dream! The deadly recipe also includes the roots of various plants. These are all ground and boiled in an elaborate ritual. The Giriama of Kenya use the roots and bark of the *acokanthera frisiorum* tree. They add the sap of the *Aloe rabainesis*, an *asapium* and an *acidpithrid*.

The Bassa do not regard their poisons as a mere concoction, but as a "person" with an individuality. When the poison is being boiled, it is addressed as a person and encouraged to come out in full strength. Incantations are shouted as the brewer tells the poison what to do. For instance, the brewer of the poison may mention the kinds of persons he wants the poison to kill. He may say: "When you touch my enemy...kill him!" "If you meet a Fulani take him out of this earth!" "Be strong! Rise up! Rise up! Rise up!" Thus for the Bassa, the poison is his messenger of death, the expression of his wrath, the enforcer of his sentence on the enemies of the community.

When the poison is ready, it is tested. The poison brewer places the edge of a knife in the poison and makes a small cut on a hen's body. The hen moves away and loses coordination within the first minute. If the poison is really "sweet," the hen should not go beyond ten yards before dropping dead. The effectiveness of this poison on human targets was mentioned earlier in the case of a British officer who died shortly after being struck in the thigh. Among the Giriama of Kenya the poison was so potent it could kill an elephant within about 500 yards and a baboon in fifteen second. The arrows are carefully dressed and the deadly liquid is allowed to settle into the arrowhead's grooves and barbs. The arrows are dressed right up to the neck, then left to dry in the sun. When the drying is over, they are carefully stored in a quiver.

Every poison brewer must prepare an antidote, called "bukwoshe," literally "the breaker of the poison." This is essential in cases of "friendly fire" involving friends, relatives or non-enemies. Because the recipes for these poisons were guarded by families, not too much is known about them. This is especially the case with the antidotes.

Quivers (called "abaguo"), were made from the young plants of the baobab tree. This tree normally has straight trunks. It is selected because the bark is impervious to attacks from weevils and wood eaters. About twenty-five to twenty-seven inches of the wood is cut, then "beaten" with a stick. A quality of the young baobab tree is that with minimum but persistent hitting all along its length, the wood can be pulled out of its bark thus, leaving a "woodless bark." As the bark dries, it forms a tough fibrous case. A round piece of wood is cut and used to form the base of the quiver. The young baobab plant is used because of the wide variety of trunk sizes. For a normal sized quiver, a plant with a diameter of three and half inches would be selected. This would take anything from eight to twelve arrows. When preparing war quivers (abaguo jasa), a larger baobab plant has to be chosen. Some warriors could carry as many as fifty arrows in extra large quivers made out of larger baobab plants. For reasons of mobility, some of the larger war quivers may have been carried by "carriers" or "auxiliaries." The quiver is covered with goatskin and straps of skin are attached to allow their being slung across the chest. When action starts on the battlefield, the quivers are pulled down to the hips or the front of the archer to allow greater access to the arrows. Some of the normal sized quivers were made out of the hollow of a bamboo stick and also covered with goatskin.

TRAINING

In my mother's clan, the Zongulo clan of Zwere, the birth of a son is marked by the making of a miniature bow, marking the child as an archer from birth. The bow then symbolizes the roles which are expected of him in adult life. From about the age of seven or eight, the child starts shooting targets with his age mates. Training begins by honing the child's skills in shooting moving targets. A long line of "baby archers" are challenged to shoot a melon rolling on the ground at top speed. From that, the child graduates into shooting birds. The young archers move in groups through the bush picking off birds and rodents. From that stage, they go on to shoot larger rodents like grass-cutters and game like antelopes, eland, impala and even buffalo.

The ultimate training ground for the Bassa archer was the hunt. I do not know how to translate the excitement of an African hunt, though those who hunt deer and elk with wooden bows will probably understand. It is like a surreal experience. There is the smell of bushfires, the rage of the crackling inferno, the shouts of excited archers as they run through the bush, even the hawks are excited and join in the hunt as they perform amazing swooping dives. In the hunt, skills are polished and perfected as the Bassa tackle fast footed impala and bush thrashing wart hogs. In the olden days when leopards and men fought for dominance in the bush, the hunt became even more intense if the anger of the "Chief" was aroused. The formidable "Chief" may scalp the unlucky hunter, but the best archer may take his hide home. It was also on such occasions that great hunting stories were born — stories of brother putting his life on the line to save brother — stories of archer facing leopard in hand to hand combat.

This was why the hunter was a member of an elite. The community admired his courage and loyalty to his comrades. They admired his pioneering spirit and his zest for new experiences and dissatisfaction with the usual, the mundane and the ordinary. For, on many occasions, it was the hunter who discovered new land, new sources of water supply and shorter travel routes. It was the hunter who knew where to hide the women and children from enemies, who challenged the others to cast away their fear of the dark, their fear (not respect) of the lions, hyenas and the animal world. He was always full of stories, entertaining children and adults alike. When aggression threatened the community, the hunter was in the fore of the defence because to him, the game of life and death was a familiar drama. Among the Bassa, a community without hunters was a community without men. Such a community would not only fall easy prey to an aggressor, but was poor in the spirit of enterprise, discovery and adventure.

One of the characteristics that made hunters valuable in the community was their generosity. I remember the first time I tasted Cape Buffalo meat was at the age of ten, when a hunter, who hardly knew me, was liberally giving out meat to children. He had taken big game and as was the custom gave out meat to the public. When a hunter killed a large animal, the village would be in a joyous mood because every member of the community was going to have a feast. The modern cash economy is placing severe constraints on this ancient custom, since meat can bring a lot of money, but hunters are still generous people.

Archery is a very important aspect of Bassa education, founded on the pillars of: (a) agricultural skills; (b) the understanding of spiritual phenomenon; (c) the veneration of the ancestors and (d) the mastery of archery. The Bassa concept of man is moulded around the symbols of the hoe and the bow. The hoe stands for agriculture, while the bow stands for bravery, courage, loyalty to the clan and the readiness to defend loved ones even to the death. Thus, archery played a role in the formation of personalities, especially the Bassa concept of "Who I am." This is very important because in their world view being biologically a man is only the beginning of manhood — a ticket from the Creator that you are eligible to begin the race for the acquisition of "manhood." The quality of manhood cannot be inherited, it must achieved, as manhood is not only a biological attribute, but a set of attitudinal dispositions acquired through bravery, valour, independence, resourcefulness, self-control/self-denial, the capacity to endure pain, the readiness to brave danger and compassion for one's relatives and comrades. These characteristics — the "way of the archer" — were incubated in the individual's psyche. This was why the bow was the Bassa man's best friend, and there was no such thing as a "man" without a bow. The symbolism of the bow as an expression of the essence of manhood is not limited to the Bassa. In Ghana, Schuurman noted that:

> "In this region as in many others, the bow and arrow are of traditional, ritual and emotional importance in the life of the tribe in general and in that of the hunter in particular, as is apparent from the fact that everybody likes speaking about the subject and telling bow-hunting stories. "Without a bow you are not a man." This statement by the natives makes it clear that the bow is not only a weapon, but also a symbol of courage and skill. The bow is regarded much more than a mere object by them...by the same token, archery is purely a man's affair...."

Among the Bassa, archery is so much a part of life that it provides many images for the transmission of wisdom. This is evidenced in Bassa proverbs. For instance, when a Bassa says, "You do not tie your arrows in the battlefield," he seeks to emphasize the importance of preparing for emergencies before they happen. When a Bassa says, "No one goes to war with one arrow," he seeks to show the importance of having more than one plan of action when embarking on a mission. When Bassa elders say, "You are shooting your arrows in the dark," they seek to caution against working without reconnaissance or enough information. When they say, "A big tree is a good place from which to shoot your arrows," they mean, the chances of success when embarking on an enterprise are improved if you have friends and connections in high places.

THE "THEFT" OF THE BOW.

I came to North America at the end of the 1980s. Before then, I had seen Sylvester Stallone fire an exploding arrow at an "enemy" in one of the Rambo movies. That was the first time I saw a compound bow. I was amazed! It was like seeing a dream bow, and I longed to possess one when I got to Canada. Being on a scholarship, I could barely spare funds to buy one, but when the tax office sent me my annual refund, I ignored my wife's pleas for a "proper wedding ring" and went to a hardware store where bows were advertised. I shoveled out almost three hundred dollars to get a compound. I honeymooned with my bow for sometime, then certain things began happening. The bow seemed to have a life of its own, a life which was being continuously sustained by lots of my dollars. When my string broke, I did not know how to make a synthetic string or get it on the bow. I had to visit the guy at the pro archery store to make my bow a bow again. That was strange, since from my background I had learned to perceive the bow as an extension of my arm — an extension of myself. When I went target shooting and my aluminum arrows became bent, I had to go again to the pro archery store to get them straightened. This, of course, costs more dollars. Then I was told that to shoot well, I needed sights with pins. All for a price. Finally, I was told that the bow which had cost me almost three hundred dollars was out of date. They said it was too heavy and I needed something made out of lighter metal. I could get a more accurate and faster bow for only six hundred dollars! At that stage, I knew something was wrong. I thought a hunter should be one with his bow — that's what makes him a hunter, a part of nature, a predator, one worthy of the respect of his peers and the community. I had an archer's heart, but the tackle manufacturers were more interested in my money than my archery.

If they were interested in my archery, they would have known that the first rule is simplicity. It is this simplicity that has made the bow so versatile and adaptable to diverse environments across continents and cultures. The mystical connection between archer and bow is broken when the archer has no part in the "birthing" of "his" bow. Throughout history, archers have in varying degrees parented their bows. If I buy any of the modern bows I concede that I have a killing machine, but true archery — as a form of interaction with nature — should not leave the archer bewildered by his weapon.

If the bow was alienated from the Bassa people the way modern archery tackle is to modern man, my tribe would have perished long ago. The bows that made them survivors for thousands of years, which protected against enemies and fed their families, were "their" bows — simple bows of wood they lovingly made for themselves.

And all of us — every one — share that same heritage somewhere in our past.

TAKE-DOWN BOWS

Jay St. Charles

For thousands of years, the wooden bow served as an essential extension of the archer's arm and will. The bow has been a treasured tool to mankind, but has also served, in a very real sense, as a companion providing food and protection. To best serve as a companion — ten thousand years ago or today — a bow must be convenient to have at one's side. It must be rugged enough to survive weather and rough handling or compact enough to be protected from the elements. But handiness, durability, and portability are not the only factors that define a good bow. The bow must also be easy to shoot and accurate under any conditions.

One solution to these criteria has been to make the bow small. A 45" to 50" bow provides a small package to stow and protect from weather, but a bow this length often carries sacrifices in the realm of shootability and accuracy. Another solution has been the take-down bow: one that can be folded or broken down into smaller parts. Utilizing this feature, the assembled bow can be any size and shape necessary to insure it is an optimum bow to shoot, yet it can be reduced in size to little more than the length of the archer's arrows.

The take-down bow is not a new concept, though in the context of the long history of archery, it is a relatively young idea. Three centuries ago the Chinese produced folding bows with hinged handles and may have developed and used them much earlier. An example of a Chinese folding bow of this type is pictured on p. 125 of Vol. 2. From the 1700's, the Japanese used a socket and sleeve take-down system much like those employed today.

References to take-down or "carriage" bows have appeared in English literature since the late 1700's. Various commercial ads appeared throughout the nineteenth century in England, Europe, and the United States, depicting a wide array of socket sleeve designs, hinged bows, and interlocking latch designs. During those times, the need existed for a more portable long bow that could easily be transported to the field or a large event in the covered carriages and rail cars of the day.

Archery became quite popular during the Victorian period in England, and the take-down bow was the center of a certain amount of lively controversy. Some complained that the take-down assembly required the bow be built around that central component and therefore compromised the otherwise pure shape and form of the longbow. Proponents insisted that if the bowyer knew his

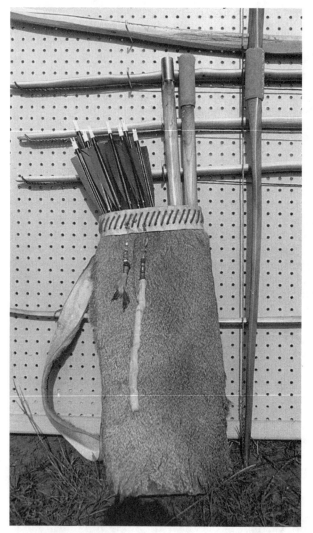

Two parts of a take-down nestled into quiver with arrows.

craft, no one could tell the well made take-down from a one piece!

The mid-1800's brought with them a surge of increased interest in target and recreational archery in the United States. Along with this interest began a prolific period for the take-down bow, and our patent system provides interesting documentation of these designs.

One of the earliest and most curious designs is a take-down center-shot bow patented by Wright and Thorne in the U. S. in 1879. This bow featured a cast iron sleeve into which round limbs were fitted. In the dead center was a 1 1/2" diameter aperture through which the arrow was shot, inserted between four small iron prongs. This was not a particularly attractive bow, despite chrome plating of the massive 16 ounce sleeve handle. A kit that accompanied this bow

ABBEY GREEN BATH ARCHERY.

J. SPREAT, UNDER THE KIND PATRONAGE OF SEVERAL GENTS, EXPERIENCED

TOXOPHILITES,

Makes Bows, Arrows, and every Implement of Archery of the first quality, and at the most reasonable Prices, in consideration of

READY MONEY.

THE NEWLY INVENTED

ABBEY GREEN JOINTED BOWS,

For Travelling;—when put together, *which may be done in one minute*, are warranted to be as firm and as elastic, as if of a single piece: and will pack with a Quiver of a dozen Arrows, Belt, Brace, &c. &c., in a small flat Case, half the length of a Bow, and about five inches wide.

N. B. The Weight or Strength of the ABBEY GREEN *Bows is ascertained by a novel Instrument.*

Ivory, Hard Wood, and Fancy Turning in General.

Ladies initiated in the use of the Bow by J. Spreat's Daughter.

An 1830 advertisement from England for take-down bows.

featured a set of arrows with bristle brush fletching, apparently to facilitate passage through the iron prong rest. The entire kit, including the bow, arrows and other accessories, was offered for five dollars.

"Jointed" bows, as some literature of the period called them, were produced by a number of makers in the United States including The Archers Company of North Carolina and the L. E. Stemmler Company of New York. A very unique design was produced in the 1920's by master bowyer and author James Duff. Duff's system incorporated a screw socket that, in addition to other alignment aspects, required the screw rotation to stop at exactly the right point to bring the horizontal planes of the two limbs together.

Wright and Thorne factory set in box, circa 1879.

Handle section of bow, showing center-shot feature. Arrows with bristles rather than feathers were used.

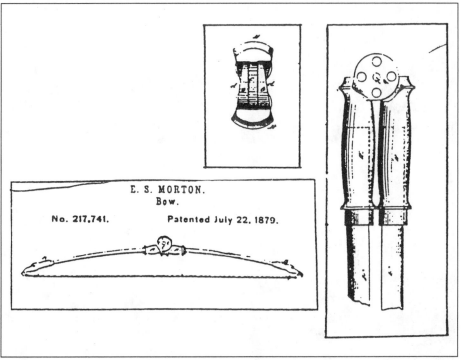

Drawings from a patent in 1879 for a hinged bow by Ephriam Morton.

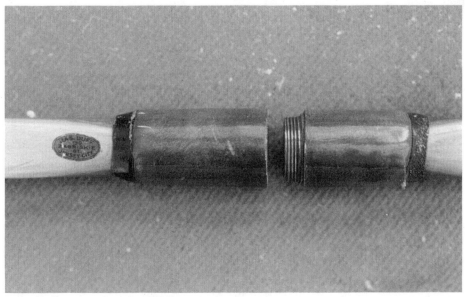

James Duff screw socket, circa 1920's.

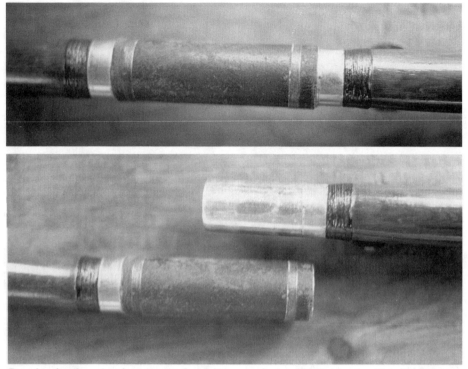

Round socketed carriage bow, mounted and dismounted, circa 1920's (courtesy Tom Baldwin).

During the 1930's, money in the U.S. was in short supply. By the early 1940's, so was gasoline and tire rubber, which resulted in bowhunters piling as many partners and as much tackle as possible into a single vehicle in order to make it to the hunting woods. Take-down bows came into increasing use by bowhunters during this period, due in part to the need to fit the most gear in the smallest space. In the Pacific Northwest, bowhunters were faced with hunting in small exclusive bowhunting areas or packing far into the back country to distance themselves from rifle hunters. Takedown equipment was convenient to pack and easier to protect from the variable weather of the region.

Two archers in the Northwest manufactured what became the very popular sleeve/socket take-down components during this period. C. M. Huntley of Oregon produced an all steel "D" section design swaged from seamless tubing. S.B. Hayden of Seattle, Washington, produced a finely crafted sleeve/socket system from welded steel tubes. These incorporated a flange around the top edge of the inner sleeve that effectively sealed the socket from the entry of water or debris. S. B. Hayden's handle components were advertised in *Ye Sylvan Archer* magazine for a number of years, and both the Hayden and Huntley assemblies were used by many different bow makers of the day.

Another method employed with success was the hinge, which in various forms allowed the bow to be folded in half rather than broken down into two

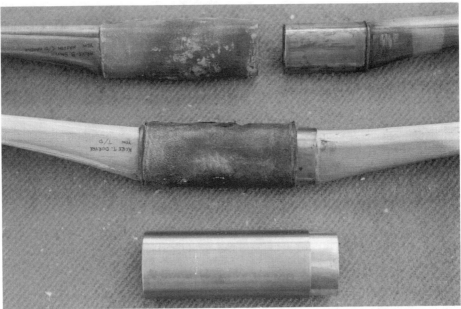

Socket and sleeve designs. Hayden handle (top), Huntley handle (center), both mid-1930's. Bottom is a modern version by Richard Dykoff.

separate pieces. Cliff Zwickey, developer of the popular broadheads, offered the Pioneer Bow Hinge. This was a compact assembly crafted of brass and steel, introduced in 1937, and manufactured through the 1940s. An interesting and thoughtfully designed hinge was developed in the mid 1940's by Barney Grenier of Michigan. The Grenier hinge had the feature of folding flat with the forward grip surface of the bow, eliminating any bulge in the handle grip area.

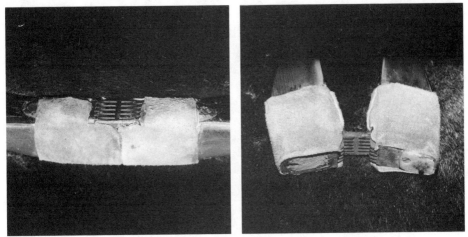

Two views of a Barney Grenier hinged take-down, closed and folded, mid 1940's.

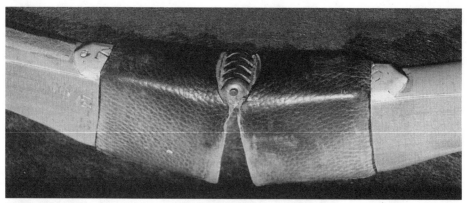

Cliff Zwickey brass and steel hinge, introduced 1937 and produced through the 1940's.

This was accomplished through a double hinging arrangement.

A variation on the hinge is the hinging latch, a design in which there is an inter-locking of hinging hooks, the two halves of the bow held together by the tension of the strung bow. The New Moon Latch, produced during the late 1940's in Indiana, was an interesting example of this type. These were precisely crafted of steel, utilizing substantial interlocking hinging hooks that combined the features of the folding and take-down designs.

Fred Bear, the tireless innovator, worked on take-down bow designs for over thirty years. He held a number of patents on these designs, the earliest of which involved several different hinging latch systems. A story is told about an early day sales meeting at the Bear Archery Company. All the salesmen from around

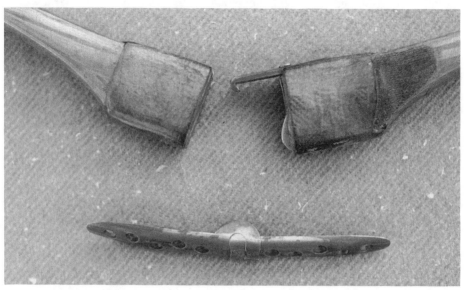

New Moon Latch components, late 1940's.

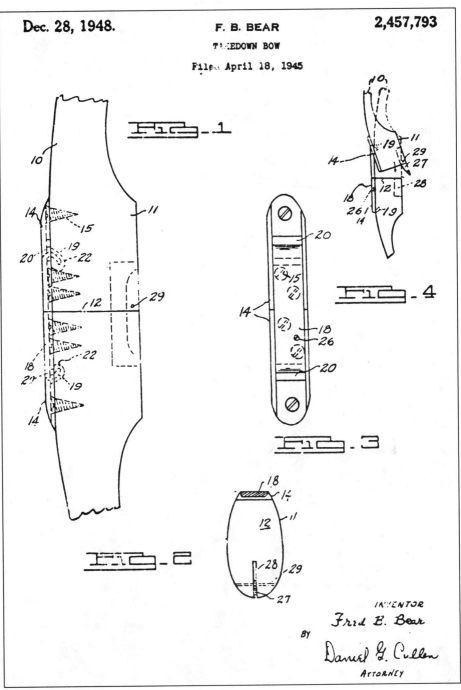

Dec. 28, 1948.

F. B. BEAR

TAKEDOWN BOW

Filed April 18, 1945

2,457,793

FIG-1

FIG-2

FIG-3

FIG-4

INVENTOR
Fred E. Bear
BY
Daniel G. Cullen
ATTORNEY

Fred Bear latching hinge patent, approved 1948.

the country were gathered to view the new products for the coming year. The centerpiece of the new line was to be a take-down bow using a secret latch device Fred had been testing. He extolled the virtues of this new system, relating to the assembled sales staff how this product was going to set new standards for take-down bows. When he was finished, one salesmen, way in the back of the room, raised his and asked humbly, "What happens to this new bow if the string breaks?" Fred immediately picked up the sample of the new bow, held it in his hand and examined it critically for a minute or so. Then, without saying a word, he placed the new bow back into its case and left the room. The sales meeting was ended. Fred literally went back to the drawing board and eventually solved the problem, ultimately producing a series of hinging latch systems, many of the early designs adapted for a two-piece style of break-down bow. The convenience and versatility of the take-down remained a major theme in the products of Bear Archery throughout Fred Bear's involvement with the company he founded.

The latest development in the evolution of hinged bows has come from the combined efforts of Rick Shepard and Jerry Brumm of the Great Northern Longbow Company of Nashville, Michigan, in their Jackknife series of bows. Introduced in 1991, this sturdy assembly combines various concepts of take-down design, incorporating a socket sleeve to secure each half of the hinge to the bow and utilizing stainless steel construction throughout.

The most common take-down system used on longbows and the static tip recurves of the past — and in modern times as well — has been the many variations of the sliding sleeve/socket system.

Ben Pearson produced a long series of sleeve/socket take-down bows utilizing an outer steel sleeve fitting over an inner sleeve with a surface of hard resin or fiberglass. These were produced in every style from self wood longbows to laminated recurves of wood and fiberglass. The Kramer family of Montana played a role in the revival of the sleeve/socket take-down longbow with the

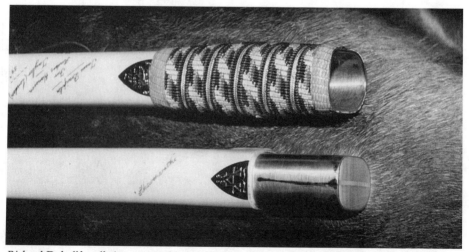

Richard Dykoff handle incorporated into self yew by John Taylor, U.K. , 1990.

introduction of their Autumn take downs in 1982. These hand-crafted bows featured a steel outer sleeve over a hardened inner sleeve surface.

At this time, a precision sliding sleeve/socket take-down assembly is being produced in several diameters by Richard Dykoff of Seattle and is currently available from a number of distributors and on a variety of bows. This version utilizes a brass inner sleeve and stainless steel outer sleeve.

Over the years many innovations have come about in take-down bow design, and the popularity of this style of bow has climbed dramatically. In fact, today the fiberglass take-down recurve is much more common than the one piece. The following passages describe an effective approach to bow construction as it applies to take-down bows. I would encourage wood bowyers to try their hand at building take-downs. You may find, as many throughout history have, that the take-down bow's features could make it your favorite.

INSTALLING THE SLIDING SLEEVE/SOCKET SYSTEM

The sliding sleeve/socket is simple, strong, relatively easy to produce, and one which lends itself to mounting and aligning with basic shop tools.

The mounting method can be applied to any simple sleeve/socket components, whether they have been purchased commercially or formed in the home shop. There is one particular alignment factor that is critical to success in the crafting of a sleeve/socket take-down bow. The limbs must always index with the axis of the outer sleeve. This component becomes the central determining point of your bow. If the limbs are tipped out of alignment with the outer take-down sleeve, the resulting misaligned handle keel or ridge will create a difficult to shoot, torque-plagued bow. Take the necessary time to make certain alignment is correct on all planes.

Although it may seem important to use some sort of shaping jig or template to assist in attaining alignment of sleeves and billets, for individual bow projects, it is possible and perhaps advantageous to depend upon alignment by eye. Most self billets vary to the extent that they will defy the effective use of a jig. Unless a great number of sleeves are being mounted on uniformly shaped bow blanks, the free hand method may be the best process to use for accurate alignment of the sleeves.

It is possible to alter an existing bow into a take down, but this is a more difficult task than beginning from a blank. There is no margin for error. If it is a favorite bow it will be much better off if left in one piece. No matter how much effort is taken to keep the bow the same, it will be an entirely different weapon when it becomes a take down. An exception would be the conversion of an unpopular, unused one-piece bow. The process will be easier if this bow has an undesirably heavy draw weight and fairly wide limbs, making it a good candidate to turn into a take-down. It can be treated as a marginally dimensioned bow blank, and with modest effort this little used bow may turn into a new favorite.

Joining billets using a sleeve/socket system effectively extends the potential length of the billets and the bow. This system of joining places the billets butt to butt, creating a stave four inches longer than one joined by splicing. A pair of billets which would be suitable for only a 64" bow might now be used to

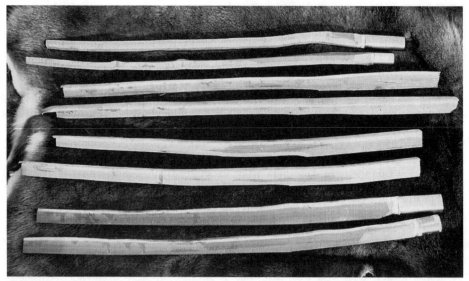

Billet selection determines the resulting backset of the finished bow. Top pair would be a poor choice due to natural deflex, the bottom two pair would be ideal for take-downs.

produce up to a 68" bow, something of a bonus from a wood conservation standpoint.

The sliding sleeve/socket take-down assembly consists of straight metal sleeves which slide over one another or a single outer metal sleeve which slides over a hard-surfaced ferrule. It is a straight line assembly, with no built-in provision for backset. If the finished bow is to have any backset, it must be in the billets naturally or set into the laminated blank by the gluing form. In the self bow, having this initial backset will make the difference between having a finished bow which follows the string a little or a lot. Much of the natural backset will have come out by the time the bow has been finished and trained to bend. While a bow can benefit in accuracy by following the string slightly, a bow which appears to be half drawn before it is strung will not likely be anyone's favorite. An ideal pair of self billets should have an inch or more of a natural backset curve.

It is optional which sleeve is used for the top or bottom limbs. By using the inner sleeve for the top limb, and establishing the center line of the bow one inch below the arrow shelf, the two halves of the resulting take-down will be equal in length. Using a 66" bow as an example, the resulting take-down will have both top and bottom limbs 34" long from nock to the sleeve butts. This mounting configuration provides the minimal broken down length for the bow. A majority of the examples of older take-down bows I have seen have been fashioned in this way.

A more significant benefit of using the narrower inner sleeve on the top limb is that better arrow clearance is created automatically. By using the narrow inner sleeve on the top limb, you place the narrowest part of the take-down assembly at the arrow shelf of the completed bow, which improves arrow flight and consistency.

If the inner socket sleeve is used on the bottom limb, and you again establish the bow's center one inch below the arrow shelf, the resulting top limb will be 4" longer than the bottom limb. Installing the inner sleeve on the bottom limb results in a more weather proof bow, in that rain water and debris are not as likely to get into the opening.

To integrate a sliding sleeve/socket system into a bow blank, the basic tools needed include a solid bench with vise, preferably a swivel base model, a sharp hand saw, a rasp, and a long straight edge.

Two power tools particularly helpful for sleeve installation are the belt sander and the band saw. Both of these tools do a more precise, controlled job than the rasp or hand saw for all but the very last bit of socket fitting. On the belt sander, a belt of 36 to 60 grit will prove most useful. A four tooth per inch, 3/4" width band saw blade is an effective configuration for wooden bow projects.

Clean all metal surfaces of the sleeve/socket components with a strong solvent such as acetone or lacquer thinner to remove any trace of residual machine oil. With a file, remove any burrs from the inside edges of the sleeves. On both sleeves, rough up the interior surfaces which will be cemented by using coarse emery cloth or sand paper to provide a clean gripping surface for mounting. This procedure establishes the final working surfaces of the sleeves and assures an optimum fit on the limb ferrules. The sleeve components are formed together in the same die, resulting in a close fit of the sleeves. There is also only one way that the two sleeves will fit together. To keep track of this match up, mark the outer ends of the sleeves with tape.

Leave the billets full width at the tip ends for now. This allows for what later may be some much needed angular adjustment. It is critical that the bow back be inserted intact inside the sleeve while fitting. Establish the final outer surface of the bow back, such as working the billets down to one growth ring or backing them with sinew, before you mount the sleeves. Do not cut into or dent this outer back area with the sleeve edges during fitting. Fit the sleeves by removing material from the sides and belly of the bow billets. Small knots or minor weakness in the billets in the handle socket area should be placed well inside the sockets or else kept at least an inch or more away from the edge of the sockets where the limbs exit.

Square the butt end of each billet so it is 90 degrees to the plane of the back. Then, using the sleeves as patterns, trace the outline of the inside of both top and bottom sleeves onto the flat surface of the appropriate billet butt. A long pencil with a sharp point works best. Allow for a hairline gap along the flatted "D" section of the sleeve where it would contact the back of the bow. The bow back needs to be treated with care throughout the mounting process. The slight gap will prevent direct contact between the metal and the back because that area will be filled with a thin layer of epoxy during the cementing process.

As a reference for seating depth of the sleeves, draw a line across the back of each limb butt. On the limb that is to receive the shorter interior sleeve, draw this line to match the exact length of the sleeve as you will be seating the sleeve to this full depth. On the billet that will be receiving the longer outer sleeve, draw your line 1/16" shorter than the half length of the long sleeve to allow for the thickness of a gasket seal for the bottom of the socket, which will be added later.

To guide the saw cuts that will be the beginning of the sleeve ferrules, draw lines on the back of your billets parallel to the center line, matching the inside width of the individual sleeves. These short cuts can be made with a hand saw or band saw. Follow the outside of the lines to assure plenty of remaining material.

The final fitting of the sleeves may be carried out using a rasp or a belt sander with a coarse grit belt. Start at the very end of the billet, cutting to trace the outline you have drawn on the billet end. Work this area until you can begin to slip the sleeve over the end of the billet. With a pencil, mark the high spots that will be visible along the back edge of the sleeve as you work it forward up the billet ferrule. Constantly check the alignment of the sleeve with the billet by sighting down the sleeve and limb, using the center lines to guide you.

The sleeve-to-sleeve fit will eventually require fine tuning before it has a smooth sliding fit but there is little benefit to performing this tuning until after both sleeves are fully mounted and cemented. The fact that both components are made of thin tubing material leaves them vulnerable to accidental deformation during the mounting process. Be careful not to force a sleeve onto the ferrule or it may bend and ruin the fit with its mate. Let the removal of wood produce the fit. When both sleeves have been fitted up to the depth index lines drawn on the back of billets, fit the sleeves themselves together partially and sight down the joined stave to check alignment. Make notations on any adjustments that need to be made when cementing the sleeves to the billets. Notes may be in the form of arrows or instructions reminding the craftsman to tilt or

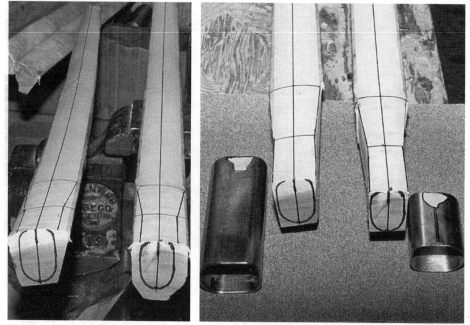

Billet butts prepared for cut-out.   *Ready for fitting.*

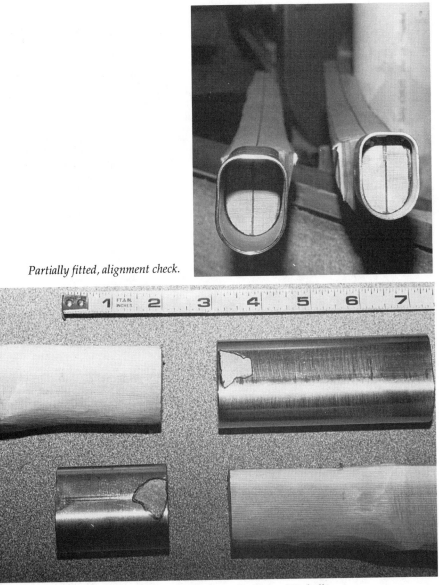

Partially fitted, alignment check.

Fully shaped, ready for cementing. Sleeve components by Richard Dykoff.

rotate a component. If you find some error, you can take care of small divergences by adding a thin wooden shim while cementing the ferrules.

Clean the sleeves thoroughly inside and out once more with fresh solvent to remove any remaining traces of oil or dirt.

The proper adhesive for mounting billets to sleeves is critical to long term satisfaction with your take-down bow. The sleeve joints are under a variety of

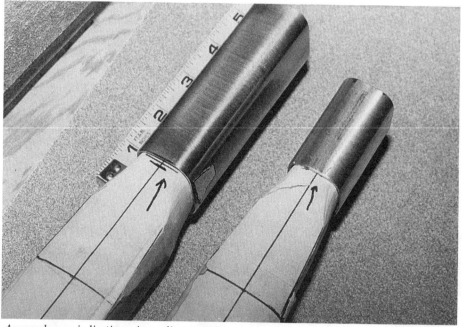

Arrows drawn, indicating minor adjustments necessary while cementing. Note lines insuring correct mounting depth at the base of components.

stresses, including impact loads from shooting the bow and the "breathing" of the bow wood as it expands and contracts from changes in temperature and humidity. The adhesive must adhere well to both wood and metal surfaces. It must fill small gaps in the mounting joint and have low enough viscosity to keep it from running out of the joints before it sets. The product with which I have had the best results is a two part epoxy from the Smooth-On Company that goes by the designation MT-13. Use of this product, or one like it which is formulated specifically for adhering metal to wood will provide solid, long term bonding of the sleeves.

Prepare your work area for the sleeve mounting process by having the items you'll needed close at hand. Although MT-13 requires 24 hours to fully cure, it can begin to stiffen within minutes, depending on room temperature. It is advantageous to mount the long outer sleeve first. This is the easier of the two sleeves to mount because of its longer sighting plane. Give the ferrule surface a good coverage of MT-13. Then slide on the appropriate sleeve and line the billet up with it. Follow the notes you made on the back of the billets earlier. Put this half of the bow aside to cure overnight. The following day, the shorter inner sleeve can be accurately mounted using the solid longer sleeve and billet to insure alignment. This "one at a time" method of mounting provides a good approach to assuring accuracy in alignment. Again, don't hesitate to check and recheck alignment between the billets and sleeves. No matter how close you shape your ferrules there is always room for final adjustment at the time the sleeves are glued.

A short time ago a customer called asking advice on how he might get his sleeves and billets apart as he had been in a hurry when gluing and gotten the assembly misaligned. He wanted to know if I had any good suggestions for removing them without causing damage to either the sleeves or the bow. The only advice I could give was to get a hack saw with a fresh blade, cut the billets off flush with the end of the sleeves, and go a little slower next time.

It is not a good idea to do any cementing with the two sleeves fitted together as epoxy can migrate easily onto surfaces where you do not want it. It would be a shame at this stage to make a one piece bow after all.

Once the cement securing the sleeves has cured, a brief session with the sanding belt or rasp will square off the butt of the inner sleeve, then a sanding block with medium grit sand paper or a flap sander can be used to remove any hardened epoxy residue from the sleeve units. If there is difficulty sliding the two sleeves together, it is likely that the side walls of the short inner sleeve have been sprung outward during its fitting onto the billet. Even when care is taken, it is difficult not to cause some slight distortion of material. The solution is to correct the shape of the outer sleeve to match the new shape of the solidly epoxied inner sleeve unit. This can be performed with very carefully applied pressure — from back and belly — with the jaws of a vise. When you feel the slightest amount of movement, back off and check directly by fitting the two units together or measure with the dial gauge. Repeat the process gently until the components regain their fit. When the sleeves fit together, polish the sliding surfaces with fine sand paper until the slide action is smooth. Take care not to remove so much metal from any surface that the fit becomes sloppy. Then polish the sliding surfaces of the sleeves inside and out with #0000 steel wool.

Before shaping the limbs, a critical detail regarding alignment of the sleeve components and the bow limbs should be discussed. As mentioned earlier, the handle assembly must be used as the central axis around which the limbs are

Flap sander is useful to help obtain a smooth slide fit of sleeve components.

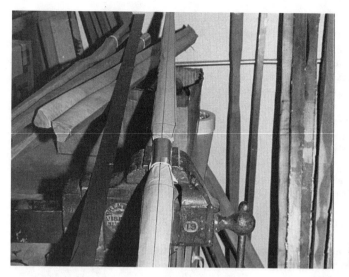

Fully joined billets, ready to shape into a bow.

crafted. This axis is pre-established by the sleeve assembly as it is the one component of the bow that cannot be altered. In the case of the one piece bow it is
possible to compensate at the handle section, shifting the axis by removing handle material from one side. When using a sleeve/socket handle assembly, the
handle section is the fixed controlling component. Because of this you must
keep an eye on how the "keel" of the handle and limbs are lined up throughout
the tillering of the bow. With this understood, the bow builder will have few
problems crafting sleeve/socket take-down bows.

With the components mounted, look down the length of the stave to get an
idea how things line up. If the lines drawn on the back match up exactly, pat
yourself on the back. If the lines don't line up, that extra width left at the tips of
your billets will now come in handy. Draw a fresh center line on the newly
joined take-down stave. To protect the bow back and help make the center line
as visible as possible, cover the back with a strip of masking tape. Note the center line of the outer take-down sleeve. As discussed, this is the center of your
bow, and the bow limbs must index from it. Using the outer sleeve center line as
a starting point, draw the layout lines that will establish the shape of the bow
back. A take-down can be patterned after any style bow you choose.

On many of the bows I craft, I draw in the widest sections of the limbs at
points 3" from the edges of the outer take-down sleeve. This widest point will be
1 3/4", if the wood permits. Out at the tips, a generous width of 3/4" allows for
slight adjustment later. Connect these points with straight lines. Also draw lines
from the widest part of the bow to the point where the billet enters the handle.
The more precisely the bow is laid out and cut, the easier it will be to craft.

In the quest to produce forgiving, easy to shoot bows, it is important to understand how much influence the basic layout of the bow has in enhancing this
quality. The general shooting qualities of a bow are improved by laying out and
building the bow to function in as straight a line as possible in the vertical shooting plane. The straighter the line that the limbs travel, the easier the bow will be

to shoot. It is not necessary to follow small side to side variations in grain in the bow limb. An old rule of thumb regarding side to side grain in a stave suggests that if the line of the grain can be kept within the bow limb inside of a 15" span of limb length, then limb integrity is assured. Although this guideline outlines the extreme case, it does suggest what is possible in bow construction. It is only fair to note, however, that the more the grain is violated, the greater the chances of wood failure, especially on higher weight bows.

Osage and yew, however, can only rarely be built as perfectly straight bows because the normally wandering grain must be carefully followed. When properly crafted, even a wildly meandering billet can produce a good shooting bow, although not easily. Many "snake" bows are beautiful and unique to build and shoot. However you choose to treat side to side grain structure, just remember that if you build bows for yourself to fit and fill your own desires, you will usually be satisfied with the results.

After the bow has been marked and cut out, keep in mind while tillering that the shooting comfort of the bow can be improved by making the handle section slightly stiffer than the limbs, the result being a gentle feel without the hand shock that occurs in a bow which bends into the grip area. Also, the mass of the sleeve assembly itself adds to the shooting quality of the bow by further dampening hand-shock vibration.

Try to work on a bow when you have an open-ended block of time and will not feel rushed. Don't try to complete the entire bow or even the sleeve mounting procedure in one session. If you run into a problem that has you a bit baffled, often the best cure is to put the bow down for the day and give yourself some time to ponder. You might be amazed at how clear things become after letting a problem bow rest for a short time.

It is beneficial to put a string on the bow at as early a stage in the tillering as possible. There is no other way to get a true picture of how the bow aligns under the stress of bending. The earlier in construction limb alignment is viewed, the earlier you can correct problems.

Once the bow is strung, hold it by one of its tips and rest the opposite tip on the floor. Sight down the length of the bow and note how the limbs line up with each other and with the center of the handle sleeve keel, the deepest part of the handle. If one or both of the limb tips are out of alignment, remove wood from the inside quarter of the belly on the side opposite to that which the tip is pointing. In other words, the limb always bends toward the weaker side, and wood should be removed from the opposite side. If the entire bow seems to wander off to one side and one of the limbs is notably stiffer, showing 1/4" or more tiller differential, it is likely that this stiffer limb is pulling the entire bow out of alignment. Remove wood from the belly of the stiffer limb first, correcting it to a closer tiller with its weaker mate.

A critical alignment check for a sleeve/socket-handled bow is made by first holding the bow in your hand as if you were going to shoot it. Holding the bow out in front of you, note the flats that exist on both sides of the outer sleeve. When these flats are held directly parallel to your line of vision, the bow string should be centered exactly in the middle of the handle. If it does not appear centered, then one or both of the limbs are misaligned and must be corrected.

Finished take-downs.

As wood is removed and the bow comes closer into tiller, gradually brace it a little higher, continually inspecting from both ends. If the bow appears to be well aligned, it will benefit from being left strung for a few minutes. This gives the bow a chance to learn to bend in a gentle, sustained manner, before it must undergo the stress of being drawn. Progress must be constantly monitored, checking tiller and draw weight throughout the shaping process.

As the bow nears completion, don't hesitate to shoot it. The draw length should be limited for the first few shots to give the bow an opportunity to get used to being shot. Check the tiller during this shooting session and plan to retiller as necessary. With the take-down handle mounted as outlined, you'll find a tiller differential of 5/16 to 3/16 greater tiller measurement for the top limb helps create a pleasant shooting bow.

It is a wise practice to seal the bottom of your outer sleeve socket with something that will act as a weather barrier and also as a pad to absorb the force as the limbs butt together upon mounting. Automotive fiber gasket material, 1/16" thick and cut to fill the bottom of the bow socket accomplishes this. You can seat this gasket by gently pushing and then tapping it home with the other half of the bow. A few drops of Loc-Tite 420, carefully dripped around the inner edges of the socket floor completes the job.

The flat end of the inner sleeve socket does not need any special treatment other than being sealed and finished. Use another few drops of Loc-Tite 420 spread around on this flat as a fast drying and very effective "pickling" finish. Be careful not to slide the sockets together until this is all well dried, or your new bow may never take-down again.

The take-down feature provides convenience and portability, while at the same time allowing the archer to maximize a bow's shooting qualities. The ability to produce your own take-down bows can add to your growth as a bow maker and also to the fine shooting stock hanging on your wall. Incorporating a sleeve/socket handle into a suitable stave or billets is not difficult if the procedure is undertaken with the same care and patience accorded any other bow building task.

A STONE AGE BOW

Tim Baker

One morning in what will some day be the ancient past three Homo Sapien Sapiens set out, stone axes in hand, for a distant stand of elm. Shade-grown, twist-free and tall, this stand held the local bow wood of choice.

Each of the three was the principle bowmaker among his people. And each had traveled a far distance to learn and share knowledge with the others. As they walked, they talked of tool stones, tillering methods, subtleties of bow design, and the endless mysteries of wood. They relished this time. For although each came from distant and sometimes opposing tribes, they could only share this depth of interest and knowledge among themselves. Bowmakers are a tribe of their own. Miles passed unnoticed, so that almost too soon the elms stood before them.

The three discussed the what-to-do's of this tree and that. Having casual mastery of their craft, they would not choose a straight tree. A true hunter does not shoot sleeping game.

In time they selected a most devious and challenging tree. Measuring three-inches in diameter and somewhat oval in cross-section, the tree was imperfect in form: if seen from its narrow side view the young elm elbowed slightly, shoulder-high from the ground. Viewed front-view it resembled a snake. "... but by placing the bow just so, the string will lay center-grip ... by placing the grip at the elbow this bow will be set back in the handle ..."

Now clearly seeing the bow resting inside, they marked the stave's length on the tree. Two-pound hand-held stone axes were brought to bear. The tree was felled, then a man-tall length hacked out of it. A stout antler tine was driven through the small log, splitting it precisely in two, both sides now suitable for working into a bow.

Their elapsed working time to this point was a mere eleven minutes!

The reader may decide this eleven-minute time is impossibly short. And he may doubt archaeology's power to determine that time.

I was amazed at this cutting speed too, but know it's accurate, because I was one of the above "Stone Age" bowyers. Here's the whole story:

Fellow bowmakers Gene Langston, James Murphy and I set out to discover just how much effort and time would be needed to make a decent bow from start to finish using only prehistoric tools.

Our tool kit was, literally, pre-human. My large-stone knapping skills are

The crudest of hand axes, scarcely more than two rocks banged together, but well able to bite through green wood. This pre-sapien level of knapping skill wastes stone, but the nature of flint-like material does insure a sharp cutting edge. "Waste" flakes can be picked through for use as various knife, plane, and scraper blades.

homo-erectine at best. But we were not interested in litho-jewelry, just a sharp edge. Any amorphous rock will make a serviceable stone blade or ax — obsidian, chert, flint, etc. Flint and novaculite, being on hand, were used here.

For felling, and crude wood reduction, blade weight is far more important than knapping skill or stone type. As heavy a blade as can be wielded with precision should be used. A two or three pound blade will do in minutes what a knife-weight blade will do in hours.

To enhance the research value of our project we decided to keep accurate times for each step. We should have brought a stop watch.

The tree was down in four minutes! A six-foot section removed in another three.

We simply — couldn't — believe it!

And our distant counterparts would have had well crafted blades, surely hafted for leverage and control. No doubt they could have reduced our time by half. Our view of the Stone Age was at the moment abruptly altered.

Moments before, this operation had had a playful air about it. But this WORKED! This was REAL.

The Stone Age had just spread its arms and encircled us. And our surroundings had set the stage: A steep, shaded slope of woods. Far below a dark creek flowed without sound, the far canyon wall a silent sheet of sun-blared forest. No artifact of man marring the primeval view, we felt connected to the ancient stone-tooled bowmen. And at heart, and in the purpose and manner of our work, we were them. With the spirits of our bowmaking ancestors now saturating the air around us we set back to work.

A patch of leather in the palm, for comfort and safety, permits a full hard swing. This three-inch tree was down before working up a sweat. But if felling a larger tree, either haft the blade for leverage, or use a five-plus pound stone and a two-hand swing.

For cleaner, less damaging entry, sharpen the antler tip to a flat wedge shape. This log was split at its center for two reasons: 1, Having been mauled by a stone ax its ends offered no sure entry point. 2, Starting at the middle increases the odds of dividing such a small log into equal halves its full length.

We had selected a small oval-sectioned tree: being small it was felled more easily, but its flat sides would yield low-crown, "big-tree" staves. This tree would therefore be split through its narrow side.

A stone-sharpened, chisel-shaped antler tip was placed at the grip and tapped in deep enough to hold in place. Its blunt top was then clubbed a single decisive blow. The antler pierced the small log clean and neatly. Several inches each side of the antler were cleaved free.

A battle-ax-shaped piece of hickory had also been prepared. Its almost-sharp edge would ax right through green elm, we had hoped. But the stringy elm shrugged off the attack. A wood ax, however, was surprisingly effective at bludgeoning off small branches. This hardwood ax finished splitting the stave in seconds. The elm's heavy wet bark pulled free effortlessly, exposing the future bow's finished back. Our little elm tree seemed positively eager to become a bow.

Reducing the half-log to front-view bow shape proceeded easily. Heavy stone blades moved with little resistance through thin-edged, soft, wet elm. With front-view reduction complete, total elapsed work time stood at just over 15 minutes. Now for tillering.

Efficient bows cannot be finish-tillered from green wood. Massive, cast-robbing string follow results. But I've found that wood can be safely taken from dripping green staves to fully cured bows in a few days' time.

This hickory axe proved useful for clearing brush, and removing small branches from our bow tree. Here it gently finishes wedging apart the antler-split log. Wood tools are easy to fashion, and raw materials usually more available than knappable stone. Only stone tools survive from the older Stone Ages. But the "Stone Age" was surely more of a wood, bone, fiber, and skin age.

During the growing season bark peels easily from the log, especially from younger trees. If cut at the very beginning, or after the end of its growth year, a full ring of summer growth is exposed. If cut during the growing season the percentage of early-wood to late-wood in the outer ring will be high if using ring-porous wood. The bow's back will then be slightly more likely to fail. This is not a big concern with tension-strong woods such as elm.

Roughing out the front-view shape. A one and one-half pound selected "waste" flake coasts through normally uncooperative elm. Work proceeded as surely and quickly as with a steel ax in cured wood.

Drying time increases exponentially with thickness—wood shavings will dry in an hour, a 4" by 4" can take well over a year. But how can you know exactly how thin to reduce a stave for drying? Simply rough tiller the bow, using the same care and attention to proportion as if finish tillering. But tiller to only *about eight inches of unbraced bend, not enough to induce lasting set.* A full explanation of quick-drying will follow.

Rough-tillering our green elm bow proceeded more slowly than earlier steps, but faster than we would have believed possible an hour earlier. Different blade shapes and various wood-removing techniques were tried. Selected blades, held at certain angles, removed long, eye-widening masses of wood. Thin, straight-edged blades served as precision scrapers. With rough tillering complete the clock stood at one hour and forty minutes.

True Stone Age bowyers would possibly have one or more rough-tillered staves dried and ready, in anticipation of a broken or lost bow. No multi-day wait for staves to dry. Such a bowyer would be deprived of a bow for only a few hours, but we must now wait four days.

A "foot-vise" made of elm inner-bark rope. Unless real muscle is put into the work rough tillering can take days. By making leg muscles resist arm muscle this rig lets the bowmaker apply as much force to the tool as his arms are able.

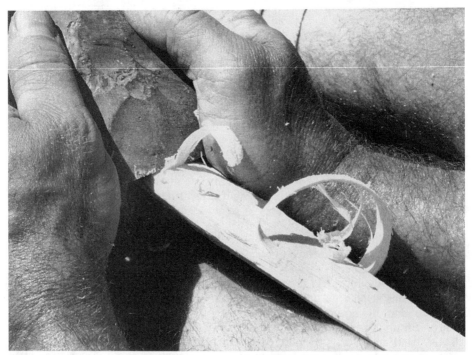

Removing bulk belly wood. On the whole, stone tools take very little more work time than modern steel tools. If time spent earning the money to buy modern tools is included we have a real horse race.

Smaller blades can be worked like drawknives and spokeshaves. Due to its flat bottom and sharp, angled leading edge, this blade works very much like a small block plane, permitting controlled reduction. By knapping, or by selecting proper scraps, an unlimited number of such "custom" blades will be available.

Here is how to quick-dry your own green staves.

Even during the pre-fiberglass hey-day of wood-based archery only a small percentage of archers made their own bows. Instead they paid about a week's wages to a professional bowyer. But much of the satisfaction of archery comes from making your own equipment.

Most archers did not make their own bows because both professional bowyer and customer believed decent bows could not be made of the common American hardwoods. And the average individual wishing to make a bow could not afford to squander expensive staves of Osage and yew learning the craft.

Volume 1 of this series inspired hundreds to become first-time wood bowmakers. And because the dark-age of fiberglass has erased much of the Osage/yew dogma from living memory, they came to the subject free of prejudice. They hadn't read the old books, so they didn't know they weren't supposed to be able to make powerful, efficient bows of hickory, ash, maple, and the like.

It looks as if the white-wood log jam is broken. The inexhaustible expanse of this continent's now-liberated hardwoods will let a limitless number of archers learn to make their own equipment.

But one more log jam remains: Archery books of the past also said or implied that if wood is to be made into a decent bow, it must be seasoned for up to several years. And this was commonly accepted.

Waiting years, even months, is a serious impediment to the average person who simply wants to make a bow. The happy truth, however, is that bowstaves can be cured in only a few days, and that this quick-drying method, if done properly, is *superior* to traditional stave drying methods.

This quick-dry method has been very hard for many "in the know" to swallow:

"Are you saying that thousands of bowmakers, over hundreds of years weren't bright enough to figure such an elementary system out? Especially since it would have saved them so much time?"

It's not that simple:

One, in the past bows were made largely by professional bowyers. Professionals had a large, full pipeline of drying wood. They didn't have to wait for staves to dry.

Two, for this quick-curing method to work the stave has to be prepared in a particular way. If done incorrectly it will warp.

Three, the quick, safe drying of staves would be no surprise whatever to countless "primitive" bowmakers of the past.

Wood can be taken from green tree to a perfectly cured, durable, hard-shooting bow in less than a week. And this method can be used with partially dried staves also.

Here's why it works:

Wood shrinks as it dries, and its outside dries faster than its inside. This means the outside shrinks faster than the inside. Something has to give. The outside gives by checking and cracking. The inside gives by collapsing wood cells.

But thin wood does not check while drying because thin wood "has no inside!"

To quick-cure a stave:

Fell, split, and debark the tree.

Reduce the stave to just over finished-bow width.

Leave the stave full width its entire length, including tips and grip.

Begin tillering as if you intend finishing the bow green. Leave tips and grip full width for now. This prevents the otherwise narrow grip and tips from warping as they dry.

Let sides be square, and belly flat — uniform dimensions promote uniform drying.

If making a 50 lb. bow, proceed until the properly-tillered blank will bend about eight inches while pushing against the grip with about 50 lbs. of force. This is not enough strain to impart permanent set, but is enough to insure the stave is as thin as it can be. The stave can now dry in the shortest possible time.

A side benefit of this drying method is that much time and effort are saved working soft, green wood. Especially if hand tools, and in particular stone tools, are used.

Once the green stave has been floor tillered, it will be very thin relative to its width. Lateral warping, therefore, is almost impossible. In fact, being so uniform in dimension, warping of any kind is unlikely.

A moderate room temperature of 70 degrees, and 50% relative humidity, will see the blank dry in about two weeks.

One hundred degree, 40% humidity air cuts drying time to about a week. A flow of air speeds drying at any temperature and humidity, just like clothes on a line. For fast, and especially for uniform drying, all parts of the stave should be exposed to a uniform flow of air.

If some small amount of warp begins to develop tie or clamp the blank to proper position. Slight natural twists and waves can also be corrected at this time by clamping. No steaming needed. Mild recurves can also be added.

Thin, uniform dimensions and an even air flow are the inviolate keys to success here. The other half of our elm log was debarked, then left as-is to dry. It soon became unusable due to twist and warp.

When dry, reduce the stave to its finished front-view dimensions, then finish tillering normally. You will now appreciate the easy-working green wood.

Here is a simple way to know when the stave is dry: Acquire a small scale of five-pound capacity. A larger scale will not give precise readings with such a low mass.

While green, the tips of the bow can be slightly recurved. (courtesy Jim Riggs)

Weigh the stave as soon as it's ready for drying. And weigh it every day or so. Weight will drop about 25% the first day, but progressively less as time passes. When the stave has lost *no weight whatever* for about 25% of the time it has spent drying, the stave is dry. For example, if a stave dries for four days, then loses no weight for one additional day, the stave is ready to work. Using a scale in place of a moisture meter works dependably only on very thin, preferably floor tillered staves. Thicker staves dry too slowly for small weight changes to register.

The stave's drying rate slows as its moisture content approaches target moisture content — equilibrium with surrounding air. A stave's speed of drying acts much like a coasting car slowing down as it reaches the bottom of a hill. But final stages of drying can be sped up by creating a steeper slope near the hill's bottom.

If drying in 50% humidity air, the stave's final moisture content will be 9%. In 70 degree, slightly moving air about five days are required to drop from 35% to 13%, another five days from 13% to 10% (the car is reaching level ground) and another several days to creep down to almost 9%. But if the second half of the drying process occurs in, say, 35% humidity the stave will think its heading for 7% and run down to 9% more quickly. Higher air speed, and higher air temperatures both speed drying, but have no real effect on final moisture content.

We dried our elm stave the Indian way, the way our ancestors likely would have when *they* were Indians in Mesolithic Europe: We used sun and wind during the day, the upper reaches of a "fire-warmed lodge" at night (my attic). Sun and wind normally damage curing wood. But this stave, being "all surface," was undisturbed.

Final tillering. The once soft and docile elm is now hard and dry. Shavings are paper thin and hard-earned. If washboards begin, scrape from another direction or change the angle of the blade.

Which is more than can be said for us. As mentioned earlier, we three "Stone Age" bowmen were from different "tribes". Gene is an ex-Army Ranger and ex-cop. Philosophically, if Gene is Terra del Fuego, I'm Portugal. Normally a small community can be powered by passing a copper wire between us. As for Gene and James, these two had manned opposite sides of police/activist lines during the late 60's. When talk strayed beyond archery the air charged up. But a mutual love of wood bowmaking acted as a ground. The ancient, soul-deep lure of the bow proved stronger than mere differences of moral philosophy.

On the fourth day in the California summer sun and Golden Gate breezes the stave's moisture content stood at 11%. Hotter, drier, more windy conditions, or longer drying time, would have lowered moisture content another point or so, but performance would hardly be affected. We were ready for finish tillering.

Ninety-plus percent of wood removal had been completed while the wood was green, taking less than two hours. Once dry, once hard, the very small amount of wood removed during final tillering required almost four hours. An extra half-hour spent fine-tuning while green would likely have saved close to two hours after the wood had dried. Still, after less than six working hours, here was a beautiful, durable bow, capable of killing any animal on the continent. It's satisfying knowing you can be booted out of civilization and have a meat-making bow in action before building up a good appetite.

Fine-textured sandstone or horsetail rush can bring the bow's surface to a modern sandpaper state. Large, coarse horsetail equals about 120-grit, younger shoots, shown here, equal 180-grit. "Boning," rubbing with bone, antler, or such, imparts a dense, primitive luster. And likely slows moisture absorption.

The stave had been positioned in the tree to take advantage of natural setback. Because of this, after several hundred shots string follow stands at just 1/2". Its snakey front view was positioned to create a near center-shot arrow pass. Despite its crude origins this is a first-class weapon by any measure.

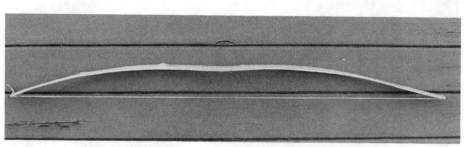

Our finished bow might have arrived by time machine. Outfitted with hand-spun flax string and flint-tipped arrow, it's especially satisfying roving the hills and creeks with this prehistoric weapon. At such times, with no proof of the present in view, brother Stone Age bowmen can be sensed walking just around each bend of the creek.

ONE-DAY STONE AGE ARROWS
ALL ARROWS AND PHOTOS BY JIM RIGGS

Turn green arrowshafts over hot coals for an hour or so, while straightening occasionally.

When straight and rigid, remove bark with scraper.

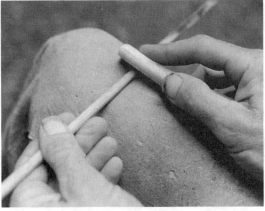

If sandpaper or some natural substitute is not available, burnish wood with smooth bone or stone to compress fibers and polish surface.

When feathers are limited, this fletching technique helps stabilize arrow. Split shaft at nock end ...

... then prepare feather and string nock as shown. Feather's spine was flattened so the split shaft will not be wedged open.

Insert feather, wrap at each end with sinew, then use hot coal to burn feather to shape.

Fletching technique with three small feathers wrapped with sinew at each end.

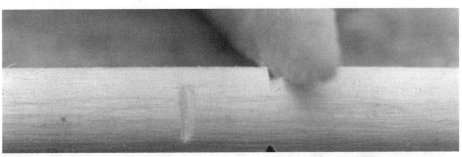

Method for cutting out notch for arrowhead or nock. Make four grooves on the shaft oriented as shown.

Make two splits from the first notches back to the second.

Break the notch out by moving it from side to side.

With a bit of cleaning, the notch is now ready for bowstring or arrowhead.

The business end of the finished arrows. Also see Stone Points in this volume.

Tim Baker shooting a Stone Age arrow from his Stone Age bow.

PREVENTING AND SOLVING PROBLEMS

Paul Comstock

In his legendary book, *Hunting With The Bow And Arrow*, Saxton Pope describes making a hickory-backed bow of eastern red cedar. After a brief description, Pope advises that all that remains for the would-be bowyer is dealing with the mechanical difficulties of the task, which "add zest to the problem."

Many bowyers know very well what Pope was talking about, since it often seems we're up to our ears in zestful problems. Indeed, the art of making wooden bows can be a never-ending problem-solving process. When a problem develops, identifying its cause is the first great challenge. Identifying a remedy or a way to prevent the problem in the future is the second. This is particularly true when we venture outside the realm of our previous successful experience. Some bowyers become adept at constructing one style of bow, or using one type of material, or one method of construction. When they try something different, it's understandable that they encounter problems they never faced before.

Confronted with this situation, the bowyer has two options. He can pronounce the problem insurmountable, throw up his hands in disgust and return to the safer, successful habits of the past. Or he can say to himself, "Some way, somehow, there must be an answer to this." Then he sinks his teeth into the problem and doesn't give up until he cracks the case.

Limitations of time and resources affect everyone's inclination to tackle new or challenging problems in one way or another. And the bowyer who sticks to one basic style or material is not prevented from becoming a talented and enviable craftsman.

But those who stick with the problem until they find a solution aren't simply making bows. They are expanding the boundaries of self-bowyery. They are discovering new options that other bowyers could use to their advantage. They have the potential to remove obstacles from the paths of other bowyers and would-be bowyers.

Few people are excited by the prospect of a broken bow. But while bows may fail, bowyers do not. Instead, they learn. My advice is always, "Try it. If it doesn't work, you'll still learn something."

Fortunately, most bowmakers I have encountered love the problem-solving process and are encouraged by the prospect of the thrill of success.

It is important to remember that despite the seemingly simple appearance of a wooden bow, there are literally thousands of possible variables in material and construction that can affect the outcome. Aside from the basic good tiller we all seek, there is no one procedure that will assure success in all possible cases. Even with the tiller, subtle variations will improve results with certain bow styles. Here we submit a number of tricks and techniques to prevent problems when we can and solve them when they occur. Keep in mind that these suggested solutions carry no guarantees. Because the list of possibilities is so huge, unforeseen factors can prevent success in some circumstances. But the solutions presented here were selected because others have used them to obtain some measure of consistent success.

Because the list of possible problems is also quite huge, no one can solve all of your problems for you. Most bowyers are ready to tackle problems, because they learn that they must.

WOOD SEASONING
In the early 20th century, white bowmakers usually chopped down a log of yew or Osage, tossed the whole log with the bark intact in a shed, and waited. And waited and waited and waited.

Finally — after all the kids grew another head taller, the hound dog died of old age, and the bowyer had collected a few more gray hairs — they split the log into bow staves.

This practice ultimately evolved into one of self bowyery's most long-lived pieces of dogma — that wood aged for several years is the best obtainable and cannot be surpassed, that its cast has somehow been magically increased during the years the wood sat around.

I disagree completely with this piece of dogma, but I do agree that letting a split log sit around several years is indeed the safest way to season wood. If nothing is being done to the wood, there is certainly little chance anything can go wrong.

Seasoning wood rapidly does entail an element of risk. But the risk is not so high that it prevents consistent success. A very large group of bowyers obtains consistent results by seasoning wood rapidly.

The old method of letting split logs season for years is not 100 percent safe in all possible circumstances. If the Osage or yew log is left outside, exposed to wide variations in temperature and humidity, the log can check deeply right through the bark. And if the log is constantly kept in a too-humid environment, a hundred years would not be enough time to reduce the moisture content to an acceptable level.

What really counts in wood seasoning is reducing the moisture content to a workable level without damaging the wood, which includes warping, checking, and decay. The optimum moisture content is 9 or 10 percent, but it is also possible to make a piece of wood too dry. If it the wood is bent when too dry, it will almost certainly be damaged.

If I cut a small-diameter tree, I typically find the stave will warp. But if the wood warps, I just steam it straight. (See "Bending Wood" in Volume 2.) While severe steam-bending weakens wood cells, I've never experienced a problem because most of my steam bends are no more than about 5 degrees. I have a couple of bows that were steamed and bent at seven different spots along their length. (This isolated steaming is accomplished by positioning only a section of the stave over a small pan of water.) The bows look and act as if they were cut from perfectly straight wood.

Checks are caused by wood shrinking too quickly as it dries. This is a problem if the wood is fairly thick, because the interior cannot dry as quickly as the exterior, or in some cases, the middle cannot dry as fast as the edges. This creates stress and the result is drying checks. If left exposed to the elements, any wood will develop checks. Under these circumstances the checks will sometimes be small, but often they are quite large.

The tendency to check will vary considerably among different types of wood. Whether the bark is left on or removed can also be a factor. If the bark is removed from green Osage orange, the log can check badly overnight when the sapwood is left on. By comparison, every elm, hickory, birch, oak, and ash I ever cut experienced virtually no checking when the green log was split and the bark removed.

Between these extremes are woods like black locust, which can easily check when the bark is removed from the green log, but not as badly as Osage. I have received reports that ironwood also checks badly if the bark is removed from the green log.

In my experience, the white woods mentioned above will not present checking problems when the wood is handled correctly. They will experience some checking at the end of the log, but this can be prevented by coating the ends with either wax, glue, or varnish. My favorite method is to simply cut the wood long. Even if the ends do check, it is fairly easy to work the narrow tips so no checks are present in the finished bow. I have even made several bows with a check squarely centered in the middle of the limb tip, with no subsequent problems save the cosmetic effect.

White woods, however, can check if the green logs are placed in an unstable environment. If they are exposed to wind, hot sun, and wide variations in temperature and humidity, anything can happen. The worst place to leave such white wood staves is outdoors, on the ground. Treat white wood this way, and it can easily check. I have always thought the best place to put such wood is in your residence, where the humidity and temperature are fairly constant, and the wood is not exposed to the sun. Damp and musty basements, searing hot attics, and drafty sheds and carports are lousy places to place a green, split white wood log with bark removed. Dampness and temperature variations will also promote decay with white woods.

Gary Davis, from Michigan, seasons green Osage in a hurry without suffering checking problems. This success depends on two elements: removing the sapwood quickly, and covering the newly exposed heartwood back with wood glue. Taking a split Osage log, he removes the bark and immediately begins removing the sapwood. He sticks with this job until it is completed, even if it takes two straight hours. He says the sapwood comes off a little easier when it is green, though it is not particularly easy to follow one growth ring (this is easier to accomplish when the stave is dry and the bowyer can take his time). The instant the sapwood is removed, Davis immediately covers the back with white or yellow wood glue to provide a moisture barrier, but says a coating of grease would probably work just as well.

If any other type of tree gives you checking problems, imitate Davis and cover the exposed back with wood glue or grease.

TILLER

The best answer to avoid tiller problems is to tiller the bow correctly in the first place. If you lack a vast amount of experience, or are working with a wavy or otherwise challenging piece of wood, the best answer is to proceed slowly. Once the limbs start bending, use only tools that remove wood slowly and check the tiller every time you remove wood. When the bow starts to show the slightest amount of string follow, it's a good plan to recheck the tiller after giving the bow a series of pulls, since wood removal might not otherwise show an immediate tillering change.

One of the most vexing problems occurs when the tiller shifts. This usually happens when the lower limb — over time — takes on more bend. The problem is most common among bows with rigid, non-bending handle sections.

The problem typically appears in the bow's first 500 shots. Sometimes it could take longer. I recently talked to a fellow I had supplied with a bow three years previously, and was aghast to find that in the last month or so the lower limb had taken on more bend!

This problem is nothing new. Study old archery books carefully and you can spot the trouble in some photos. In *Archery Tackle* by Adolph Shane, a fellow in a Boy Scout uniform on page 96 is shooting a bow that appears to suffer from this affliction.

Typically, the bend in the lower limb increases to a certain point without further change. But there is no guarantee the condition will not worsen. At best, this problem hurts the cosmetics by giving the bow an uneven appearance.

I have given this problem a lot of attention, but still cannot say I have anything better than strong suspicions about what is happening. I suspect that:

• Lower limbs inherently experience more strain than upper limbs.
• Uneven compaction of the limbs' bellies is often responsible.
• Uneven moisture content in the limbs is often responsible.
• The method used to string the bow may be responsible.

My suspicion that lower limbs experience more strain is based mainly on the fact that this problem almost always appears in the lower limb. The archer always pulls the string at a point higher than the spot where he holds the bow. As a result, the section of string from drawing hand to upper nock is usually shorter than the section of string from the drawing hand to the lower nock. At first glance, this would seem to place more strain on the upper limb. But if the string creates a leverage effect on the nocks, then a longer lever creates more energy than a short lever. And the string from drawing hand to lower nock is longer. Leaving aside the accuracy of my diagnosis, one way or another the upper limb is almost never the problem.

The long-standing habit of making the upper limb about 1/4-inch further from the string that the lower limb is often enough to prevent the problem. But even bows made this way can sometimes end up with too much bend in the lower limb.

Another step that can be taken is to make the lower limb slightly longer than the upper. I have a copy of an old advertisement for Ben Pearson Archery, when the company was selling only wooden bows. Measuring the limbs in the photo shows the lower limb is longer on each bow. This trick made sense to me when I realized that while hunting, my bow's upper limb often tangles in branches and the lower limb seldom touches the ground.

I have never seen this problem occur in a board bow, only in bows made from log staves. This is an interesting clue. Because of a log stave's subtle contours, it often happens there will be more natural reflex in one limb than the other. If the more-reflexed limb is the lower limb, it will tend to be cut slightly thinner than the upper to create an even tiller. If this happens, the thicker wood of the upper limb will acquire slightly more string follow than the lower limb — in the beginning. To state it another way, the lower limb can bend further in the beginning with less string follow because its limb is slightly thinner. This difference may or may not be visible. But when it happens, the lower limb is experiencing less compaction on the belly than the upper limb.

This situation does not remain constant. As water seeks its own level, strain searches for a weakness. The thinner lower limb is inherently weaker in our example. When the bow is thoroughly broken in, ultimately the lower limb will be bending more. The very same thing can happen if the lower limb has a section with a trace of excessive bend not present in the upper limb. A spot too flat in the lower limb could also cause the same result.

I have successfully avoided this problem in long-lived bows by studying the stave carefully. If one limb is more reflexed than the other, I made it the upper limb. If one limb is more deflexed than the other, I made it the lower limb.

I have also steamed a slight reflex into an upper limb near the handle, leaving the lower limb as-is. Yet to be tried on my list of experiments is making the upper limb about 1/8th of an inch wider than the lower. All of these stunts are designed to make sure the lower limb is not thinner than the upper in the new bow.

You may be inviting this problem if you always lean your bows against a wall, with the lower nock on the floor. Tim Baker says he has found moisture content of wood on the floor will — over time — be about 1 percent higher than wood several feet off the floor. Higher moisture content in the lower limb will create excessive bend. To avoid it, store the bows in a horizontal position. If they lean against the wall, turn them over regularly so the upper and lower limbs each spend the same amount of time on the floor. If you are fairly certain you have this problem, try the moisture-reducing method in the upcoming section on string follow.

When the bow is being strung, it is customary for the string's loose loop to be around the upper limb. The string is usually secured to the lower limb with a small loop, or a timber hitch. Under these conditions, it often happens that the lower nock will be positioned against the foot by its very tip during stringing. By comparison, the archer tends to grab the upper limb several inches below the upper nock to bend the bow during stringing.

If this is performed habitually — particularly with the step-through method — the lower limb is being loaded with more initial bend than the upper limb.

This initial bend will be maintained as the bow is used, putting more strain on the lower limb.

I have seen smart archers check their bow after stringing and push their knee against the upper limb belly to flex it, increasing its bend before shooting.

I think a simpler solution is to make the string loop secure on the upper nock, and loose around the lower limb. In other words, hold the bow upside down when stringing it. In this manner, if extra bend is given to one limb, it is given to the limb that can stand it: the upper limb.

If the upper limb is loaded with too much initial bend during stringing, a few draws will usually return an even tiller — a situation that seldom occurs with the lower limb.

Oddly enough, this entire problem seems confined to man-sized bows. Shorter bows typically take on higher levels of string follow, reducing the odds that the lower limb will develop more set than the upper limb.

If a bow has this problem, what to do? Carefully reducing the belly of the upper limb may solve the problem. I have corrected uneven tiller by steaming a slight recurved kink in the last few inches of the limb that's bending too much. This will work if the limb tip is rigid enough. I have also accomplished this on a sinewed bow using hot air from a space heater. But that approach requires a cautious touch and a limited bend to avoid cracking the belly wood.

Many have solved the problem of uneven limbs by shortening the weak limb. If the bow is shorter than the archer, I would avoid making one limb more than two inches shorter than the other, to reduce problems from excessive strain.

Another tillering problem is a hinge, a spot that bends excessively.

Tim Baker corrected one hinged spot in a bow by piling lots of sinew on the back at that spot. The finished sinew backing at this point was 3/8-inch thick.

Primitive technology writer John McPherson fixed a bow by reducing the belly and gluing on a thin splint over that section of the belly. Once this was accomplished, he retillered the bow.

Such a belly splint could have ends that feather in thickness. Since the belly is under compression, it would be possible for the splint to have square ends, with the reduced belly cut to accommodate the splint. However, a square-end splint poses potential difficulties. If the splint has to be forced into the cut limb, it is already compressed and may crumble during bending. If the splint is too small for the space, the limb may develop a hinge at that spot.

This bow by Tim Baker shows that to correct a hinged limb, a considerable amount of sinew has to be applied on the back of the hinged spot.

BROKEN BOWS

Even when a bow breaks outright, it is occasionally possible to salvage it. The handiest method is to splice on a new limb to replace the broken one. I did this with the second Osage bow I ever made. John Strunk has done it several times, even using Osage for one limb and yew for the other.

It is probably easiest to accomplish when the original bow came from a single stave, and the handle is thick enough to allow splicing. Given a good bandsaw and a careful eye, it would be possible to cut a spliced handle apart along the original glue line, and then splice on the new limb.

During this process, the bowyer will at one point have a limb that is thoroughly broken in, while the other limb has no set. This could invite the problem of the new limb ending up with too much bend. To make the new limb match the old one in string follow, I put the bow on the floor belly-up, stood on the handle, slipped a cord on the new nock, and pulled and pulled until the level of follow matched the older limb.

Tim Baker advises that if the bow makes a clean break at the handle, it may be possible to square the broken ends and fit them into a short piece of pipe. They could be glued in solid, or one limb could be left unglued to create a take-down bow.

SPLINTERED BACKS

If an unbacked bow develops a slight splinter on the back, simply gluing on rawhide or covering the back with sinew is often enough to fix the problem.

If the splinter is severe, Tim Baker recommends first working the splintered spot down to the ring beneath it, then filling the spot higher than the surrounding wood with sinew. Then, he says, sinew back the whole works.

I gouged out a bad splinter on one bow, filled it with sinew, and sinewed the entire bow. Over the splintered spot I applied extra sinew that left a long ridge of the stuff in the finished back, running along the center of the limb. The spar varnish I put over the back cracks continually at this spot, signaling that sinew there is strained mightily. But thanks to the trick, the bow is still a bow and not firewood.

If you have bamboo or a suitable piece of hickory, a more reliable method may be to plane the entire back flat and glue on the backing. If the wood of the bow is fairly weak, like cedar or birch, the hickory or bamboo should be as thin as you can conceivably get it. If such backing is too thick, the weaker belly wood will be under too much compression, resulting in a number of frets or chrysals on the belly. This danger is much lower with highly elastic Osage and yew as well as the particularly resilient hickory.

If the center of your bow's back is higher than the limb's edges, you have a good option available if the bow splinters in the middle of the high crown. Grab a scraper and decrown the back until the splinter disappears. (See "Design and Performance" in Volume 1, or "Ancient European Bows" in Volume 2.) You may as well do both limbs evenly, to avoid having to retiller the belly of one limb. I did this with one bow. When the splinter disappeared, the decrowned flat edge on the back was an inch wide, still narrower than the two-inch limbs. The bow fell from 60 to 57 pounds, which I considered a fairly modest drop. I was also able to raise a knot on the back in the process.

FRETTING AND CHRYSSALING

If a section of limb is severely fretted on the belly, it is possible to imitate McPherson and replace the fretted section with a splint. Keep in mind frets occur because the bow is tillered badly, or the thickness is tapered badly, or the bow is overstrained. Unless the original problem is diagnosed and dealt with, more frets could show up on the splint.

Another answer is possible if the fret is small or faint, or where the limb is chrysaled (a number of small, short frets). Take a stout needle, small knife, or

Here is a good patching job by John McPherson. At top is the scooped-out belly and plug, before gluing. The center photo shows the plug glued into place and sanded flat. The whole works was wrapped with sinew when finished. Such a patch can be used to repair a fretted belly.

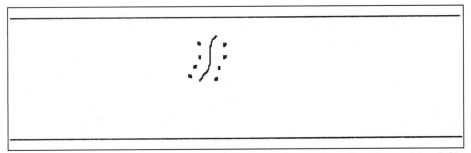

Pin holes made with a stout needle or sharpened nail can reduce compression when positioned this way on either side of a fret.

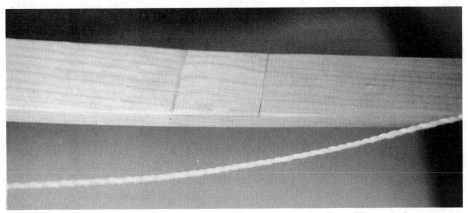

A belly patch that replaced a bad fret on a bow repaired by Doug Walters of Irmo, S. C.

sharpened nail, and create several shallow holes along either side of the fret, so the holes form lines parallel with the fret. This reduces compression on the fret. If you try to simply sand a fret away, the spot will fret worse. If you run your finger across a fret, you can feel the pinched wood rising above the limb surface. Press the holes in with the needle, and steel wool the fret smooth. If the fret is still smooth after shooting, you have stopped the fret in its tracks. This trick was described in Roger Ascham's *Toxophilus*, written in 1545 A.D. I confess, however, I read the ancient, tortured English of those sentences about 10 times until I finally figured out what Ascham was talking about.

If you check the limb with a pair of outside calipers, you will typically find that the section of the limb on the nock side of the fretted section is too thick. In other words, if the limb thickness tapers from handle to nock, there will be insufficient taper in that spot next to the fret on the nock side of the limb. Scraping the section down and rechecking it with the calipers can arrest a fret. Long frets often go deep into the limb. If the limb begins to take on more bend at a fret's location, the limb is rapidly moving toward fracture.

CRACKS AND SPELLS

Wooden bows often develop cracks in the limbs' sides or bellies for a variety of reasons. Typically, the crack was in the wood, but hardly visible as a result of splitting out the stave. A crack is easy to distinguish from a drying check, because the drying check follows the grain perfectly. The fibers have not ruptured at a check, only separated. A crack, by comparison, will cross the fibers and sometimes cross the rings. A crack has ruptured the fibers. If a crack appears closer to a bow's back than the belly, it is similar to a splintered back. Since the wood there is under tension, a crack that does not follow the grain closely will likely pull apart over time. Cracks are less likely to be pulled apart on the belly side, which is under compression.

Sinew and hide glue are the natural bowyer's equivalent of baling wire and duct tape. Odds are good that a heavy wrapping of sinew and glue will arrest a crack on the belly. Wrapping cracks closer to the back is a riskier proposition. For best odds of success, treat such a crack like a back splinter.

Gary Davis has dealt with large knots on the side of a limb by cutting them away, leaving a V-shaped hollow. He has done this when the bottom of the V does not significantly cut through the back's outer ring. He then glues in a plug with strong epoxy, and smooths the whole works. This has potential for dealing with a short crack near, but not on, the bow's back. It is a good plan to wrap the plug and surrounding limb with sinew and hide glue.

Steve Allely, another fine craftsman and a co-author of Volume 1, puts hide glue in a crack before wrapping the limb. He does this by warming up the limb, daubing glue over the crack, and blowing on the glue until he sees it sink into the crack.

Tim Baker says silk makes an effective binding, since the silk can be stretched during wrapping to create tension. The silk can be soaked in hide glue, and the ends of the wrapping must be tied or twisted (similar to a string serving) so the tension is not lost.

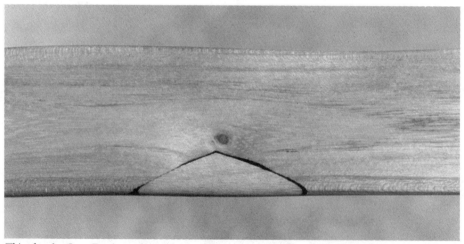

This plug by Gary Davis can be used to replace a knot or crack on the belly side of a limb. The plug was cut at an angle, so the outer ring was violated only slightly at the limb's edge.

Thin grades of cyanoacrolate woodworking glue are very effective at sinking to the very bottom of a crack. If you buy cyanoacrolate, make sure you also buy a bottle of cyanoacrolate solvent. In a span of two seconds, you can literally glue your thumb tight to the bow limb with a powerful cyanoacrolate glue. When you have a bottle of solvent, you won't have to worry about wide-eyed nurses staring as you walk into the emergency room with a 68-inch piece of wood glued to your hand. The solvent will soften the glue enough to free you, usually in under 60 seconds.

Ralph Lelii used stainless steel pins and metal cement to repair a nasty crack in a 35 pound bow. The finished repair job is shown here from back (top), belly (middle), and side, which also shows the crack.

Clear epoxy glues, sold in tubes with a 12-hour drying time, are very runny. They can sink deeply into a crack before the glue sets up.

If a crack threatens to ruin the bow, it seems appropriate to attempt any method, however desperate, to correct the situation. After all, if the bow is on its death bed, you have nothing to lose. One successful example of this attitude is a bow made by Ralph Lelii of Neshannock, Pa. He made a sassafras bow that revealed a nasty crack running diagonally from the back to belly. The crack was in the board used to make the bow, and opened visibly as the bow was drawn.

Lelii saved the bow by making it draw only 35 pounds, and pinning the crack with five short pieces of 3/32nd-inch stainless steel welding rod.

He drilled holes from back to belly through the crack, and glued the pins in with JB Weld, a glue made for bonding metal. He warmed the bow with a hair dryer before applying the glue, and clamped the crack closed until the glue dried. The pins were applied after the bow had been backed with rawhide.

At this writing, Lelii has counted 800 arrows shot through the bow. The crack has remained closed, and there is no deterioration around the glue or pins.

A "spell" is an old term for a feathered section of grain that lifts up on a bow's belly. Spells are typically caused by one of two problems. The first is a bad taper. This usually develops at a raised handle section, when the thickness taper has been cut too sharply. If such a spell covers most of the belly's width, it may eventually develop into a crack that sinks deep into the handle. You can eliminate this problem by covering the too-sharp taper with a splint.

When I did this, I cut the splint to about 1/4-inch thickness and boiled it for 20 minutes. Using padded clamps, I yanked the splint from the pot and quickly clamped it to the bow, so the wood would conform to the contour near the handle. After it dried, I epoxied it on and rasped the whole works smooth. This splint was about four inches long and created the gradual taper the wood should have had in the first place.

The second type of spell usually develops in white wood that has suffered some disease or other mild deterioration. I have dealt with these spells by digging out all the loose wood with a knife tip. Then I fill the hole with sawdust, soak it with cyanoacrolate, and sand it smooth when dry. Sometimes it takes more than one application.

If you have slight or moderate gashes in the belly from sloppy woodworking or using the wrong tool, you aren't the first person to make this mistake. I was surprised to find that filling these blemishes with epoxy and sanding them smooth made a very durable patch.

HANDLE SPLICES

Most problems with handle splices occur in the novice's first attempts. Reliable splicing methods are described in Volume 1, but eager novices often fail to take seriously the need for adequate equipment and technique.

Virtually anyone who cuts many handle splices is going to use a good bowmaking bandsaw. No other power tool is going to do the job justice. Cutting the splice with a handsaw is a possibility when the bowyer has a good sharp saw, can cut a straight line, clamps the wood in a vise, and exercises large amounts of patience and care.

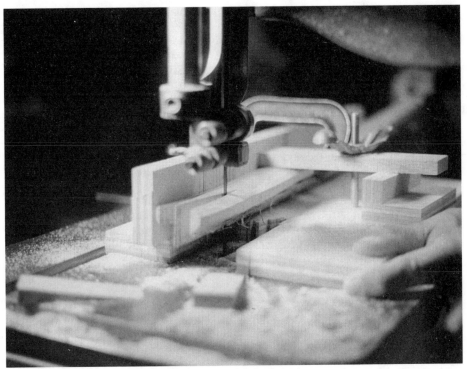

A jig like this can be used to obtain perfect cuts for a handle splice.

A band saw alone is not going to guarantee happy splicing. The trick to cutting a handle splice is making sure the distances between the cuts are the same on both back and belly. Since each cut requires a separate pass on the saw, it is imperative that the wood be at the same angle for each cut. If this is not done, the cuts will be wider on one side than the other.

Some step must be taken to ensure the handle section does not wobble in the slightest on the saw table. This could be done by making sure the belly side of the wood is perfectly flat and square. If you plan to cut very many splices, it would be worth your while to make a splice-cutting jig. The illustrated jig design was conceived by Dean Torges. I went to a hardware store, bought the metal fixtures I needed, and made one like it. The jig will hold wood well, particularly if irregular pieces are secured with a clamp or shimmed with small wedges.

An ace-in-the-hole for the splice-cutter is to boil the splices and clamp them together when hot and wet. This can easily force irregular cuts to mash together for a closer fit and better glue line. Unclamp the splice after 24 hours and let it dry thoroughly before gluing. The first splice I ever cut was made with a circular saw and hatchet, and a more gruesome-looking mess can hardly be imagined. But boiling and clamping created a good fit out of the original nightmare.

If you use this boiling method, gaze down the bow from one end to make sure the billets are lined up straight as soon as you are finished clamping. If they are not, the wood should still be soft enough to allow you to push the handle section to the left or right to correct the trouble.

If using a Z-shaped cut, I would make the handle at least an inch wide and 1 1/2 inches deep. Using a W-shaped cut creates more gluing surface and permits a less bulky handle. Torges uses the W-cut to create handles so trim it's hard to imagine they were spliced at all. These handles are 1 1/4 inches wide and deep at their thickest, and 1 1/8 inches in diameter on either side of the grip.

Drilling a hole through the spliced section and gluing in a 5/16th-inch wooden dowel has been said to strengthen splices. If the dowel is glued in correctly, the technique does no harm. But rest assured that if you insert such a pin and do not glue it in place, the stressed handle will break right at the hole. This can happen even if the rest of the splice has been properly glued. This happened to me and convinced me the pins provide no real advantage.

If you glue a splice so the resulting bow is crooked in the handle, it's still possible to fix the problem if you used a good epoxy glue. I steamed such a handle straight right at the splice. Weldwood Resorcinal was the glue used.

Practicing splicing by cutting scrap pieces is a good idea to increase odds of success with actual billets.

STRING FOLLOW

For a hunting bow, I have always considered excessive string follow to be more than two inches from the back of the handle after the bow has been unstrung overnight. Much more than that and cast per pound will be adversely affected, because the bow will be robbed of adequate tension early in the draw.

String follow under two inches, and particularly under one inch, can actually be an advantage. For example, many suspect a little string follow makes accuracy easier. A slight amount of string follow often signals the bow is properly designed: that is, the limbs are not so massive that they include excessive, cast-robbing weight. Incidentally, I measure string follow not by placing the bow's back on the floor, but by tying a string between the nocks, with the string going straight down the side of the bow. I think the method is a little more precise.

If the bow follows the string excessively because it has been overstrained, there are a limited number of options that may or may not work.

One would be to heat and straighten the bow, and then back it with sinew. Placing a wood backing on could also work, provided the belly wood is strong enough in relation to the thickness of the hickory or bamboo backing. Weaker woods require thinner backings of hickory or bamboo.

Either way, it is conceivable to bend the bow into a slight reflex before applying the backing. To prevent belly fracture, I would heat the bow first with a hot box or some other artificial dryer. A slight backward bend will crack most bows on the belly.

I have been able to reduce string follow by steaming a reflex into a solid-stave bow at the handle. This will only work well if the bow is fairly rigid at the handle. Odds of success are probably better with a longer bow.

One possible cause of string follow is excessive moisture, which is not too hard to correct. If this is the problem, the wood was probably too green in the first place, or the finish was not adequate for the job, allowing the moisture content to rise under humid conditions.

If you are fairly certain you have this problem, sand any finish from the bow's belly. Clamp the limbs straight against a plank and place them in a hot box or stovepipe dryer for 48 hours. Then put a reliable finish on the belly. I was able to reduce string follow in one bow by an inch and raise its weight by five pounds with this method. Moisture content was this bow's only problem. It was wide and long enough, and well-tillered.

Read again about cable backings in "Design and Performance" and "Other Backings" in Volume 1. A modest cable backing of linen or silk can cut string follow by an inch if your bow can accommodate the cable.

Excessive string follow is typically caused by a design or construction error. Such errors include a bow too narrow for the draw weight or wood species, a bow too short for the draw length, a bow that has been overdrawn or over-strained during tillering, a bad tillering job, or a crown on the back that is too high. Another frequent cause for novices is stringing the wooden bow too high. Between 5 and 6 inches from the belly side of the handle is plenty, even for a man-sized bow.

If the bow is man-sized, and if the string follow is not caused by the bow being too narrow for the draw weight, then the weapon can often be improved substantially by recurving the ends. Be warned, however, that if the bow is particularly short, or excessively narrow, then recurving the ends could simply make it explode on the first draw because of excessive strain created by the recurves.

I steamed three-inch static recurves of about 25 degrees on a 50-pound, 66-inch bow that followed the string three inches. The weight jumped to 56 pounds and the string follow fell to two inches. The bow was transformed from a limp wall hanger to credible hunting weapon. The recurved bow was not over-strained, because its original problem was being pulled too far, too soon during construction. The "Recurves" chapter in Volume 2 provides guidelines for the process.

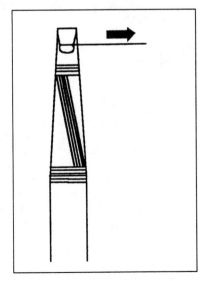

Here is Dan Perry's method for repairing a warped wooden recurve. The bow is secured to a bench with a clamp or vice, then a cord tied to the tip of the warped limb. The cord is pulled until the tip is slightly past the center line, then secured. Next, long strands of glue-soaked sinew are wrapped, one at a time, once around the limb and then laid diagonally on the back of the warped section as illustrated (viewed from bow's back). Once the diagonal strands are in place, the loose ends of sinew are wrapped with more sinew. The limb is left clamped and tied until the sinew is completely dry.

While low string follow helps ensure a lively, efficient weapon, keep in mind that string follow is relative and only one of several factors that can be used to judge a wooden bow. In a hunting bow, string follow can be fairly high and the bow will still be very lethal, as long as the draw weight is high enough.

For a good example, look in Saxton Pope's *The Adventurous Bowmen* for a photo of Arthur Young holding two jackals he shot. His bow — which appears to be about 62 inches long — is unstrung and appears to follow the string in excess of three inches. Judging from the text, this weapon almost certainly pulled over 80 pounds. With it, Young was virtually flawless. In moments of the highest tension and excitement, when the shot was difficult and required split-second timing, Young's arrows performed breath-taking deeds time and again.

I could be happy forever with a bow following the string three inches, if I could accomplish everything with it that Arthur Young did!

The main advantage of low string follow is that the bow is not badly affected by small variations in draw length. Such variations are more troublesome in a bow with high string follow, since a greater percentage of the bow's energy is stored in the last stage of the draw.

LIGHT BOWS

If you make a bow that is lower than the draw weight you want, there are several possibilities. If the bow is long enough, you can shorten it. Taking an inch off each end could raise the weight by five pounds. Exactly how much the weight increases will depend on the bow's draw weight and dimensions.

You could also reflex the handle or recurve the tips, if the bow is long enough. Gluing sinew on the back can increase draw weight. So can applying a wood backing.

A modest cable backing of linen or silk — about 1/4-inch thick — can raise a bow's weight by five pounds. If the bow will allow application of a husky cable, the weight could increase by 10 pounds.

Recurving, as discussed in the previous section, is also an option of the bow is long enough.

Another option is to give the light bow away and make another, chalking it up to experience and the learning process.

Building a wooden bow to a specific draw weight involves many challenges and nuances. If you are careful to never pull a bow past its final draw weight, it is possible the finished bow will lose weight later if the strain of use exceeds the strain of construction. This is particularly a risk with a wooden hunting bow, which must withstand long stringing times, unfavorable temperatures and humidity, and thousands upon thousands of shots.

A wooden hunting bow must be, as Saxton Pope put it, "broken to the string" during construction. In other words, the ideal is that during construction, the bow attains the same amount of string follow it will have after months of regular use. A bow that is not broken to the string adequately during construction can only lose weight after a period of constant use.

On the other hand, if you make an excessively heavy bow, and then lighten it to the desired draw weight, the finished bow may have too much string follow. If an eighty pound bow is lightened to fifty pounds, the weapon will have the string follow of an eighty pound bow.

The best answer may lie somewhere between these two extremes.

The main question is: How upset do you get if and when this happens to you? Some people accept a certain loss in draw weight as normal. Personally, I can't stand it. If I make a bow that pulls 60 pounds, I want it to continue pulling 60 pounds forever.

If you share this prejudice, several approaches are possible.

Working in the bowyer's favor is the fact a bow can be bent when the draw weight is quite high and the bow will not be damaged or take on excessive string follow, *as long as the bow is bent a small amount* on a tillering board, with a tillering string. For example, it could take 100 pounds of tension on a tillering string to move the limb tips four inches on a tillering board. Yet — barring some extremely serious problem — the bow will not break nor take on excessive string follow from such a bend.

It is my practice that once a new bow seems to have an adequate tiller, I bend it on the tillering board so the limb tips move four inches — no matter how heavy the bow is. Then I let it sit that way an hour. This step goes a long way to prevent the finished bow from losing draw weight.

A critical phrase in the preceding paragraph is "adequate tiller." If you can tell the tiller is bad, correct it before you do anything else. If the tiller is uneven or if there are hinges or flat spots in the limbs, draw weight can continue to drop in a finished bow because some of the wood is overstrained and string follow can increase.

My experience suggests that a very practical alternative is to never stress the bow during construction more than 10 pounds above the desired finished draw weight. This is a particularly safe procedure at draw lengths at least two inches under the desired final draw length. In other words, if the finished bow is to pull 60 pounds at 28 inches, then it can safely pull 70 pounds at 26 inches. Then the bowyer can reduce the weight and increase the draw length. This assures the bow is adequately broken to the string, and at the same time creates no excessive string follow, when all else (i.e., moisture content, tillering, etc.) is OK.

Reducing this basic concept to a simpler application, make the finished bow 5 pounds heavier than the desired draw weight. Then either shoot it 400 times, or draw it 400 times.

Another factor is stringing time. A finished wooden bow can be expected to be strung six hours during hunting. If properly designed and built, such stringing time will not increase string follow or injure the bow. So if this is the goal, let the bow sit braced for six hours and then shoot it a few dozen times before you conclude it is still 5 pounds too heavy.

Here's another expression of the same basic idea: Make the bow 10 pounds too heavy while pulling at least three inches under the final draw length (to be on the safe side). Then draw the bow 400 times. Then lighten the bow, if needed.

Reducing the draw weight without changing the tiller is a delicate operation. For a reliable approach to this job, read about the rasp and scraper in the "Tools" chapter in this volume and read the "Tillering" chapter in Volume 1.

It is possible to learn the draw weight of a bow under construction without stringing the bow. This can be done when comparing two bows of the same length, using the same tillering board and the same tillering string.

For example, we take a 66-inch finished bow and pull the string to a notch on the tillering board. Using a spring scale with a hook, we see how many pounds it takes to pull the string out of the notch. Then we take our unfinished 66-inch bow and pull it to the same notch. The finished bow draws 60 pounds and it took 40 pounds to lift the tillering string from the notch. It takes 55 pounds, or 15 pounds more, to pull the string from the same notch with our unfinished bow. This tells us that if pulled to full draw in this condition the unfinished bow would pull at least 75 pounds, or 15 pounds heavier than the finished bow.

SLOW CAST

If a bow is excessively light or has excessive string follow, cast is adversely affected. But it is also possible for a bow with adequate draw weight and little string follow to have relatively poor cast. There can be several causes.

If the bow's limb tips are excessively heavy, the bow cannot reach its cast potential. I have long operated under the rule of thumb that limb mass weight must be minimized in the last four inches of the limb. If the limb tip appears particularly massive, my approach has been to string the bow and draw pencil lines outside the string loops. In other words, I mark off the wood of the tips that is not directly supporting the string. Then I trim the excess wood away from the nock and taper the last four inches of the limb from this narrow tip to the limb's edges. It has been my experience that if the bow has the correct tiller, narrowing the last four inches will not change the tiller. Thinning the belly of the limb tip, however, could increase the bend. It is more effective and safer to narrow the limb tip. If the tiller will allow it, the limb tip width can be tapered back more than four inches.

I have long favored pin or shoulder nocks, simply because they are a relatively easy way to keep tip weight down. But nocks cut into the side of the limb are also effective, as long as the tip is relatively narrow and light.

Some may doubt the effectiveness of this approach, particularly if they read what *Archery, The Technical Side* (1947) has to say on the subject. The authors used a light bow shooting light arrows for their test, which yielded no particular advantage for lighter limb tips. My own tests on the subject,

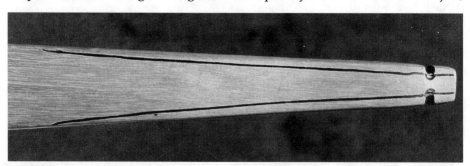

Tip of an Osage bow with lines drawn showing where wood should be removed and new nocks cut. As much as 200 grains per tip can be removed, which makes a noticeable improvement in cast and a corresponding reduction in hand shock. Osage is strong enough that very narrow, delicate tips with nocks can be used, as illustrated. Weaker woods require slightly wider tips or tips tapered to a point with wrap-on nocks.

conducted before I wrote *The Bent Stick*, showed that removing excess tip mass on a heavy hickory flatbow shooting arrows weighing more than 500 grains increased cast significantly.

Tim Baker has pursued the subject even further, checking the results with a chronograph while using a large number of bows for his sample. The results have been so compelling that Baker typically narrows limb tips to a point 1/8th inch wide, tapering the width a foot or more down the limbs. To maintain an adequate tiller, he gives these narrow tips sufficient thickness. Many of these bows have tips so narrow that wooden nocks can't be cut in. Baker instead typically uses a wrapped tip to provide a shoulder for the string.

String stretch is very damaging to cast. This problem usually occurs when a nylon string (such as artificial sinew) is used. By using Dacron or linen, the problem is easily avoided in strings of reasonable dimensions.

Those interested in wringing every possible foot-per-second out of a bow will prefer a continuous-strand string with no twist whatsoever in the strands, using as few strands as possible. However, using a twisted string with Flemish-spliced loops is a sensible compromise in the interest of durability, particularly if a few more strands are added. Such a string will still allow a robust, working hunting bow to remain quite deadly. My attitude has always been the bow can't kill anything with a broken string.

By the same token, those interested in maximum cast will aim during the draw and shoot with no hold after anchoring. Chronograph tests by Tim Baker show a noticeable loss of cast occurs in the first second of the hold.

I shoot with no hold after the anchor, but this was not always the case. Many need to anchor and correct their aim before shooting. While there is definitely some loss of cast caused by holding, I would not term it a serious loss as long as the hold is five seconds or less. Saxton Pope used a shooting machine to determine that the hold had to be increased from 5 to 15 seconds before the arrow dropped significantly at 60 yards. If you need to use a two or three-second hold to shoot well, my advice is go right ahead and let your conscience be clear. The hunting capability of a well-made bow — long enough for the draw length and wide enough for the draw weight — will not be adversely affected by such shooting.

While I am strictly a field shooter, it is noteworthy that Dan Perry of Salem, Utah, an accomplished flight shooter, is more critical of holding before the release. Perry believes that the cast loss of a two-second hold is unacceptable. He also points out the longer the hold, the more stress on the bow, with string follow increasing proportionally. Perry has produced bows with extremely high cast per pound by paying attention to such details. He holds four national records and three world records in National Archery Association flight shooting for natural materials bows. They include a shot from a 50-pound wooden bow that sent a 180-grain arrow 295 yards, 2 feet, 3 inches.

A bow excessively long for its draw length, or excessively massive for its draw weight, will not be as efficient as one with a more optimum design. But this can have its compensations in terms of increased durability and stability. By comparison, the more efficient bow could be permanently damaged by being overdrawn an inch, while the more massive or excessively long bow would not be troubled. Bowyers are frequently faced by the choice of such trade-offs, and should design the bow to meet their own priorities.

NOISE

Compared to the violent ka-boing of glass-laminated recurves or the explosive blast of a compound, wooden bows are soft-spoken and quiet creatures. Even so, the archer may find he has noise problems.

One type of noise problem is string twang, most common with a sinew-backed and/or recurved bow. String silencers are an easy way of dealing with a twanging string. The standard commercial varieties of string silencers do the job, but many purists prefer to tie on or twist into the string bits of hide with the fur attached. These silencers look quite appropriate on a wooden bow. If using a heavier arrow is an option, they can also reduce twang since more energy is absorbed by the heavier shaft. If using a particularly high brace height, lowering it a bit will increase the distance in which the string is pushing the shaft, also imparting a touch more energy into the arrow.

Arrows rattling against the bow handle are a typical problem for the novice shooting a wooden bow. Assuming the archer is using arrows matched for the bow, I think the best answer to this arrow rattling problem is to improve one's shooting style until the rattling ceases. I had this problem the first few years I shot before it ceased permanently.

I submit that a wide variety of shooting problems can be cured by improving the shooting style. These include hitting to the left, erratic arrow flight, and great inconsistencies in windage or elevation. At one point or another, I had all of these problems (and others). Refinements to my shooting style cured them all. This was accomplished by a years'-long effort to eliminate needless movement and find a method that would create the greatest amount of shooting comfort and the least amount of shooting strain. These things provide greater amounts of stability, conducive to straight, clean, and true arrow flight.

Problem is, this did take several years for me, and no doubt it could take several years for others. Those who switch from a modern glass-laminated bow sometimes find their old shooting style is next to worthless with a wooden bow. I did. So while I would urge an archer to continue working on his shooting style, I would also urge him to resort to expedients as long as he needs them.

In the case of arrow rattle, modify the arrow rest and/or arrow plate. Gluing on bits of hide with the fur attached makes a fairly good muffler. Thicker or softer pieces of leather could accomplish the same thing.

INCONSISTENT SHOOTING

The problems one can encounter when learning to shoot consistently can be so varied it would take a book to begin to address them in a thorough way. There are, however, a few common pitfalls that quickly lead to bad shooting.

One is using a bow that is too heavy. Since accurate shooting requires the bow to be held still during the shot, pulling too much weight will cause jitters and shakes, making an accurate shot impossible.

Arrow spine can be another problem. More than a few shooters need to shoot arrows spined about five pounds under the wooden bow's actual draw weight.

The only answer to this problem is to experiment with different spined shafts, keeping in mind that some trouble with shooting form or technique — and not arrow spine — may ultimately be the answer.

Those dissatisfied with commercially available arrow shafts can make their own, as described in the "Arrows" chapter in Volume I. And those who are convinced that slight irregularities in arrow spine are their problem need only to buy or make a spine tester, make their own shafts, and sample different spines. If they are still dissatisfied after this effort, the next experiments should be with variables in shooting form.

Recently, I was visiting with Jim Hamm at a traditional archery tournament in Michigan when a fellow with a beautiful Osage flatbow and a large frown approached.

"I'm about ready to quit archery and take up interpretive dance, so I hope you guys can help," the disgruntled bowyer said, "I've tried everything and still can't get my arrows to fly right."

After he correctly answered our questions about arrow spine, brace height, nocking point, and release technique, Jim told him, "Let's go down to the range where we can watch you shoot."

As we left, Jim grabbed a handful of his own arrows from his quiver. We discovered the man did, indeed, have arrow flight problems, with one arrow fishtailing off to one side of the target, the next flying perfectly, then the next corkscrewing wildly.

"Here, try some of mine," Jim said, handing the man an arrow. He nocked it, drew, and released. The arrow flew like a dart into the center of the target. With raised eyebrows, he reached for another arrow and repeated the performance. After shooting six times, all with perfect arrow flight, he finally exploded, "What's the deal?" A grin threatened to split his face.

The deal was simple. The feathers on Jim's arrows were a tall 5 1/2-inch shield cut, while the shooter's arrows sported low-cut 5 inch parabolic fletching, fine for a center-cut recurve or longbow, but without enough wind resistance to stabilize an arrow from a non center-shot self bow. Slightly larger feathers can magically correct arrow flight problems. Yes, they reduce arrow speed slightly, and yes, they are slightly noisier, but these are cheap prices to pay for proper arrow flight and consistent accuracy.

When test shooting a set of arrows, it is important to shoot on a still day. Crosswinds can effect arrow flight but the worst situation is a tailwind. When the wind is moving the same direction as the arrow, the arrow, in a sense, flies in a vacuum, with greatly reduced wind resistance against the feathers. Naturally, the arrows flit about like bats. If you want to see some hilarious arrow flight, try shooting in a 30 mile an hour tailwind.

I have urged friends with shooting problems to experiment with shafts up to two inches longer than the draw. Several have reported, particularly when shooting broadheads, that this step created improvement. Some archers are horrified at the notion of shooting a too-long arrow. But a host of ancient and modern aboriginal archers — as well as the pioneering Thompson brothers — successfully used arrows six inches or more longer than the draw. As I said to my friends: if it helps, you can't argue with success.

Many archers can shoot well with no arrow rest and no nocking locator on the string. Those who use these aids need to experiment with different heights of the nocking locator — as do shooters of modern bows.

WEATHER EXTREMES

Many wooden bow shooters fear carrying their weapon in the rain because of possible water damage to the bow. I know a couple of people who refuse to hunt in wet weather for fear of bow damage. The fear is a real one, since water can create cracks or splits around knots, loose spots in backings, and a drop in cast and poundage from damp sinew.

Whether a hunter intentionally wants to go into the rain is his choice, but anyone can get caught in the rain unexpectedly, to say nothing of heavy fog, snow and mist.

I have always thought the best answer to wet weather is to create a bow that can stand it. And I mean stand it for hours or even days on end. When wet weather is present or threatening, the archer can pick up his all-weather bow and continue on his merry way. My nomination for an all-weather bow design is a man-sized straight-limbed, unbacked bow. For such a bow, my ideal would be a stave with no knots in it anywhere. Failing that, I would select a stave with as few knots as possible. Tiny, almost invisible cracks can appear in and surrounding knots. Under dry circumstances, these knots are seemingly unaffected and never deteriorate. This condition can change in minutes if water works its way into these tiny openings. They can quickly enlarge and send a crack traveling into nearby wood. For these reasons, I would attempt to avoid knots. If knots are in the back, I would raise them at least 3/16ths of an inch, to avoid any small openings around the knot. For the same reason, I would select a stave clear of drying checks.

If you are forced to carry a bow containing knots or checks, it might be a good plan to smear lard over them if wet weather threatens for extra insurance. I would recommend lard for this task, because it is the most tenacious, water-resistance grease I have ever used. I covered a piece of wood with lard about a year ago and the stuff looks like it was applied yesterday. I carry some lard in a 35mm film canister in the bottom of the quiver.

I would cover this all-weather bow with some finish containing a varnish. Pure oil finishes such as linseed oil and tung oil have failed me badly when faced with water. I would reject any finish that cracks under bending, or that fails to bead water. I would apply at least four coats and keep paste wax constantly over the finish.

I would also reject the idea of putting a leather grip on the handle. Leather soaks up water like a sponge and stays wet for hours. I have never found any finish that even comes close to preventing this.

Two remaining options are to leave the grip as bare wood or wrap the handle with a rattan grip. The rattan I have used is the cane used to weave seats in wooden chairs. Robert Elmer tells about using cane for a grip in his 1926 book *Archery*. I use rattan almost exclusively and love the stuff. (The bow on the dust jacket has a rattan grip.) The finished grip can be heavily varnished, the finish seeping under the rattan before it dries, sealing hidden but exposed surfaces.

Grips wrapped with rattan are much less affected by rain than a leather handle grip. These bows are all unbacked, making them more robust under wet conditions.

The finished product soaks up virtually no water. Of course, the advantage of a rattan grip is lost if you must pad the handle under the grip with leather strips or some other soft material. I have never quite understood why such padding is needed with a narrow, deep handle, since I can easily mold such a handle to fit the hand comfortably. It is a simple task to round off the sharp corners of the handle's back and belly. One might fear touching any of the outer ring in a bow's back, but rounding off the back corners hardly requires destruction of the outer ring. I have routinely performed this operation on handles of English bows that work slightly in the handle, and the bows suffered no ill effects.

To apply rattan, soak it in hot water for 30 minutes. Towel it dry and wrap it around the handle. Cover the loose end used to begin the wrap with succeeding revolutions. To close the wrap, stick the loose end through the final two revolutions, and pull it tight. Don't cut the loose end off until the grip is completely dry. The rattan can easily unravel it you cut the loose end off when wet, as the rattan shrinks as it dries. When the handle is dry, a sharp knife will remove the loose end. I typically apply some cyanoacrolate glue to the overlaps at each end of the grip. This step is not 100 percent necessary (Elmer didn't do it) but I figure it's a little extra insurance. When the glue is dry, I smooth the cane with 100-grit paper and varnish the grip.

If anyone is worried that cane lacks adequate gripping texture, they can accomplish the same goal by wrapping the grip with heavy cord, and varnishing the finished product.

For the archer who prefers a softer grip, one compromise would be to wrap the grip with a tied-on piece of long suede. If the bow gets wet, the suede can be removed until it dries.

It is also possible to use a wood-backed bow for an all-weather design, particularly if the backing is applied with epoxy glue. Of course, the bowyer must take care to avoid possible compression problems mentioned earlier.

If it makes sense to have an all-weather bow, it also seems a good plan to carry a few all-weather arrows. Goose feathers stand up well in water, and it's worth having a few shafts fletched with them. They are a bit more delicate than turkey feathers, fraying and losing bits of vane easier. Even so, I tend to carry at least one shaft with goose feathers, in case the weatherman lets me down. A reasonable all-weather arrow can use turkey feathers if the vanes are an oversized (about 3/4-inch tall) straight or shield cut. If the feathers are soaked and matted, such large vanes can still provide enough resistance to steer the arrow. A goose feather can probably do the job better, but oversized turkey feathers are better than nothing and it's a small compromise to have at least one in the quiver. Needless to say, the arrow shaft must be finished as carefully as a wooden bow to protect it from water that could warp the shaft.

Tim Baker has purchased silica crystals, and tossed a bag or two in his bow case if he thinks he will encounter continually damp conditions.

Another wet-weather option is to wrap a cord or rattan grip with a long piece of tied-on suede. If it gets soaked, remove it until it dries.

Depending on where your bow was made, and where you take it, it is possible to encounter an environment so dry that the moisture content will fall dangerously low. If this happens, Baker predicts, the first clue is the bow's draw weight will increase noticeably. If you encounter this situation, a good plan would be to place the bow in a humid environment. If you think you might experience this, it may be worthwhile to carry a lighter bow, just in case. The longer and wider the lighter bow, the greater the odds of it surviving in such an environment. The same can be said for bows used in subzero temperatures.

Dan Perry once lost one of his favorite yew bows by shooting it in too-cold weather. He said the first warning sign was the bow suddenly became harder to pull. A fraction of an inch from full draw, the bow broke. A friend accompanying him was carrying a yew bow that survived. It was longer, wider, and thinner than Perry's bow.

Perry says that in cold weather, some archers rub the bow to warm it up, or begin the draw with a series of short pulls. He thinks these tricks are of little real value, when compared to an adequate cold-weather design.

He warns that stringing a bow that is too warm can also cause damage. So can putting a strung bow in an enclosed car in summer. He recommends padded cases and shade to prevent problems with heat.

A wooden bow that is drawn too quickly may break when it could survive by being pulled back somewhat slowly, Perry says. This view varies considerably from my experience with a score of bows, which I used to draw with a violent jerk as a matter of routine. The possible reason for these divergent experiences may be the temperature extremes to which Perry is accustomed.

ARROWS AND POINTS

It's a safe rule of thumb to advise beginners to break or discard any cracked wooden arrow. I would do this, also, when the crack follows grain that runs sharply across the shaft.

However, if a shaft is extremely straight-grained, it can conceivably be repaired if it cracks. This is particularly true of shafts made from a small branch, cane, or bamboo, when the crack is not too long. Putting some glue in the crack and wrapping the shaft with sinew is usually enough to keep the crack closed. It is also possible to wrap the shaft with sewing thread, putting varnish or glue on the wrap. I would limit such repairs to short cracks, since longer cracks can warp the broken halves, making it difficult or impossible to straighten the repaired arrow.

Shafts with somewhat crooked grain make less durable practice arrows than shafts with straighter grain. For this reason, I tend to save these marginal shafts for hunting arrows, assuming I can make them perfectly straight. A practice arrow will be shot hundreds of times, while a hunting arrow will probably be shot only once, if at all. The lucky arrow that sinks into the side of a deer is usually going to end up broken, anyway. And the unlucky arrow that misses may be permanently lost.

Being a flintknapper of limited skill, I occasionally produce an arrowhead that has a small stack on the side that I can't chip away. I have always feared that such a lump, however small, may hurt penetration. So I grab an abrasive stone

If the grain is straight and the crack not too long, a split arrow can be repaired by gluing the crack closed, wrapping the shaft, and replacing the nock.

and grind the stack smooth. I think the best plan is to produce a stone-tipped arrow that will spin straight on the tip when finished. At least if the arrow misses, you'll know it wasn't because the point was on crooked. In my experience, stone-tipped arrows that spin straight cut a beautiful straight line through the air.

If cutting or enlarging an arrowhead notch in the shaft with a sharp knife, it is fairly easy to cut the notch snug enough to hold the head in place for a test spin or two. Even when wrapped, the point can be wiggled to produce a straight spin when the sinew is wet. I have found such an arrow placed carefully aside will also spin straight when the sinew is dry. Putting glue or pine pitch mixed with charcoal into the shaft's notch also helps the process (see also Stone Points in this volume for hafting techniques).

Making your own steel hunting points is an admirable challenge. Veteran broadhead maker Martin Kruse has some tips for producing durable steel points. He says broadheads that break or bend too easily can be remedied by using a suitable grade of steel, or steel that was properly hardened and tempered. Kruse advocates high carbon steel for broadheads. He says steel's quality can be tested by touching it to a spinning grinding wheel. Good steel will throw off a complex, multi-pointed spark shaped like a star burst. After the blade has been through any necessary shaping and/or drilling, Kruse advocates heating it to a cherry-red, and quenching it in oil. Once this is accomplished, the blade can be tempered. Heat the blade slowly as the metal changes from straw to bronze to purple to dark blue to lighter blue. When the dark blue starts to lighten, quench the blade again. If you plan to solder the blade into a ferrule, Kruse recommends a low-temperature solder, like Kesters, to preserve the metal's temper.

OTHER NUISANCES

Jay Massey wrote in Volume 2 about the love-hate relationship many archers have with their quivers. The only quiver design that hasn't prompted me to curse and gnash teeth is one similar to that worn by Art Young in photographs in *The Adventurous Bowmen*. It is a parallel-sided leather tube about four inches in diameter and deep enough to reach the fletching. It can hold a dozen arrows and is worn with the arrow nocks about shoulder high. I have seen some shoulder quivers that weigh a whopping four pounds. A Young-style quiver weighs about a pound. Some quivers are loose and floppy bags, but Young's tube is rigid and keeps its shape.

Some quivers spill arrows everywhere if the archer reaches down to scratch his knee. Because of its length and small diameter, a Young quiver has to be practically upended to spill arrows. I hunt with one made extra-long, to cover all but the last two or three inches of the fletching. This keeps arrows more secure and helps protect the fletching from tree branches.

Young was photographed with this quiver in Africa in 1925. At the time, he was a seasoned veteran of many hunts in rough conditions in Alaska and the western states. It is no surprise to me that the quiver he carried in Africa worked so well. Doubtless Young carried nothing but broadheads in this quiver. If I feel compelled to carry field-tipped arrows when hunting, I equip them with plastic nocks so touch can distinguish them from the wooden nocks of my hunting arrows.

Anyone who ever stitched together a wallet in summer camp can figure out how to make a Young-style quiver.

Roving, or stump shooting, was a great pastime in the pre-fiberglass era. Saxton Pope heartily endorsed it to familiarize the archer with shooting at unknown ranges over uneven ground. Those who try it today may become discouraged by the dirt or mud that can accumulate on the arrows if shooting on damp ground. To deal with this, the old-timers made a tassel out of yarn, and hung it from the belt or quiver. A tassel will wipe arrows clean, and when the dirt dries, it falls from the tassel. A good-sized tassel will clean as many dirty arrows as a roll of paper towels and still be usable.

Arrows with pointed field tips often meet an early death during stump shooting, since a glance off a small stone can produce a powerful sideways force that can snap the shaft behind the point. A square-ended blunt usually lasts longer. I am also fond of gluing .38 Special or .357 Magnum cartridge brass onto the end of the stump-shooting shaft. This allows a point to be glued on without cutting any of the underlying wood, making it slightly stronger. If you can find thick-walled bamboo of a proper diameter and spine, it can produce an extremely tough arrow when tipped with a blunt point. Thinner-walled cane is also particularly tough if a small dowel about four inches long is glued into the point end for an insert.

❖ ❖ ❖

If you are a veteran bowmaker, you may be experienced with some of the tricks in this chapter and no doubt have learned others on your own. If you are a novice, let this chapter be an example of the virtue of persistence. If you want to be a wooden bow enthusiast, you can't be a quitter. Never give up until it's hopeless, and then give it another try.

WOODEN ARROWS

Gabriela Cosgrove

Nothing makes a bow shoot more accurately than a perfectly matched set of arrows. I have produced arrows commercially for over ten years and developed some "tricks of the trade". This is not the only way to make arrows, so don't be afraid to experiment, but the described methods have proven successful and consistent.

Though you can start with an elaborate set-up, I suggest being a little conservative in your first attempts at arrow-making. Some basic supplies needed to make arrows: shafts, spinemeter, grain scale, nock-point taper tool, sandpaper, steel wool, paints and thinner, dip tubes, crester, cresting brushes, hot-melt ferrule cement, fletching cement, fletching jig, feather burner, nocks, points, feathers, broadheads, and this book.

WOOD

Throughout history, many types of wood have been employed to make arrows. We use Port Orford White Cedar but are always experimenting with alternatives. This wood is not as abundant as in years past due to demand overseas and the fact that this tree is not replanted after being harvested. I understand the shafting manufacturers only use trees which have been down for 30 to 40 years and had the bark and sapwood rotted away.

Other woods available in shaft form that we have found to be satisfactory are fir, birch, Sitka spruce and certain pines. Fir is abundant and works well for archers who are interested in arrows with a heavier grain weight. The only problem is that this wood is not being produced in large quantities, and the growth rings do not usually run as straight as cedar. Birch is inexpensive and can be purchased in most hardware stores. While it is not generally considered as one of the better shaft materials, it makes a tough, durable arrow of a heavy grain weight. As for Sitka Spruce, this wood is a very good alternative to Port Orford cedar. The characteristics are basically the same as cedar with the advantage of a little heavier grain weight. This wood is abundant, we just need someone to begin producing commercial shafting from it.

We are presently producing quality arrows out of Highland Pine which comes from British Columbia. We are very excited about this wood because the characteristics are so like cedar except the shafts are a bit heavier and the growth rings are noticeably straight. Spine-wise, they are very similar to cedar.

Whatever wood you decide on, make sure to select shafts that are as straight-grained as possible. The grain is the lines where the yearly growth rings show on the sides of the shaft. Ideally, the grain should run straight from one end of the shaft to the other. This is very important in the production of a superior product. Shafts with excessively crooked growth rings or growth rings which do not run from one end of the shaft to the other should be discarded.

There are different styles of shafts from which to choose. The most common and least expensive are parallel, in which the diameter of the shafts is the same throughout their length. Another shaft type is barreled, in which the diameter is smaller at both ends than in the middle. Its basic use is for target archery and flight shooting and tends to be less durable. The footed shaft — in which hard-wood is spliced on at the point or pile end — adds grain weight and durability. They are somewhat time consuming to build yourself and very expensive to purchase. They make an attractive, durable arrow and are reminiscent of days past. The final design is a tapered shaft, which is narrower at the nock end and wider at the point end. The tapering of the shaft allows the nock end of the arrow to clear the bow more easily, resulting in better arrow flight. This eliminates drag, the fletching lasts longer, and also reduces weight — which produces a faster arrow. The tapering allows the arrow a much quicker recovery rate after it bends around the handle of the bow. The faster the recovery rate, the more stable the arrow.

Shafting can be purchased from any number of companies. The shafting depends on your needs and the amount of money you wish to spend. Some shafts are randomly spined and not grain weighed, and are the least expensive, while some are hand spined and grain weighed in matched sets. This eliminates a great deal of time, and you don't end up with several groups of shafts of different spines and grain weights. The more closely matched the arrows are, the more consistently they will fly.

To be able to match the shafts yourself, you would have to start with a fair amount of shafts, 200 or so, to end up with a well-matched set. If going to all the trouble and expense of making your own arrows, be satisfied with the raw materials you start with, so you can take pride in the finished product.

SPINING SHAFTS

The spine is the strength or degree of stiffness of the shaft. You will want a certain spine for your draw weight and draw length. This spine is determined by using a spine meter. When spining a shaft, always position the shaft so that the growth rings run up and down (12 and 6 o'clock) since this is the strongest side of the shaft. The spine of the shaft is determined by the amount of bend, or deflection, when a 2 pound weight is hung from the center of the shaft while the shaft is supported on two points 26 inches apart. Spine meters generally measure in 5 pound increments, and this is how arrows should be spined and separated. Examples: 50-55#, 55-60#, 60-65#, etc.

DETERMINING THE SPINE FOR YOUR BOW.

There is no steadfast rule to follow when determining what spine shaft will shoot best out of your bow, but here is a general guide for determining spine:

Spinemeter, used to determine stiffness, or spine, of each arrow shaft. Two-pound weight is hung from center of shaft and the amount of shaft deflection measured on gauge at right.

Start with your bow weight when drawn to 28 inches. Add 5 pounds of spine for each inch of draw over 28 inches. For arrow length less than 28 inches, subtract 5 pounds of spine per inch of draw length. Add 5 pounds for heavy broadheads (those over 110 grains). Add five pounds for extra fast recurves.

This gives a starting point for selecting the correct arrow spine for a particular bow.

There are many variables to take into consideration, such as recurve or long-bow, Flemish string or Fast flight, custom bow or factory bow, long or short draw length, heavy or light broadhead. Let's say you need to determine what spine to shoot out of a custom longbow drawing 50 pounds at 28". This long-bow has a Dacron string and 125 grain broadhead. Using the above formula, this bow requires a 55 pound spine arrow — 50 pounds for the weight of the bow plus 5 pounds for the heavy broadhead. If this bow had a Fast flight string, it would need five pounds more, or a total of 60 pounds.

A bow of a different design might need a different spine shaft, even though it has the same weight at the same draw length. Let's assume you want to deter-mine what spine shaft you need for a custom recurve drawing 50 pounds at 28 inches. This recurve has a regular Flemish string and a broadhead that weighs 125 grains. Using the same formula, this bow, due to the extra speed of the recurves and the heavy broadhead, requires a shaft with a spine of 60 pounds. A Fast flight string needs at least 5 pounds more spine. If this 50 pound bow had a draw length of 30 inches without a Fast flight string it would need a 70 pound

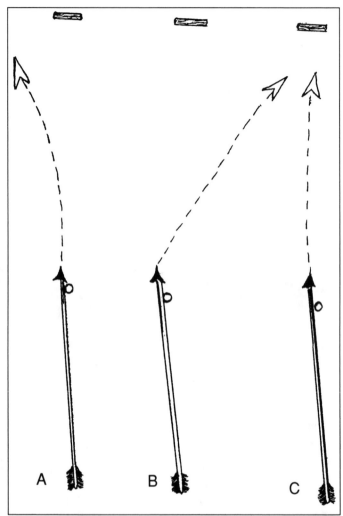

Arrow spine as it relates to archer's paradox, or the bending of an arrow around the handle of a non-center-shot bow. A) the arrow hasn't enough spine, or is too limber, and shoots left. B) the arrow has too much spine, or is too stiff, and shoots right. C) arrow spined correctly bends around the handle and flies straight to the target.

spine — 5 pounds extra for the recurves, 5 pounds for each of the two extra inches of draw over 28 inches, and 5 pounds for the heavy point.

These examples are for centershot bows, or those which are cut out to allow the arrow to travel along the lateral center of the bow. For those shooting self-bows which are generally not centershot, *spine is even more critical because of the archer's paradox.* Spine should be reduced about 5-10 pounds below the examples already given, to produce a shaft which bends a bit more easily around the handle. **Archer's paradox** is defined as the flexing of the shaft around the handle of the bow. If an arrow is underspined, it will strike the target to the left or "nock left". If an arrow is overspined, it will strike the target to the right or "nock right", assuming you are a right-handed shooter. For left handed shooters, this rule would be reversed.

Finding the correct shaft for a particular bow and release technique sometimes takes a bit of experimentation. This is part of the beauty of making your
own arrows; you can easily try different spines and fletching combinations until
perfect arrow flight is achieved.

WEIGHING SHAFTS

Now that your shafts have been spined and separated into matching bundles,
it is time to grain weigh them. It is important to have shafts both spined and
grain weighed for a perfectly consistent set. If this is done, you can expect the
same performance from every arrow. Most arrowmakers weigh their arrows +
or — 5 grains (which is actually a 10 grain span). On your first attempt at grain
weighing, you will notice that in any given spine there may be as much as 150
grains between the heaviest and lightest shafts. With such variance, you can see
why arrows that are only spined and not grain weighed may fly higher or lower
depending on their actually physical weight since speed, and point of impact, is
determined by the weight. A lighter arrow flies faster, while a heavier arrow
flies slower but has more penetration.

There are different types of scales on the market for determining shaft weight.
The three most common are the balance beam powder scale, spring scale, and
electronic scale. While balance beam powder scales are accurate grain scales
designed for weighing gunpowder, they also can be used to weigh shafts. The
only drawback to this scale is that it is somewhat slow to use. A spring scale is
the most common and affordable type of grain scale on the market — fast and
relatively accurate. The electronic scale is fast and extremely accurate which is
reflected in its higher price.

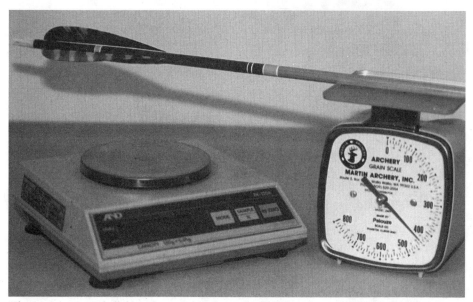

Electronic grain scale (left) and a spring scale, used to weigh and match arrow shafts.

PREPARING THE SHAFTS

After selecting the shafts, examine them to be sure there aren't any split ends or cracks. Check for smoothness (no gouges or rough spots). This is the time to weed out any which won't make a satisfactory arrow. I would rather spend a little extra time in this area to avoid any mishaps in the steps ahead.

Sometimes, all the work that has gone into building an ultimate beautiful set of arrows is "shattered". For this reason, always start with 13 arrows and avoid the possibility of having to go back and try to duplicate the 11 other shafts. If, after straightening, there are still 13 arrows, the extra becomes a flu-flu.

Sand the shafts smooth with medium or medium-fine grit sandpaper (220 to 400) or steel wool. Sight down the shaft to check for straightness. If the shaft stays bent in the opposite direction when you flex it with the palm and forefinger, it is referred to as a green shaft. Discard it, for no matter how much you adjust it, it won't stay straight and isn't good for anything — except maybe a tomato stake. Which, by the way, I make a pretty good return on in our yearly garage sales.

At this time we are interested in the serious straightening. This is one of the crucial steps in the production of quality arrows. To straighten an arrow shaft, first sight down the shaft and locate the bends. While still sighting down the shaft with your right eye and holding the shaft with your right hand, gently

Straightening the shaft by sighting down it and bending crooked areas with the heel of the hand.

flex the shaft in the opposite direction of the bend. Rotate the shaft while still sighting down it. If you still find a bend, slide the left hand which is cradling the shaft to the bent spot. Position your hand on the far side of the bend and give it a gentle flex in the opposite direction. This procedure may have to be performed two or three times to remove the bends. Next, sight down the opposite end of the shaft and repeat this process. Make the shafts perfectly straight before continuing.

Sometimes arrow shafts are bent near the end. Depending on your arrow length, you may be cutting off all or most of this bend. This is fine as long as the remaining shaft is straight.

NOCK TAPERING

Sight down the shaft and choose the straight end for the nock taper. This makes it easier to get the nock on straight since the crooked end, if any, will be cut off when installing points. Nock ends can be tapered with an inexpensive hand-held tapering tool or a power tapering tool. There is a considerable difference in cost between the two, but both work fine. Put a slight taper on the point end of the shaft to help paint and sealer run off more freely.

STAINING AND SEALING

If the shafts will be stained, purchase a stain compatible with your paints and glue. Staining brings out the grain configuration in the wood and gives a richer

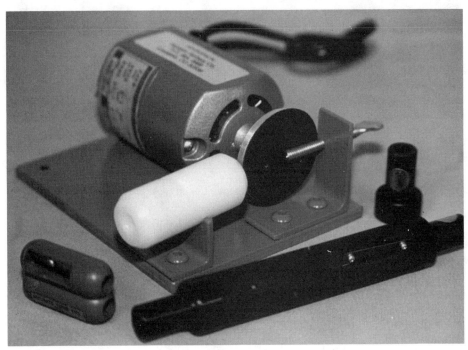

Tapering tools; power and pencil sharpener types.

Dipping shafts in sealer.   *Hanging shafts to dry.*

appearance. I suggest using a lacquer base stain, which can either be rubbed on or put in a dip tube into which the shaft is inserted. Wait about 20 minutes for the stain to dry, then rub to a brilliant shine with #1 medium steel wool.

If the arrows aren't to be stained, this is the time to dip the entire shaft in a clear lacquer to seal them. I like to seal the shaft and then steel wool with fine steel wool. This makes the shaft smooth and more accepting to the crown dip.

PAINTING SHAFTS

There are various items that can be used as a paint dip tube; pop bottles, golf tubes, aluminum piping. Something narrow is probably best for someone only interested in making arrows for himself and a few friends. If you purchase a dip tank, you will need enough paint to fill a tank. Corks can be purchased at hardware stores to seal most openings.

Decide on the colors to be used. I have only had experience with lacquer paints and know that they are compatible with my glue. These are most readily available from Bohning Co. Ltd. or as automotive acrylic lacquer. If you are in doubt about the compatibility of your products, try building one arrow first. Rushing into arrow-making with incompatible paints and finishes may become a nightmare when they adversely react with each other and leave the finish bubbled, wrinkled, or curdled.

CROWN DIP

This is where you can let your imagination take off (especially if you don't have enough ventilation). Which brings up an important safety point. Many of the paints, glues, and sealers used in arrowmaking are toxic when used in an enclosed area. Always follow directions on the products and use them with adequate ventilation.

Decide on the length of the dip. We generally put a 10 inch dip on the nock end. The easiest way to do this is to construct a jig and make sure all shafts are even. Then run a pencil or marker of some kind across all the shafts at one time. Leave them in the jig and put alligator clips or clothes pins on the point end. We've made a rack in our dipping room from which to hang these clips. Another way to mark the dip is measuring down each shaft to the correct length and marking each one individually.

Proper consistency of the paint is obtained by pouring it into a cleaned and dried gallon milk jug then adding about one third lacquer thinner. Shake container well to mix paint and then allow it to set until the bubbles have dispersed, usually 20 minutes or so. A good trick to help this along is to tap the bottom of

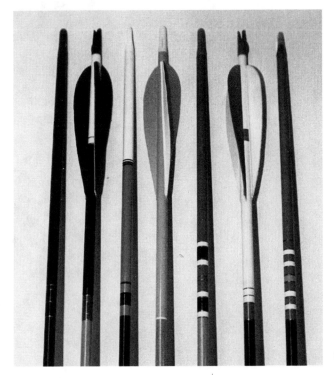

Crown dipped arrows.

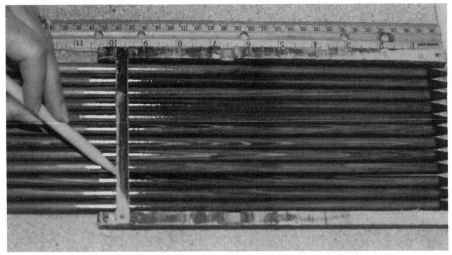

Marking length of crown dip.

Crown dipping shafts.

the milk jug on the floor to make sure there aren't any bubbles on the sides or bottom. When there are no bubbles, pour the desired colors of paint into dip tubes.

It is better to give the arrows four or five thin coats of paint rather than one or two thick coats. Wait about 20 minutes between coats. If bubbles develop in the tubes during the dipping process, either scoop them out or tap the tube on the floor and wait a few minutes before proceeding. If bubbles develop on the shaft during dipping, touch the bubble with a finger or use a straight pin and pop it. Then immediately give the shaft another coat of paint to smooth it out.

Never try to dip arrows on a very humid day or when temperatures are under 70 degrees. The best facility would be one with a furnace or air conditioner to control conditions. A humid day will cause the colors to look cloudy. A product called Blue-Clear can be purchased from Bohning Co. which removes most of the clouding and makes the arrow colors more brilliant.

When the dipping is complete, wait at least 24 hours before attempting to crest them.

There will be a finish-coat of polyurethane applied later.

CRESTING
This entails a certain amount of skill and technique which is only acquired with practice. Consistency is the biggest hurdle. The crest can be as simple or elaborate as you like and can help identify your arrows and be your "trademark".

You will need at least a couple of brushes. I like the ones made of sable hair, purchased from an art store where there is a larger assortment from which to choose. The brushes I use the most are a 1/2" brush and a hairline brush, both with soft, fine bristles. Take care of your brushes and they will virtually last forever.

Paint specifically made for cresting is available, but it is just as easy to use the dipping paint. Save a little before it is thinned for dipping. If the cresting paint does not apply smoothly to the shaft, add a few drops of thinner at a time. If too much thinner is added just leave the lid off overnight so some thinner can evaporate.

The easiest way to crest arrows is with a cresting machine that costs around $60. It consists of a motor and chuck on a board, essentially a tiny lathe. If your crest is simple enough and your hand steady enough, it might be possible to spin the shaft in your hand and get good results.

One way to insure uniformity in the crests is to decide on a pattern and make a template to attach to the crester. This way, all the shafts will have their crest in the same area. Another way is to put the shafts back in the jig that was used for marking the dip. With a ruler and a straight-edge mark the shaft with the amount of lines desired.

We hand crest hundreds of arrows a day, so we have installed a heat lamp above our cresting machines to accelerate the drying process. This way, we can put on our wide bands and not have to put the shaft in a rack or other means of storage until they are dry and ready for the pin stripping. This drying time usually takes about 10 to 20 minutes. While cresting, always be sure to angle the brush so the cresting paint flows in a downward motion. This insures the paint flows smoothly.

When all of the shafts are crested and completely dry, dip the entire shaft in polyurethane as a sealer coat. When this sealer is dry, the shafts are ready to nock.

NOCKING

This procedure is very important for optimum arrow flight. Before proceeding, take a moment to nip-off the dried drops of paint formed by the dipping process that are at the nock ends of the shafts. When applying the nock to the shaft, align the nock so that when the arrow is nocked, the growth rings on the end of the shaft are at right angles to the string. This makes for a sturdier shaft, and if all the shafts are nocked in the same way the chances of all your arrows flying the same are enhanced. This is called nocking across the grain.

After we have glued the nock on but before it is dry, we insert the point-end of the shaft into our cresting machine (backwards) and watch for any nock misalignment. If the nock needs to be adjusted, if it does not spin true, put a light pencil mark anywhere on the nock for a reference point and adjust the nock. Spin the shaft in the cresting machine again to recheck alignment. Sometimes this takes a few tries.

Snap nocks, left and right, and speed nock, center.

There are several types of nocks on the market, but the two most popular types are Snap nocks and Speed nocks. Snap nocks are designed to clip or snap on the string and hold snugly. Speed nocks fit loosely on the string and usually have an indicator that can be used to locate the cock feather without having to look at the arrow. Selecting between them is simply a matter of preference as both work well.

CUTTING THE SHAFT

First, determine your draw length. Different length arrows can be tried or, better yet, a friend can watch you shoot and advise as to the length of draw. Starting from the bottom of the string groove in the nock, measure forward the proper distance. Be certain to add enough extra to accommodate the point taper, as the draw length is measured to the *back* of the point. Experiment on some scrap material to determine the length of this taper. Once the correct length is marked, cut off the shaft. Power cut-off saws are available and are handy for making stacks of arrows. If only a few are being made, a hacksaw works just as well. To prevent splitting, cut lightly all the way around the shaft with the hacksaw before cutting off the excess.

FEATHERS

Besides having all kinds of shapes, colors, and sizes of feathers to choose from, there are also left and right wing feathers. There is an old rule of thumb which says that if you are a right-handed shooter you should use left-wing feathers, and if you are a left-handed shooter you should use right-wing feathers. We have used both and have found little or no difference in arrow flight.

Most often, 5" die cut parabolic or shield shaped feathers are used. If you're having a problem with arrow flight or stability, you might find that a four fletched arrow or a larger feather will help. For this, full length feathers are required rather than pre-cut feathers.

Different shapes can be attained by either using a feather chopper or a feather burner. Feather choppers are available in an assortment of shapes. Some of the choices are 5" high parabolic, 5 1/2" high or low parabolic, 5" shield, 5 1/2" shield, bananas, or what is called a traditional cut. All do a fine job with a little practice and are less costly than purchasing pre-cut feathers. They are also less offensive to anyone within a 1 mile radius of your home than burning feathers.

A feather burner, aside from the smell, is the most versatile because it offers a limitless variety of shapes and sizes. Size and shape of the fletch can be adjusted

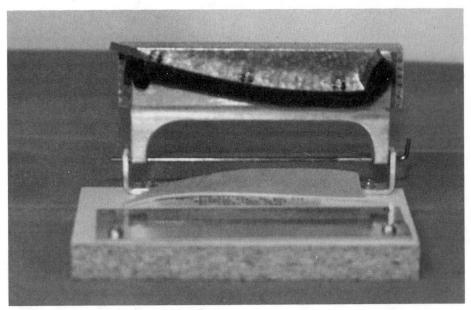

Feather-chopper with shield-cut feather design.

Young feather burner. Wire burner can be shaped for any style fletch you wish.

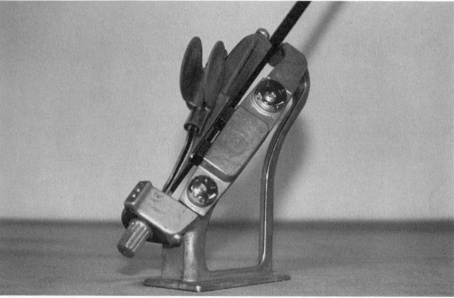

Bitzenburger fletcher.

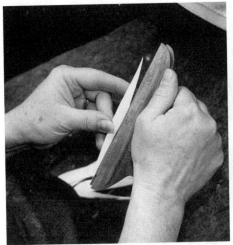

Place the feather in the fletching clamp.

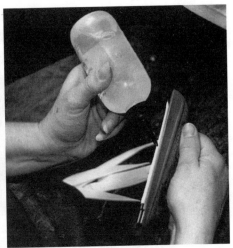

Use a small bottle with pointed tip to apply glue to the spine of the feather.

to different bows and different arrow spines and weights. With this method, the feathers are burned to shape after they are glued on the arrow.

When preparing full length feathers, select the middle part of the feather where the quill is neither too thick or too thin. It is better to get one good quality fletch rather than two that are not uniform.

There are an assortment of fletching tools on the market. I am familiar with only 3 and am partial to one — the Bitzenburger Dial-0-fletch, the most versatile and precise fletcher available.

When fletching, decide what distance from the nock to set the feather.

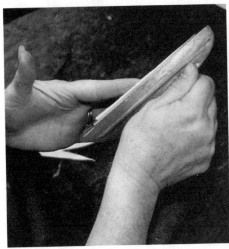

Spread the glue evenly with a finger.

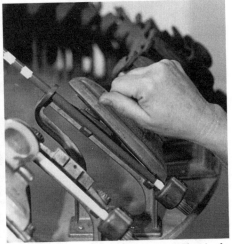

Place the clamp with the prepared feather in the jig.

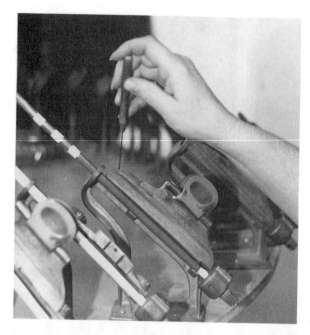

An awl or small screwdriver is used to insure the front and rear of the feather are firmly seated against the shaft.

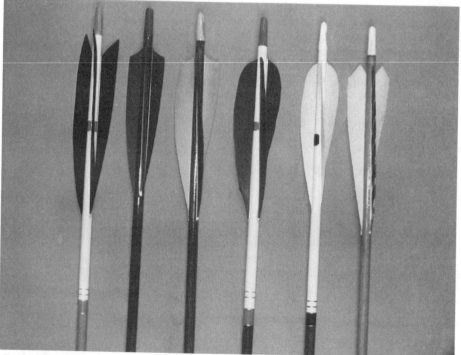

Feather shapes can suit individual tastes.

Determine this by holding the arrow on the string with the shooting hand and seeing how far up the shaft the feathers need to be to clear the fingers, usually about 1/2 inch from the nock. Mark the shaft at that point and set the feather in the clamp accordingly. Use this mark to position all of the feathers in the clamp.

Fletch-tite glue is used to hold the feathers to the shaft. It can be purchased in tubes or in cans that are poured into small bottles. I have more control of glue flow with the small bottles. Whichever you choose, try to obtain a steady, even flow onto the feather's base. If you apply excess glue to the feather, just run your finger along the length of the quill to even it out. Then apply the clamp and feather to the shaft. About 20 minutes is all that is needed for the feather to be set enough to remove the clamp, rotate the shaft, and go on to the next feather.

When all the feathers are attached, there will be a "nub" of quill at the front of the feather that needs to be removed by shaving or grinding. Taper this nub so it is a smooth transition from shaft to feather. After this is done, place a little dot of glue at the spot to keep the feather from lifting, which prevents the quill from running into your hand as the arrow leaves the bow.

ATTACHING POINTS

There are a few different hand held tools for tapering the front of the shaft. Most common are the hand held "pencil sharpener" types. There are also power tapering tools which are great if you have a lot of arrows to taper.

Glue and heat sources for attaching points to arrows.

Whatever tool you use, begin with a scrap shaft for practice and check the length of the taper. Save this for a template to be used in future tapering. Different points and broadheads have varying lengths of ferrule taper. Try to make the point tapers as long as possible, as this adds strength and you won't get a "shock absorber" effect when the arrow hits bone in a game animal. Points will also be easier to install straight.

When attaching points, a source of heat is required, either an alcohol burner or propane torch. Keep a jar of water handy for cooling off points and a cloth for drying points after they are attached. With hot-melt glue stick in hand, heat the glue. Apply a small amount of the glue to the tapered end of the shaft. Very quickly, hold the steel point with a pair of pliers and run it over the flame. When it's hot, attach it to the shaft. Twist the point on the end of the shaft to distribute the glue then push the point against something solid to seat it down all the way. Spin the shaft and sight down it to see that the point is on straight. If not, use forefinger and very quickly — so as not to burn yourself — push in the direction needed. If the point does not move, reheat it by running across the heat source and re-melting the glue. Start the process again.

A broadhead can be mounted with the blade turned at any angle, with the most common being horizontal or vertical in relation to the nock. Whatever angle you choose, mount all of them the same. That way you are seeing the same thing every time you draw a shaft and look at the target. Make sure the broadhead is mounted straight by spinning the shaft and watching the very tip for any wobble.

✧ ✧ ✧

Every archer and hunter wants to shoot with pin-point accuracy, and matching arrows exactly to a bow, along with months of diligent practice, is the way to achieve it.

Anyone who refuses to follow the crowd and makes his own wooden bow from scratch wants his tackle to be personalized and unique. This, too, can be achieved by making your own arrows.

CUSTOM SHAFTS

Gene Langston

When it comes to making arrows today, the basic procedure is simple: take a wooden shaft, glue die-cut feathers and a manufactured plastic nock on one end and a machined steel point on the other. If quick-drying cement is used, it's possible, I suppose, to turn out this kind of arrow in about ten minutes. Considerably less if you're going for a record.

Few traditionalists, however, are satisfied with such a hasty arrow. Most go a step or two beyond the basics and at least add a finish to the shaft to protect it from the elements, whether that finish is bear grease or polyurethane. Many stain and crest their arrows, and some perfectionists might crown dip their shafts, or perhaps splice different-colored feather sections into their fletch to give their arrows a personalized, custom touch.

But that's about as far as they go, and for a very good reason: that's about all that can be done with a self-arrow. And what kind of arrow do you get for this minimum amount of work? An excellent arrow, assuming that you use reasonable care when assembling the components. When it is straight and correctly spined for your bow and tipped with a true and proper head, this arrow is the apex of self-arrow achievement. Making such an arrow is an accomplishment of which one can be justifiably proud, because it will shoot as well as the finest arrow of any material that you can buy. You can consider yourself to have graduated *cum laude* from the School of Shafts.

But now to graduate school, where the real work begins.

Regardless of how good self-arrows are (and they can be excellent), the finest arrows have always been footed arrows. Robert Elmer describes them as the *ne plus ultra* of the arrowmaker's art. The quality of a well-made footed arrow makes even the best self-arrow seem plain and pedestrian by comparison. Looking at well-made representatives of the two, you can easily see the difference in quality. While a self-arrow satisfies the honest needs of the archer's heart, a footed arrow answers a need deeper and much harder to define. They are soul-satisfying with a particular beauty that is unique.

When I talk about footed shafts, I'm not simply talking about the cane arrows footed with a hardwood foreshaft often used by American Indians. These arrows were previously covered in Volume I. I'm talking about the highly-refined English-style footed shaft, which I think is the finest arrow the world has ever seen. These arrows, which were so popular in the 19th and first part of the

20th Century, are products of what has been called "Archery's Golden Age." Footed with purpleheart or beefwood and nocked with buffalo horn, they represent the arrow brought to uncompromising perfection made possible only by the use of steel tools in the hands of craftsmen whose livelihood depended on the quality of their work.

Note, however, that while I said the English footed shaft is the "finest," ("fine: finished; brought to perfection; refined") I did not say it was the "best." There is a very clear distinction between the two terms, as there is between silk and wool. Most would agree that silk is finer; which is "best" would depend on the purpose for which it is being used. While a footed shaft is unquestionably finer than a solid fiberglass shaft, for example, it is not best for shooting carp.

As beautiful as it is, the footed shaft is also practical, which is why it was such an ancient, widespread practice among American Indians. There are aboriginal European footed arrow shafts in existence to prove that the practice took place over there as well. Stone-Age cultures tend to share more similarities than differences, and attaching a hardwood foot to a softwood arrow seems an obvious, arrow-saving solution. In *Toxiphillus*, Roger Ascham mentions "pieced" arrows, as does Gerevase Markham in his century-later effort, *The Art of Archerie*. In both cases, it is clear that they are talking about footed target shafts.

In England during Victoria's reign, archery made its first "modern" comeback, and both bowyers and arrowmakers flourished. Footed shafts became extremely popular during that time and were imported to America, especially after the Thompson brothers published their famous articles in *Harper's Magazine*, which were later collected as *The Witchery of Archery*. During that time, tournament shooting was archery's dominant form, and during the last part of the 19th and the first part of the 20th, no serious tournament shooter would consider shooting the York or the American Round with self-arrows. It was felt that the up-front weight enhanced an arrow's flight characteristics. Footing was also a common practice when repairing self-arrows, not only making the arrow stronger, but increasing its value as well.

Footed arrows remained popular as long as wood arrows were popular. After World War II, however, several factors spelled doom for footed arrows. Manpower shortages caused the price of labor to rise steeply, which made labor-intensive footed shafts practically unaffordable. American archery tastes changed. The 100-yard American Round was replaced by Field Archery with shorter distances and rockier courses. Bowhunting became very popular. Neither field archer nor bowhunter particularly relished sending an expensive footed shaft toward a target when the odds were pretty good that it could be lost or broken.

Another factor that helped doom the footed shaft was the advent of the "dowel" arrow, or the finished cedar shaft with which all of us are familiar. Previously, arrow shafts were planed out of boards, a procedure requiring tools, materials, and skills that were not the property of the average archer. It took about an hour to make an arrow in this manner, and understandably, most arrows were made by professionals.

Once dowel shafts were accepted, they changed the face of archery. They were so easy to make into arrows every man became his own fletcher.

Aluminum and fiberglass arrows were introduced and touted as the perfect arrow shaft material. Cedar shafting became cheap and, like every other thing that is inexpensive, lost respect. Those who shot cedar would often make a new arrow rather than spend a few minutes searching for one that was lost. To put things in perspective, consider this: ever since most of us can remember, a cedar arrow shaft has cost less than a cup of coffee at a fast-food restaurant.

But that was then: this is now. The price of dowel arrow shafts is skyrocketing, and it looks like the wood arrow will finally get the respect it deserves. And if you're going to shoot wood arrows, why not shoot the finest? Not that footed arrows are for everyone or for every shot; they emphatically are not. They are not for those who would walk away gladly from a shaft buried under the grass, nor are they for those who plan to salute the rising sun each day with an arrow fired symbolically into the blue. They are much tougher than softwood self-arrows, but cannot be shot into granite boulders with impunity. And they're definitely not for those who think custom arrows are the solution to accuracy problems caused by poor form or a bad release. Footed arrows are for those who simply want to shoot the finest arrow they can make.

And they *can* be made, at home, by anyone who has a reasonable degree of proficiency with tools. By this, I mean anyone who is at least as handy as I am. Most people on the planet qualify.

In fact, to the politically correct, I suppose I would be known as "Tool Challenged." I can often be seen in hospital emergency rooms, grimacing in pain, or limping down the corridors of clinics to have yet another part of my body repaired. When we come in contact with power tools, we Tool Challenged people sometime earn nicknames we don't particularly relish, like "Scarface," or "Lefty," or "Three-finger Joe." So, if I can make a custom footed shaft and escape relatively unscathed, anyone can.

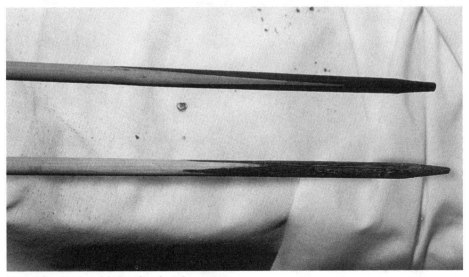

Two-splice (top) and four-splice footed arrows.

THE TWO-SPLICE FOOTED SHAFT

The two types of footed shafts which are the most common are the two-splice and the four-splice. The two-splice is the simplest and the oldest. It is perhaps slightly stronger, and it looks great. It is the kind I make most often because of its simplicity and durability.

TOOLS

I've intentionally tried keeping the described methods as simple as possible, using a minimum number of widely available tools, so that anyone who wants to can make footed shafts.

Unless you're extremely skilled with a fine-toothed saw that will cut to the required depth, you'll need access to a band saw to cut the hardwood to dimension and to cut the footing slots. If you don't own one or know a friend who does, get a millwork shop to do it for you. The footings *must* be cut uniformly. Consistency here is the key to success. You can do everything else with hand tools.

You will need three 1-1/2-inch C-clamps to hold the footing to the shaft while the glue dries (A pair of Vise-Grip pliers is a good substitute for a C-clamp). You'll also need a small, fine-cutting plane, such as a palm plane or something even smaller. I bought mine at a hardware store for, as I recall, less than five dollars. The man who sold it to me called it a "thumb plane." It looks like something you could get at a woodworking or a model shop if your hardware store doesn't have it. Despite the fact it's simple-looking and relatively inexpensive, it

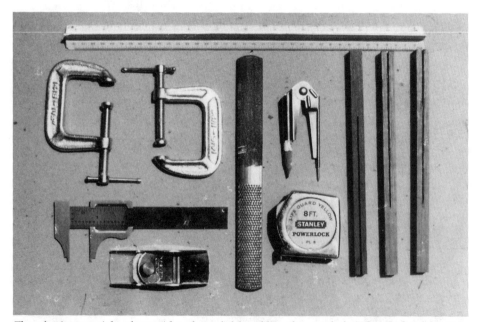

Three footings, at right, along with tools needed for adding them to shaft. "Thumb plane" is at bottom left.

is a high quality tool and will peel extremely fine shavings from the hardest hardwood. It'll last a lifetime.

You'll also need sandpaper, a wood rasp, a compass for drawing circles, a ruler and a pencil.

In the first part of this century, most fletchers used casein glue for footing arrows. Made from milk protein, it was the strongest glue available that was also waterproof. It was used in the World War I aircraft industry to hold the wood and fabric airplanes together. Casein glue is made up in dry form and mixed with water. You can buy it, mostly at woodworking supply stores, but there are alternatives that are stronger, simpler, and easier to use. I wonder if the white woodworking glue you get today isn't an updated version of casein glue, since one brand is put out by a milk company. In any case, the white or yellow wood glue you can get at a hardware store works great and gives an absolute bond.

Another alternative is hide glue. It isn't waterproof, but some of the old fletchers preferred it because a significant part of their work involved repairing broken footings and they felt a joint glued with casein was a bit too "permanent." I find hide glue messier and more difficult to work with than just about any other kind of glue, and for footing arrows, I don't use it. On the positive side, it is very strong and you can make it yourself. Volume I has a section on glues, so you can refer to that if you have any questions about strength or suitability. Epoxy works, and is in fact is what I use for four-splice footings, but for two-splice footings it's more expensive than wood working glue and not any better.

You will also need full-length shafts and hardwood for footings. Beefwood and purpleheart are the woods most commonly used. I've used both, and from the way it works under the plane, beefwood might have a slight edge, but not enough to worry about. Osage is excellent, walnut is pretty good, and other hardwoods will also work. Even some light-colored hardwoods will make good footings, but they lack the color that gives the desired contrast for the most attractive footed shafts. And since it's the same amount of work, why not make something that's beautiful as well as durable.

GETTING DOWN TO BUSINESS

Cut the footing material (or have it cut) in small billets 7/16-inch square by 7 1/2-inches long. These dimensions assume that you're resawing (splitting the thickness) of a hardwood plank for the footings, which results in the most footings from the smallest amount of lumber. Such planks are usually exactly one inch in thickness, and the above specifications allow for the saw blade kerf. When measuring, make sure you make allowance for the width of the blade.

Now that the footing billets are sawn to dimension, on one end of each billet directly down the center cut a 5 1/4-inch slot with a fine-tooth saw with a thin blade. I tried this by hand once using a hack saw with the blade turned sideways. It was a difficult task, and I recommend using a bandsaw.

On the opposite end of this footing, locate dead center by carefully drawing two lines diagonally from the corners. Where the lines cross is the center. Put the point of the compass on that intersection and describe a circle of shaft diameter. In other words, if using a 11/16-inch shaft, make that the diameter of

"Reed" of the shaft (top), or the edges of the yearly growth rings in the shaft. "Rift" of the shaft (bottom), or the flat view of the yearly growth rings. Reed and rift are two ancient terms that are the least confusing when describing growth ring orientation in arrow shafts.

the circle. This circle will come in handy later as a guide when planing the footing round.

Next, measure five inches up from the end of the arrow shaft and mark it lightly all the way around at that point. Call this line A. Then, identify the "rift" and the "reed" of the shaft . The reed is the shaft's strongest aspect, where the grain runs in parallel lines for the length of the shaft. It is where, on a properly fletched arrow, the cock feather lines up. The reed lies against side of the bow when shooting. The rift lies at 90 degrees from the reed and is where the growth rings run out the shaft. The rift of the shaft should rest on the arrow shelf or on your hand when the arrow is nocked.

On the end of the shaft, make a pencil line across the center, from one side of the reed to the other. Call this line B. Using the plane, start at line A, the line you drew five inches up the shaft, and plane the shaft down on both sides toward line B until you have a wedge tapering to a knife-thin edge at line B. The sides of the wedge should be level, but it can be slightly concave from front to back. (To make this clear, imagine that the shaft has a nock already mounted; in order to make the wedge, you will plane away wood on the top and bottom of the shaft, from reed side to reed side). The end of the wedge, at line B, should be as thick as the bottom of the slot in the footing in which it will fit. If it's thinner, you won't have a good glue joint and might even have a void you can see through. If it's thicker it can split the footing.

Now, prepare the other shafts in the same manner, taking care to taper them uniformly so you will have the same hard-to-softwood ratio in each finished shaft.

Before we go any further, let's stop and review what we've done. We have several 7 1/2-inch by 7/16-square hardwood footings with a 5 1/4-inch slot cut down the center of each. We have the same number of arrow shafts that have been tapered into a wedge for the last five inches of their length. This wedge is cut in such a manner that if we nocked the shaft the flat part of the wedge would be on the top and bottom of the shaft.

Fold a piece of 150 grit aluminum oxide sandpaper with the grit side out and insert it in the first few inches of the footing slot. Pinch the slot together slightly and draw the sandpaper through it for a few strokes to smooth the inside of the slot somewhat. This insures a better glue joint. Don't overdo it or you could round off the edges and get a bad fit. A little is enough in this case.

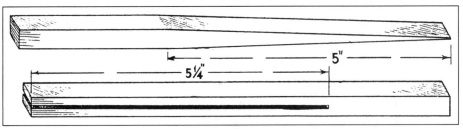

Slotted foot (bottom) and the front of the arrowshaft tapered with a plane to wedge shape.

Now, take one of your C-clamps and screw it down tightly about a quarter-inch below the bottom of the slot in the footing. This is to prevent the footing from splitting when the wedge of the shaft is forced into the slot.

Apply glue liberally to the wedge of the shaft and insert it into the slot. Hold your fingers on either side of the slot to keep the shaft centered in the footing. As the shaft slides home, it spreads the wings of the footing apart and tightens up.

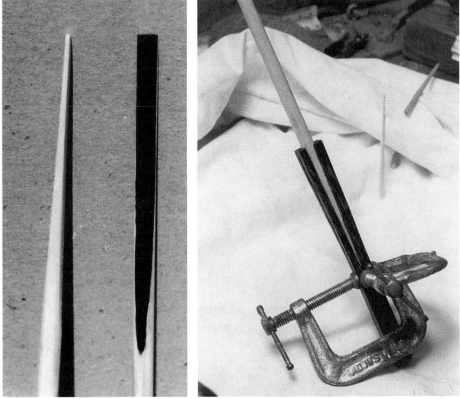

Two views of tapered arrowshaft. Dark stain added for clarity.

Wedge of arrowshaft inserted, with glue, into slot in footing. Note clamps in place to prevent splitting of footing.

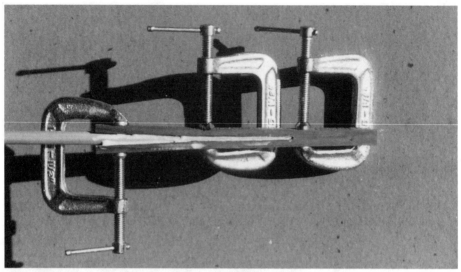

Once shaft and footing are aligned, two more clamps are added.

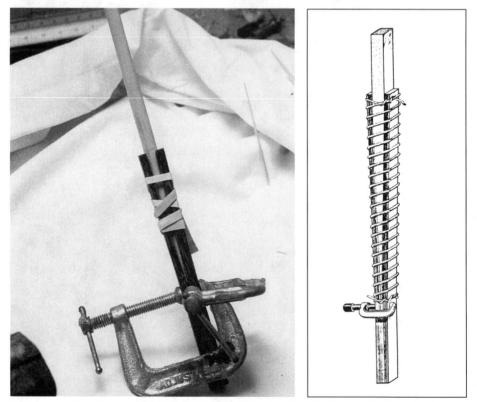

Two more options for securing shaft and footing while glue dries. Rubber band, left, and string.

Since it's important to insure that the shaft is firmly seated at the very bottom of the footing, you might have to gently tap it home with a piece of wood or a rubber hammer, all the while guiding the shaft with your fingers. If it's crooked, pull it out and start again. You can check for alignment by noticing the fit on both sides of the footing. It should be the same. When everything is lined up, wipe off the excess glue and hold the shaft to the light. Sight down the shaft and all sides of the footing. Does it look straight? If it's crooked, you'll never get your finished arrow to come out straight. There is plenty of time before the glue dries, so use it now to get everything lined up.

When you're satisfied, put the other two C-clamps on the footing and tighten them, but not so tight you crush the shaft. Don't worry about scarring the footing; you're going to plane away the outside anyway. Now let it dry overnight.

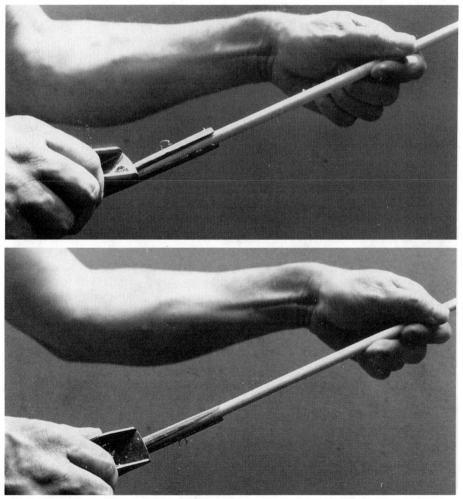

Planing away the "wings" of the footing.

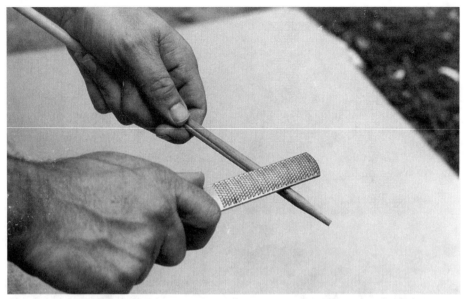

Once most of the excess footing is removed, switch to a rasp to prevent gouging the shaft.

After everything is dry, remove the clamps. If you have a bandsaw or table saw, carefully cut away the excess material where the wings flare out and save yourself some time. If not, you can use the plane to cut them off — which works fine, too. Using the plane, cut back toward the nock-end of the shaft with a light stroke. Before cutting toward the shaft, however, wrap a rubber band around it about a half-inch from the footing. If you use too long a stroke, the bottom of the plane rides on the rubber band and prevents the plane from cutting into the shaft above the footing. As you remove material from the back of the footing, you'll see the top of the wing begin to taper into a point. You're getting close. Cut as closely as you dare, but don't cut into the shaft. A fine rasp or file is good for the final shaping. Then, reverse directions: start planing toward the pile end of the footing. Sight down the shaft now and then to make sure you're not cutting the footing crooked. Here's where that circle you drew earlier comes in handy; plane toward it, using it as a guide both for correct diameter and roundness. Continue checking the roundness for the entire length of the footing as you remove wood. If you have a caliper, well and good. If not, you can use an open-end wrench to check the dimension. Check often to prevent cutting dips in the footing. You can also use your senses: roll the shaft on a flat surface, feel it to see if it is round, eyeball it, whatever it takes. You'll probably be surprised at how close you can get just by using sight and touch. If you find the first few shafts have a few flat places and aren't totally cylindrical, don't worry about it too much; they will shoot just fine as long as they're straight.

Continue removing wood, but keep in mind that it's a whole lot easier to take it off than put it back, so be careful now that you're almost finished. When you get the shaft down to the desired diameter and as round as possible with the

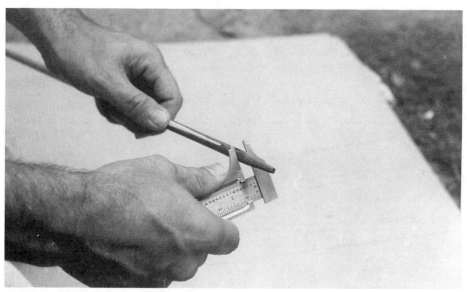

Checking for roundness with caliper.

plane and rasp, sand it smooth, cut it to length, dip it, nock it, crest it, feather it, and shoot it.

THE FOUR-SPLICE FOOTED SHAFT

For years, I felt that making the four-splice footed shaft was a woodworking task roughly equivalent to carving a living room suite out of a solid block of oak with a broken beer bottle and a Swiss Army knife. It's complicated-looking, this four-splice footing, and I could find no reference source in any of the old archery books on how to make it. I ran different scenarios through my mind innumerable times, each time becoming stuck on some particular point that prevented me, in my thoughts, from creating that simple and elegant joint that resembles the splice of a pool cue. I supposed that it took exotic tools of which I could only dream.

From joining billets for self-bows, I suspected the four-splice joint was some form of double fishtail splice, since a two-splice footing is nothing but a single fishtail. Working under this faulty assumption, I soon learned that if I used a double fishtail splice the points would be of uneven thickness, which worked, but made the footing appear ungainly. And take my word for it, it ain't no picnic cutting a double fish into a 11/32-inch shaft, especially for one who is Tool Challenged!

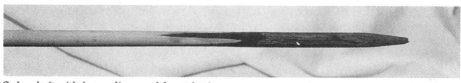

Cedar shaft with four-splice purpleheart footing.

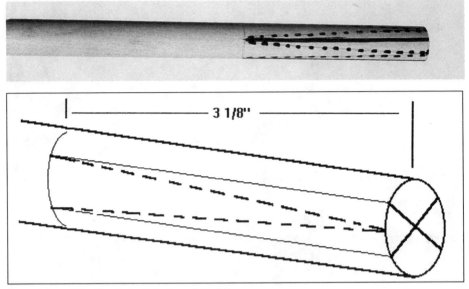

Layout for cutting the shaft. Cut along dotted lines.

Finally, I stumbled on the answer, and, like many things in traditional archery, what had at first seemed complicated and impossible turned out to be ultimately very simple.

Actually, there are two methods of making a four-splice footed shaft. The first method described is the older and can be accomplished entirely with hand tools. It also allows a longer, better-looking splice, and it yields a joint comparable in strength if not simplicity to the two-splice shaft. It is more complicated in the telling than in the doing, especially until you've done a few and come up to speed.

To use this method, measure from one end of a raw arrow shaft the length you want to make the splice. Between three and four inches is a good place to start (I use 3 1/8 inches for nostalgia's sake; the old footed shaft I destroyed to figure out this method was of that length). Draw a pencil line around the circumference of the shaft at that point. This is Line A.

Next, draw a mid-line across the end of the shaft, directly across the grain. Mark a second line at right angles to this one so that the two lines intersect in the center of the shaft, making a cross. Extend each line down the shaft until it intersects Line A. You will find that you can do this quite easily freehand by using your thumb and middle finger for guides. In effect, you are dividing a 3 1/8 inch section at the end of the shaft into quarters, but you don't need to do a lot of complicated measuring to accomplish this. If the lines appear equidistant apart to the eye, the "cornea caliper," that is sufficient.

If, however, you are one of those people who have an affinity for measuring things and want the exact measurement for quartering the shaft, recall from high-school geometry class the formula for finding the circumference of a circle.

(If, like me, you slept through geometry, the formula is C = pi d. You then divide this by four.) For an 11/32-inch shaft, this is .26 inch; for a 23/64 shaft it is .28, and for a 5/16 shaft, it is .24. But when it comes to wood, it's unrealistic to think in terms of hundredths of an inch, so a quarter inch is close enough.

With your pencil at the end of the shaft, once again visually divide each of the sections you've just marked. Make a small pencil tic mark at the end of the shaft centered between each of the lines. This mark should be the approximate width of your saw blade, probably about 1/32-inch wide.

Now, to make the cut for footing the shaft. The four parallel lines represent

Beginning cut on shaft.

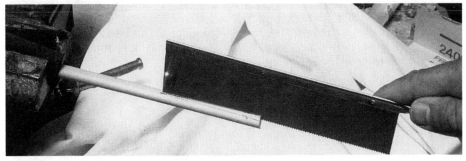

Finished cut on shaft.

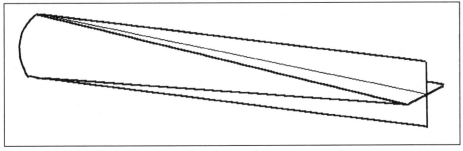

Leading edge of the shaft after saw cuts have been made.

the parameters or boundaries of each of the four splices, or "wings" you are about to cut. The tic marks at the end of the shaft represent the point of the splice. Secure the shaft in a padded vice so that one of the tic marks is on top and well-centered.

Use your thumbnail as a guide. Place it on the tic mark, and, with a fine-tooth backed saw, start the cut on the right edge of the mark. Hold the saw so that it is at 90 degrees to the diameter of the shaft, and angle it to the right so it meets the boundary line where it crosses Line A. You needn't pencil-mark this; your saw blade will serve as a straightedge. The cut will be shallowest at Line A, becoming increasingly deeper as it approaches the front end of the shaft.

After making this cut, move your thumbnail over and start your second cut in the same way as the first, except begin on the left edge of the tic mark and angle the blade to the left.

Do this all the way around, rotating the shaft. Make sure you are at all times sawing at **right angles to the diameter of the shaft.** It is easier to cut each wing partially, rotate the shaft, and then cut the next. After all eight cuts are partially made, go back and finish-cut each section, watching the end of the shaft to make sure you don't cut past center. When you are through, the end of the shaft looks like a +, (a "plus" sign.) This "plus" should be the same thickness as your saw blade for the best fit. It should certainly be no thicker; if so, it could split the footing.

Clean up the cuts with a sharp pocket knife. The very back of the cut where it tapers to nothing is usually where this is needed most.

Next, prepare the footing. Take a six-inch piece of footing material, 3/8 X 3/8, and saw a 3 1/8 inch slot directly down the center. Rotate the material and saw another identical slot at right angles. Place two C-clamps just below the slots and tighten them to prevent the footing from splitting. Use a couple of small wedges (splinters or toothpicks will do) and wedge the mouth of the footing slightly open to expedite the insertion of the end of the thin, fragile shaft.

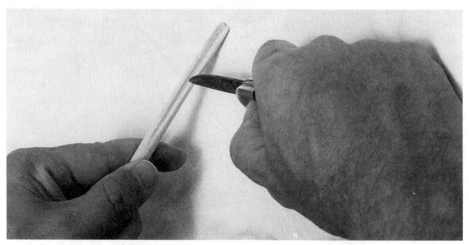

Carefully cleaning the cuts with a pocket knife.

Slots cut in footing.

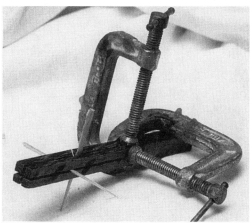

Clamps in place to prevent splitting and small wedges to hold footing open to accept shaft.

Apply glue liberally to the shaft. Although wood glue works well, I use epoxy here because it fills small voids that may have resulted from a less than ideal saw cut. Insert the shaft into the footing for an inch or so, remove the wedges, and force the shaft to the bottom of the footing. Wrap a rubber band around the joint to hold it tight until the glue dries.

After it is dry, the finishing process is the same as with a two-splice footed shaft. Remove wood with a plane and wood rasp until the footing is perfectly round and the points taper nicely and sharply. You might even find this easier than with a two-splice taper, since, as the splice is shorter, there's less wood to remove.

This method also works when attaching sectionally square shaft stock (called "stickers") to sectionally square footing. It is, in fact, somewhat easier to make the splice, since you don't have to deal with cutting into the round shaft. You can save finishing time it if your stock is only slightly larger than the dimension you intend for your finished shaft; 3/8 stock for a 11/32 shaft, for example.

You can often buy 3/8 dowels in cherry, walnut, and sometimes even more exotic hardwoods from hardware or woodworking stores. The method I described above will not work well for attaching round-to-round; the shaft invariably breaks. If you must use round stock, there is a quick method for doing so.

A bowyer friend of mine, Jerry Fisher, came up with this solution. The principal is simple: cut a V-notch in the shaft material, rotate it 90 degrees, and repeat the process. Do exactly the same thing with your footing material and join the two together. This process is quick if you're good with a bandsaw, which Jerry is.

The width of the notch should be one quarter inch, as discussed earlier. The length of the splice can be any depth you can confidently cut, but the deeper the cut the more acute the angle at the tip of the splice, and the more difficult it becomes to get a proper fit. Two inches is about the limit using this method.

Uniformity is necessary so that every splice, on both shaft and footing, is

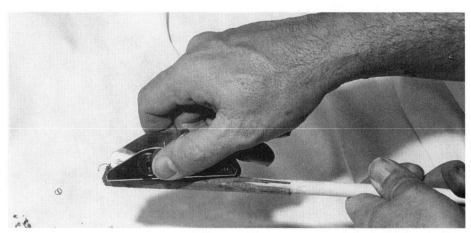

Planing away excess material.

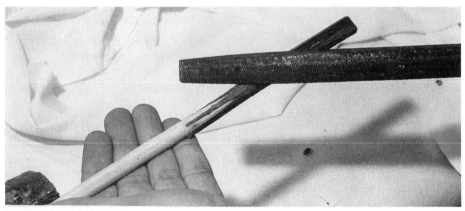

Rasping to finished diameter.

exactly the same. If you have a good eye and a steady hand, you can make a template for laying out the notch and then mark the material and saw out the splice, either by hand or on a bandsaw. Use a six-inch strip of any thin, hard material for the template; ideal is stiff, clear plastic because you can see pencil lines through it, which helps with alignment. Make it six inches long so the other end can be used to make a nock-insert template, which we'll discuss later. The template will be a V-slot, a quarter of an inch wide and two inches deep.

Line up the notch template so the point of the V is at the center of the shaft and the mouth of the V is aligned with the sides, and mark it with a sharp pencil. Rotate the shaft exactly 90 degrees and mark it again. Before marking and cutting, I wrap a strip of two-inch wide masking tape around the end of the shaft. The tape helps minimize splintering, and it is easier to see the pencil mark on tape than on the bare wood.

To make sure you're rotating exactly 90 degrees, you can make this simple index jig: take a two-inch square piece of hardwood a half-inch or so thick.

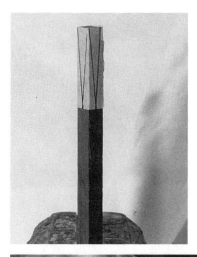

Purpleheart footing with cuts laid out on masking tape.

Making the cuts with a bandsaw.

Finished footing.

Draw an X, corner to corner, with a fine-point permanent marker so you can see it clearly, locating the center. These lines will serve as your index guides. Now, drill a hole of shaft diameter where the lines cross. Insert the shaft in the hole, and make a mark on it adjacent to any one of the lines on the index jig. Use the template to mark the V-notch, and rotate the shaft so the mark you made on it is adjacent to the next index line, thus rotating it 90 degrees. Mark that notch also, and you're ready to cut.

If using a bandsaw, leave the shaft in the jig, securing it with rubber bands. This insures that the shaft is square to the cutting table and gives a better fit. Carefully cut out each V-notch; if using a hand saw, start all four cuts for a depth of about an inch before sawing out the first notch; if you saw out one notch and then go back to saw out the other, you'll find that the top of the shaft

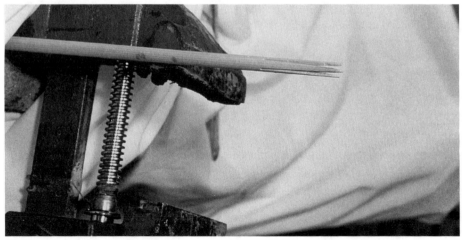

Finished shaft, ready to accept footing.

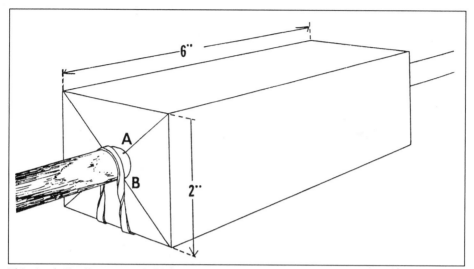

This simple jig allows you to hold the arrowshaft steady while bandsawing. The rubber band holds it in place. The crossed lines at the end allow you to rotate the shaft exactly 90 degrees. Mark the shaft at line A, make the cut as described in the text, then rotate shaft until mark lines up at B.

is so thin and unsupported that the saw blade will chew it away. Hardwood doesn't exhibit this characteristic as much, but care is still necessary. As a further preventative measure, come in a bit from the edges of the shaft before starting the cut.

If you've done everything properly, you will have a four-pronged affair that looks vaguely like a flower petal with four sharp points. You then repeat this process with your footing material stock. And if you did everything right, you're ready to fit the two together and join them.

Usually, however, you haven't done everything right, especially on your first shafts. And it's a bit more difficult than it sounds. For example, when you try to saw the V-slot into a round shaft, you have to fight the optical illusion the roundness gives. There is a tendency to rotate the shaft as you cut, which will make the splice uneven and give a poor fit. When trying to cut soft Port Orford cedar shafts in the round, the saw blade chews out chunks near the apex of the splice, which can cause the points to be of uneven lengths. I keep an emery board on hand to finish the points and bring them up sharp. After you make a lot of cuts, you'll probably get experienced enough that you don't need it.

You can also make a jig that allows you to hold the shaft securely and cut the notch accurately. The jig, which is an extension of the one described above, is a modification of a nock inlay jig (which will be discussed later) and can do triple duty as a nock-slot jig as well. I've included a drawing of the jig to help you make one. In my jig, I drilled two shaft holes, one larger than the other, in case I wanted to foot some really big shafts, but the larger one was superfluous. You can modify these plans to your needs.

Take a block of well-seasoned hardwood and mark a line directly down its center lengthwise. Then, mark lines at right angles to this centerline for the shaft

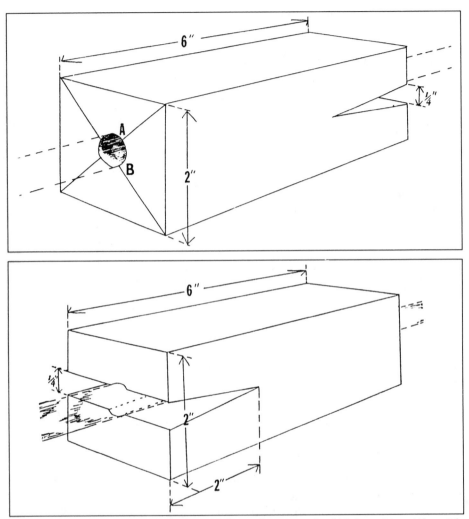

Two views of same jig modified by having a V slot cut into one end, which is used to cut the notch with a thin-bladed hand saw or a bandsaw. The slot is 2 inches deep and 1/4 inch wide, slightly smaller than shaft diameter.

holes. Do this on both top and bottom of the block, because you'll need the lines later as a reference. Drill shaft diameter holes from top to bottom of the block, using a wood bit (which gives you a cleaner hole) and, if possible, a drill press or some other method to insure straightness. Next, drill two holes, 5/16" diameter, about a half-inch in from the edge of the block and 2-1/2 inches down from the top, passing through the block from side to side. These holes are for the quarter-inch bolts and are mostly for alignment; you're going to clamp the jig in a vise which will hold it together. You could just as well substitute wooden pins for the bolts.

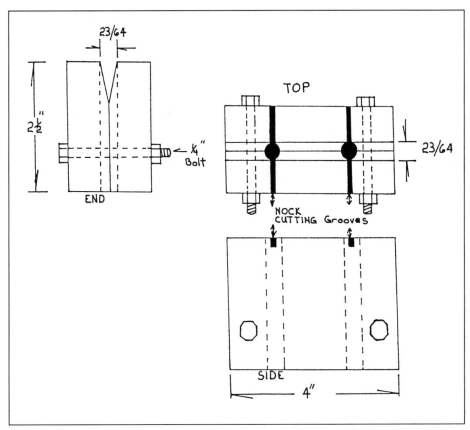

23/64

2½"

¼" Bolt

END

TOP

23/64

NOCK CUTTING Grooves

SIDE

4"

Schematic drawing of jig.

Next, draw two lines, an eighth of an inch on either side of the center line and parallel to it. This will be the width of the V-notch, a quarter of an inch. On one end of the block, measure two inches from the top directly down the center and make a small mark. This will be the depth of the V-notch. Mark and saw the notch out of the block with either a stiff-backed hand saw or a bandsaw (keep in mind that the notch must be slightly less in width than the diameter of your shaft hole).

Once you've sawn and removed the V-shaped wedge, draw a straight line from the bottom of the notch to the bottom of the jig and saw along this line until the block separates into two pieces. Take each side of the jig, and inspect the angle of the V-notch you just sawed. You might have to smooth the sides of the notch with a fine rasp or a file and sandpaper.

To cut V-notches in your shaft, place the shaft in the blocks and turn it so you can see the pencil lines drawn earlier on the bottom of the jig. If drilled properly, the pencil lines will exactly bisect the center of the holes like crosshairs. Make a small pencil mark on the shaft directly in line with one of these perpendicular lines which act as indexers in the same manner as in the index jig described above.

Now, place the jig in a vise and saw along the angle on both sides, cutting out a V-shaped wedge. Turn the shaft until the pencil mark on the shaft lines up with the next "crosshair," thus rotating it exactly 90 degrees.

When making the cut, use a hand saw with a very thin blade. You will notice that because the jig is tight and the shaft wood is soft, the blade binds at the bottom of the cut. A thin-bladed saw, such as a Japanese "razor" saw, does a nice job.

Next, cut the V-notch in the round footing and join the two together. I recommend epoxy exclusively for this job, since there are bound to be some voids that need to be filled. Overall, I would rate this joint as somewhat weaker than the other method, although it is a practical way of joining round-to-round stock. It is faster, once the technique is learned. Practice cutting V-notches on junk stock until you're adept at it. Like everything else in traditional archery, practice means perfection.

NOCKS FOR CUSTOM ARROWS

Now that you've taken care of the business end of the arrow, it's time to pay some attention to the nock. Here your choice is very wide, ranging all the way from the plain but serviceable to the ultimate custom nock, the horn insert. Somewhere in the middle is the plastic nock, which I feel is certainly a viable choice, although some would disagree.

Actually, plastic nocks have a lot going for them. They're cheap, easy to carry in your pocket, last a long time, and you can get them just about anywhere. If you happen to break one in the field, all you have to do is cut away the broken one and glue on another in a matter of seconds. They're offered in a wide variety of colors, shapes, and sizes, from translucent jewel-like snap-on numbers that grip the string to index nocks that allow you to nock an arrow without looking at it. And they only cost a few cents each. Cheap, versatile, and available. No wonder they're so popular.

They do have some disadvantages, though. Cold weather can makes some of them brittle, weather changes can affect the glue used to hold them to the shaft and cause them to pop off, and many times they just don't fit the string, being either too tight or too loose. Mix a too-tight nock with cold weather and you are asking for a broken nock and a potentially hazardous condition, either to yourself or to your bow.

Perhaps the biggest problem with plastic nocks is the problem of nock misalignment. If you don't get the nock taper accurate with a good tapering tool, then the nock will be off-center, the arrow will leave the bow askance, and you'll never get accurate arrow flight. And good tapering tools are few and far between, although some improvements have recently been made in that area. Nock misalignment is bad enough with field points, but it becomes much more pronounced when you glue a broadhead on the arrow.

There are excellent alternatives to the plastic nock, and I will present them here so you can make your mind up about using them, or perhaps which of them to use. And sometimes, especially on custom footed arrows, plastic nocks would simply be...well, wrong. After making a set of beautiful purpleheart-footed shafts, you probably would not want to affix a yellow-green Bjorn-type nock.

As far as accuracy goes, these alternatives are at least as reliable as plastic nocks, and possibly more so because the nock is cut directly into the rear of the arrow. Nock alignment is relatively easy to achieve along with better arrow flight.

There are several methods of nocking an arrow other than using a pre-manufactured plastic nock. Listed in ascending order of difficulty (and in my mind, desirability) they are as follows: self-nocks, reinforced self-nocks and inlaid nocks. These are the ways arrows used to be nocked, but with the advent of the plastic nock, these methods fell into disuse. Not because they were ineffective, but because of cost and convenience and the other advantages listed above.

THE SELF-NOCK

The self-nock, the easiest and most primitive method of joining string to arrow, is how arrows have been nocked from the dawn of time. While a custom arrow probably wouldn't be nocked with a self-nock, the principals of the self-nock are the same as the other methods, which is the reason I included it. You simply cut a slot *across the grain* of the shaft about a quarter-inch deep. It takes only seconds to make an arrow nock in this way. Jay Massey talks about self-nocks in Volume I to the extent that little more need be said here. Jay likes the self-nock much better than I do, possibly because his arrow wood, Sitka spruce, is better than mine. I've had worse luck with them and have in fact broken several self-nocks when I used them, either through striking the nock with another arrow or for some other reason. With a self-nock, the main challenge is sawing the slot straight, and this can be accomplished by either making a jig or modifying the one described earlier. You do this by simply sawing a nock guide slot across the center of the shaft hole. The conventional tool for sawing the nock is three hacksaw blades taped together, but if you use a thin bowstring this will be somewhat too big, so experiment before you merrily saw all your nock slots too large. Far better to have to widen a too-narrow slot than to saw it too wide. When you finish sawing the slot, you can round off the bottom with a small round file.

If you use tough hardwood arrows, like birch or hickory, a self-nock might be all the nock you need. However, nocks take quite a beating from the impact of the string, and as I said, I've broken several. One way of reinforcing self-nocks is to tightly wrap the shaft beneath the slot with silk string or sinew. This might help some, but not much, and it's an unsatisfactory measure at best. A better means of reinforcing the self-nock is needed to lessen the chance of breaking a nock and possibly doing damage to the bow.

THE REINFORCED SELF NOCK

Fortunately, such a method exists, and it requires only a couple of minutes more than a self nock. Take the nocking jig and at right angles to the nock slot and centered on the hole, saw another slot, 7/8 to one inch deep and somewhat narrower, perhaps only two hacksaw-blades wide. Saw this slot in the shaft first, *parallel to the grain*. Then, insert a snug-fitting piece of reinforcing material, say a thin slice of hardwood or horn or fiber, into this slot, glue it in with a good-quality glue that is compatible with both the wood of the shaft and the reinforcing material. After it's dry, cut the nock in the manner described above at right

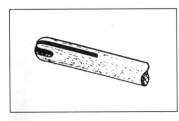

Nock reinforced with fiber.

angles to this reinforcement. What results is a tough, stiff material against the string held in place by a strong glue, reinforcing the self-nock and keeping it from splitting. War arrows recovered from the *Mary Rose* had nocks reinforced in just this way. It works great and you can also leave just enough material sticking out on one side which, when rounded off, will allow for a cock feather index.

What kinds of material make a good reinforcement? Anything tough and hard which can be glued to wood. Exotic wood works well and looks good, too. Another excellent material is a strip of cow horn sawn from the large end, where it's thinner. You can boil it in water and press it flat in a vise and then let it dry into a narrow sheet to make it easier to handle before sawing to the correct dimensions.

Another once popular reinforced self-nock is the shouldered nock reinforcement. Unlike the nock reinforcements just described that strengthen the nock internally, the shouldered nock reinforces the nock from the outside. It is simply a short, thin-walled tube of hard material that is the same outside diameter as the arrow shaft. It fits flush around the end of the shaft.

The nock is then sawn in the conventional manner, across the grain and the tube. Aluminum, hard rubber, bakelite, and fiber were once marketed for this purpose. I have personally used this method only once, when at a yard sale I found some small, hollow tubes of very dark, purple- and black-streaked dense wood that were part of a wind chime. The diameter was almost exactly the outside diameter of my arrow shafts, 23/64. I fitted 3/4-inch long sections over the end of the arrow shaft and in no time flat made some very fine looking arrows. Possibly some kind of small, hollow bone would work as well. Such a nock is very little trouble to fit and looks both unusual and fine.

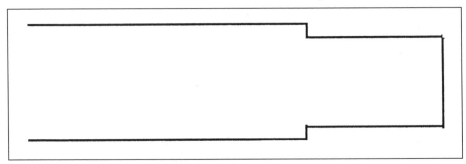

End of shaft prepared to accept shouldered nock.

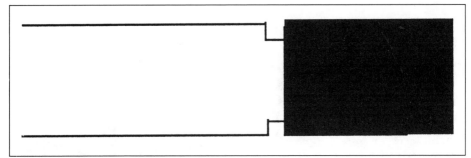

Glue thin-walled tube over end of prepared shaft.

Shouldered nock complete with slot sawn through tube and shaft wood.

THE INLAID NOCK

The third method of making nocks is more difficult. It's also the toughest and by far the most beautiful; it's the way the highest quality arrows were made in the old days. If done properly, the finished result will be an enduring arrow nock of which you can be proud. I'm talking about the nock insert, also called the inlaid nock, where a wedge of wood is cut from the end of the shaft and replaced with a same-sized wedge of harder material. The nock is then sawn into this hard insert. It's slightly tricky, but not beyond the average person's skills.

The traditional materials used for making insert nocks were hardwood, horn, and, later, fiber. Hardwood is the easiest to obtain and the easiest to work with, too. It was also the material most commonly used in America back when such arrows were the pride of the fletcher's art.

As in wood for footing a shaft, almost any close-grained hardwood will do. The most beautiful results come from the exotic woods, though: purpleheart, ebony, beefwood. You don't need much of it for making nock inserts, and you can pick up the quantities you need at arts and crafts stores fairly cheaply. If there's a dealer in exotic hardwoods near you, check with him. He might have leftovers he'll sell you, but when you're buying exotic hardwoods, don't look for it to be cheap (notice I said "leftovers," not "waste." With exotic hardwood selling from $7-$19 per board foot, there is no such thing as waste). Expect to pay

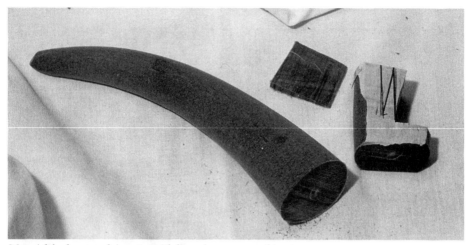

Material for horn nock inserts, with lines drawn on masking tape.

about the same price per board foot for exotic leftovers as you'd pay for a full-sized board, but since you only need a small amount, the total cost will be quite affordable. You can, of course, use scrap from arrow footings and match the nock with the footing. Or you can use a different colored hardwood for a contrasting effect.

The other traditional natural material for nock inlays is horn. Beauty is a matter of taste, but to me horn is easily the most beautiful of the insert materials. English fletchers used it on their finest arrows almost exclusively, but it was never widely used in this country for some reason. Its relative rarity as a nocking material and difficulty to work made it very desirable to archers and horn-nocked arrows were correspondingly more expensive.

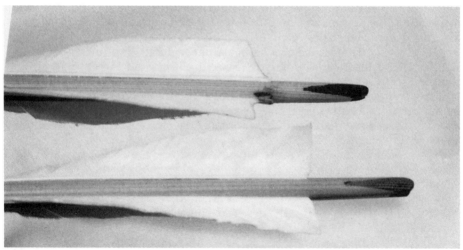

Completed purpleheart nock inserts.

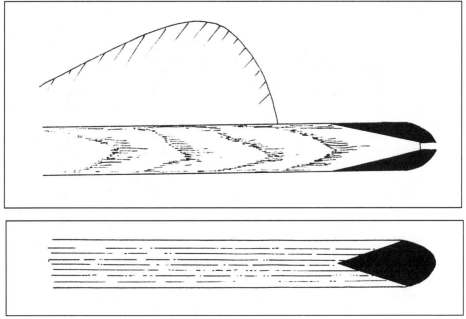

Nock insert viewed from the rift side (top), and reed side.

Robert Elmer felt buffalo horn (as in water buffalo) made the best, but it was very hard to come by even in his day. However, cow horn makes excellent nock inlays and is readily available. Cow horn can be bought in many places that cater to buckskinnners, such as Tandy Leather Company. I use the big end of the horn for making nock reinforcements, the small end for making horn tips for English bows, and have plenty left over for nock inlays. It is a bit difficult to work, but the results are outstanding.

The third substance, fiber, is much easier to work than horn and (to me) better looking than hardwood. Actually, Elmer preferred hard fiber to steer horn, although he doesn't say why. Archers used hard fiber for a variety of things, including bow-backing. The fiber with which I am familiar is paper or linen cloth laid in a resin matrix, and is known as phenolic. It is used in the communication industry as an insulator because it is too dense for radio waves to penetrate. The resin is made of carbolic acid, which is obtained from coal, wood, or other organic substances. This hard fiber is a rich tan-brown color. Pliable when green, it hardens when heat cured and becomes extremely dense. I hadn't seen phenolic fiber since I took apart our old Philco radio when I was a kid. In fact, I thought it must be long out of production, replaced by some modern synthetic high-tech equivalent. Then, as luck would have it, I found several blocks of phenolic at a junk store not long ago. For less than two bucks I bought enough scrap to make several hundred nock inlays. I called around and found that it is sold by the sheet in a wide range of thicknesses, ranging from 1/32 of an inch to more than two inches. A 3' x 4' sheet of linen-base phenolic 1/32-inch thick sells for about forty dollars, so it isn't inexpensive. If you're interested in phenolic, look in the Yellow Pages under "Plastics."

If you use fiber for nock inlays, make sure you run the "warp" of the fiber lengthwise down the shaft, and not across it, which could weaken the nock slightly. It really makes a strong, fine-looking nock insert, one with a rather quaint look of the 1930s to it.

Other materials will work well as nock inlays. I've often thought about using micarta, the material used in knife handles, as nock inserts, although I haven't laid my hands on any yet. If you know a custom knife maker, he might let you have his scraps for nock wedges. The stuff is easy to work, comes in beautiful colors, is practically indestructible, and looks a lot like old-time fiber.

Regardless of whether you use hardwood, horn, or fiber the method is the same: saw a V-notch into the shaft with the grain and then fit a wedge of insert material into the shaft and glue it. After it's dry, trim it up, saw the nock slot, and file it to shape.

For cutting the notch, you can make a jig similar to the one for four-splice footed shafts, or you can make a template and cut out the V-notch freehand. I started off with a jig and then switched to freehand because the notch is really very simple to cut. The depth of the notch isn't as great as with a footing, and the tolerances aren't nearly as critical. You can usually clamp the thin, soft wood of the arrow shaft tightly enough to compensate for minor lapses in your saw cut.

To mark the inlay notch, make a template 1/4 inch wide by 1 1/8 deep (use the other end of the footing template if you like). Mark the shaft so that you're cutting the V-notch from *reed side to reed side, with the growth rings.* I emphasize this because until you cut a few shafts, it seems a bit confusing and directly opposite what your common sense tells you about nocks.

Now, carefully saw down the angle of the V-notch on both sides. If you did everything right, you'll have a perfect notch in less than a minute. The edges will be fuzzy because the wood is soft, and the saw blade pulled out wood fibers, so clean up the outside of the saw cut with fine sandpaper. If you didn't do everything perfectly, you can use 100-grit sandpaper to correct a multitude of errors. Just especially careful at the apex of the V or you'll round it out, which might make an unsightly gap at the bottom of the inlay.

At the top of the notch, the ends of the shaft will come to rounded tapers that do not quite come to points. They should be even, but if they're not *exactly* even, don't worry about it too much because you're going to remove them eventually when you cut in the nock slot.

Now, using your template, mark your inlay material for cutting. If you are using horn, cut or file it into a rectangular shape so you can mark it more easily. With hardwood or fiber, this task will be much simpler. Cut the inlay material in the V shape; depending on its thickness, you might be able to get several nocks from one cut. Try it for fit; it should be right on, but if it's very slightly too large, open the notch in the shaft with sandpaper. If way too large, file the insert wedge into shape. Never force a wedge even a little bit because you'll split the shaft. Now all you have to do is glue the insert, applying slight clamping pressure to bring the sides of the shaft in line with the insert wedge or perhaps wrapping it with string or a rubber band. Before you glue, however, test glue a scrap piece to make sure the glue you're using is compatible with your materials. I usually use epoxy, but carpenters' glue works fine. If you decide to use epoxy, read the package, some of the faster drying kinds are not waterproof. Avoid the "instant glue" type of "super" adhesives. They're very useful in other applications, but they are not as stout when subjected to moisture.

When everything's dry, file the excess insert material into the same diameter as your shaft and using your jig as a slotting jig, saw the nock slot.

File and rasp the outside end of the nock into a graceful shape, slightly flat on top so it's easy on your fingers. Use a thin file or sandpaper glued to a flat stick to even up the inside of the nock slot, if needed. To finish the bottom of the slot, use a small chainsaw file.

Now that you've finished with the nock, here's the point where you decide whether to taper the back end of the shafts from, say, 11/32 to 5/16. Many archers claim better flight and better performance with broadheads when using tapered shafts. I like them okay, and think they fly well, but have not been able to observe enough of a performance advantage over parallel shafts to cause me to take the time necessary to taper them. The original reason for tapering parallel shafts, which has been largely forgotten, was to bring individual shafts to a standard weight within a set of matched arrows by removing material at the back of the shaft, and that, in my opinion, is still the most viable reason. Still, some very knowledgeable archers will shoot nothing else, and for them, tapered shafts unquestionably work best.

You can taper shafts for about eight or nine inches from the nock without affecting the spine. Using a fine file, a scraper, or very coarse sandpaper, such as the kind used to sand hardwood floors, you can bring the taper down very quickly. If you are using horn or hardwood nock inserts, it is a good practice to file this to the desired diameter first and then taper the shaft toward it so as to maintain the shaft's roundness. Once the taper is completed, you're ready to finish the shaft.

Sand the shaft with progressively finer paper and polish it with 0000 steel wool. Some hardwoods, like purpleheart, get a deeper color if you let the shaft sit a few days before dipping. Avoid getting finish on the inside of the nock slot.

When setting the cock feather, look at the nock end of the shaft and notice which direction the rift points run. They will run in opposite directions on "top" and "bottom" of the shaft. Mount the cock feather so that when the arrow is nocked, the rift on the *bottom of the shaft,* where it rests on your hand or the arrow shelf, points back *toward you.* All old archery books recommend this in case the shaft breaks when you release the string. If so mounted, they say, the jagged edges of the broken shaft will go up instead of down into your arm. I have never broken a shaft in this way, nor do I want to, so I cannot personally testify to the advantage of this procedure, but I follow it religiously. It only takes a second.

Now that you've made a fine set of footed arrows, you probably want to keep them that way by performing regular arrow maintenance. This includes touching up the finish occasionally and keeping the feathers from getting ratty. I use a polyurethane finish on my arrows because I feel it is much tougher than anything else available, including commercial fletching lacquer. If the shaft gets nicked or dinged or the finish starts to wear off, I simply hit it with sandpaper and steel wool and dip it again, field point and all, right up to within a quarter of an inch of the feathers for as much protection as I can get. Dampness can cause terrible harm to an arrow, and I try to eliminate any source of it whenever possible. This is why I do not use shellac, which offers less protection.

Feathers can be cleaned while on the shaft with soap and still retain their oil and stiffness, if not done too often. Do NOT use detergent, which removes too much oil. I rub soap over the feathers and gently scrub them against my hand. It's a good idea to keep arrows in a red cedar arrow box to keep the feathers from being eaten by moths. When gluing feathers, make sure your glue will stick to the dip material. Use Duco if you're going to dip with polyurethane, use commercial fletching material if you use lacquer.

Many people straighten arrows by sighting down them and bending them with their hand, or by holding them over a heat source. This doesn't work for me. I can never figure out how much counter-bend to put in the arrow and often bend it too much in the opposite direction. Also, for those "compound bends" where the arrow bends in two directions, it's quite difficult to use hand pressure to straighten a shaft. So, for some time now, I've been straightening my arrows with a screwdriver.

Actually, you can use any hard, round object. One of the best arrow-straighteners I ever used was an S-hook from the end of a black rubber tie-down. The way you use it is simple. First, you locate the outside, or the "high part" of the bend. Usually, but not always, it will be directly in line with one of the hen feathers. You then stroke the outside of the bend with mild downward pressure, varying the pressure according to the severity of the bend. It doesn't take much pressure or many strokes with a cedar shaft, about three or four will probably do it. In a very short while you will get a feel for how much pressure it takes and how many times to stroke it. Starting out with this method there is a tendency to overdo it. Too much and you'll bend it back the other way.

I think this compresses the shaft fibers slightly and this causes it to straighten out. However it works, it works wonderfully, is quick, and once you get the hang of it, very precise. Also, arrows straightened in this manner stay straight longer, or so it seems. It also works with hardwood shafts, although you have to apply considerably more pressure.

So there you have it; a complete guide to custom wood arrows. If making a set of custom woods seems like a lot of work, you're right, it is. But only if you think of these arrows as temporary things to be used up, like beeswax and bowstrings. They are not; they have permanence. So in a sense, they are lifetime investments, just like your bow. And if given the proper care and the respect they deserve, you can pass them along to your grandchildren.

STONE POINTS

Scott Silsby

After reading three volumes of *The Traditional Bowyer's Bible*, the idea undoubtedly has dawned that making an entire archery system is no small undertaking. Unfortunately, it won't get any easier here. But you'll find encouragement in your efforts by reflecting on the fact that of forty thousand or so generations of Homo Sapien S. that have preceded you, all but a handful mastered flintknapping in one form or another.

Working out new tools and techniques sometimes took hundreds of thousands of years between technological steps, but the time between steps decreased as our ancestors put the emphasis on thinking through the system rather than just banging on rocks like so many monkeys on typewriters. It's true that any idiot can break a rock; chimpanzees have been taught to make crude flaked pebble tools. But to make an arrowhead of a quality worthy of taking game you'll need to develop an understanding of how certain rocks and minerals fracture and cleave.

There are two approaches to teaching this craft. One is to instruct the student in the process of fashioning a tool. The other is to explain the how, who, what, where, when and why of it all so the student can go off on his own and advance his skills independently. I've included both. As you get into knapping further and gain experience, you'll find a good many of the explanations take on new meaning.

KNAPPABLES

There are over one hundred elements that singularly or in combination make up approximately five thousand minerals. These minerals singularly or in combination make up an astronomical number of rocks which are classified in a few different ways depending upon the branch of science to which the classifier belongs. Therefore, all fine-grained siliceous rocks bedded in limestone or dolomite are chert to the geologist and petrologist. The same rock becomes flint when it's described by an archeologist studying the English flint mines. Avoid getting caught up in the semantics of descriptive meaning and remember that a knappable stone knaps as well by any other name.

Arrowheads can be made from a very wide range of materials. If you're going to stick to the ancient methods of flaking you have a fairly easy to follow set of criteria when choosing the stone to be used. The material needs to break with a

Spall of very fine-grained flint from Central Texas. The use of a hard stone hammer caused the accentuated ripples in the fracture scar, making it look like a conch shell. Hence the term: concoidial fracture.

conchoidal fracture, which is to say it breaks like glass. The finer the grain of the material, the more distinct the fracture tends to be, but sometimes finer grained material will be weaker. Fortunately, knappable material is strongest in compression, or crushing strength, which is a very favorable attribute for an arrowhead to have as most of the abuse occurs as compression when the point strikes the target. Experienced bowhunters tend to amass collections of steel heads whose points have bent upon impact with bone. Stone points often fracture at the tip when hitting bone, then continue an angular penetration, cutting with an irregular but sharply snapped tip. Keep in mind stone points such as spears, darts, and arrowheads have been taking game for hundreds of thousands of years. Bronze, wrought iron, and steel points replaced flint because they can be mass produced cheaply and efficiently, whereas a well made stone point is a time consuming, high skill item. Economics, not performance, drove stone

A partial representation of 11,000 years of point types from the Mid-Atlantic region. Triangle in center of lower row is from European Contact Period, made of gunflint from a ship's ballast from England. From its right is a wrought iron trade point made in England and found in Tennessee, crudely made and much-used "gin bottle" glass from near the Falls of the Potomac near Washington, D.C., a Bear Razorhead found in Virginia along with ancient stone points, and, at far right, a modern-made flint hunting point. We've come full circle.

Chalcedony *Southeast, PA*	*Flint* *Abingdon, VA*	*Chert* *Flint Ridge, Ohio*	*Prase "Green Jasper"* *Normanskill* *Formation* *Greene Co., New York*

Opal *Idaho*	*Jasper Credi* *Arlington, VA*	*Jasper* *Front Royal, VA*	*Quartz* *"Bull Quartz"* *"Vien Quartz"* *Adams-Franklin* *County, PA*

Quartzite *Arlington, VA*	*Sard* *(Brown Chalcedony)* *Front Royal, VA*	*Basalt* *Wagner, AZ*	*Obsidian* *Glass Mtn., CA*

Limestone *Front Royal, VA*	*Metabasalt* *(Greenstone)* *Blueridge Mtns, VA*	*Metarhyolite* *Caledonia, PA*	*Horntel (argillite)* *Byram, NJ*

Knappable stone is found throughout the entire U.S.

Metamorphosed volcanic Rhyolite spall, southeast Pennsylvania. (photo by Jack Cresson)

points out of the marketplace. It is left to you to produce a point worthy of this ancient craft.

There are few regions in the United States that don't have a knappable stone within a day's travel. You may have to track down sources by contacting local colleges with a mineralogy/geology program, rock shops, fellow knappers, and flint dealers, but if you persist, you'll succeed. Rockshops are listed under Lapidary in the phone book.

Volcanic glasses and related types offer the possibility of the sharpest edges. When flaked to its optimum, it can be five hundred times sharper than a new razor blade. The hitch is you've got to perfect a technique that produces this edge. An improperly made obsidian point is no better than any other poorly made point. It will also be the weakest, as obsidian, along with the opal family, are weak stones. As one well-known knapper, Dr. Errett Callahan, has pointed out, "easy to make, easy to break".

Another exceptionally sharp stone is the crystalline quartz family of vein Quartz, Quartzite and silicified Sandstone. While most flint family stone contains a good bit of fibrous chalcedony, the crystalline quartz material is made up primarily of fragments of hard crystal fragments and grains in a frozen jumble. It ranges from sandstone through metaquartzite with the desirable knapping grade lying in the middle range, usually called orthoquartzite. All these crystalline quartz family stones will, when chipped, expose numerous edges, some as sharp as obsidian, others acute corners of semi cleaved crystal fragments. It will scratch flint and saw obsidian in half if you have the patience. When broken on the edges it exposes fresh edges and grains equally as sharp.

Being considerably harder than most other knappable stones, it holds its edge better and cuts through dirty surfaces without losing its sharpness, though its hardness makes it more difficult to work. Silicified varieties knap more like flints. Some of the more common silicified types are known as: Hixton from Wisconsin, Tallahatta from Mississippi, Alabama and Spanish Diggings from Wyoming.

During the invasion of the new world, many Native American groups were cut off from their stone sources and displayed a remarkable ability to adapt unfamiliar materials to their knappables list. Bottle glass, ceramic insulators, window glass, and ballast flint were all used.

Again, it is best to pay little attention to what a particular stone is called, its mineral environment, or composition. Instead focus your faculties on its performance. Is it hard? How much strength do flakes possess when attempts are made to snap them like a toothpick? Do flakes feather out when struck from a mass, leaving sharp edges? Even if these edges are irregular as in quartzite, are they sharp? How much force is required to get flakes to release from a core when struck? Once you're satisfied the stone meets your minimum needs, you'll want to lay in a considerable amount for practice.

Try not to mix different types of stone when learning, as each type will often, but not always, give different results to the same applied technique. *Stick to one type and grade of material, and you will get a standard feedback to your successes and failures.* If you cannot differentiate material failure from technique failure your learning experience will be strewn with difficulties.

The late Ron Baltzley and his son-in-law levering out a large boulder of metamorphosed Rhyolite.

Arrowhead made of "Johnstone", or the author's favorite term, "Thunderchert", both names to describe toilet bowl ceramic. This point took around forty minutes to make.

Today, flat window glass is an excellent material on which to learn, as it is cheap (or free), readily available, consistent, and flakes fairly easily.

TOOLS OF THE CRAFT

At any big gathering of knappers you always run into at least one knapper who has an impressive array of tools and "gizmos". Count on these tools to be used very little. It's human instinct to seek the short cut and almost inevitable that you'll try some gadget or trick that allows you to bypass the needed understanding and patient repetition of process in order to master the craft. Here you will have to trust me as my list of tools is rather simple.

Antler billets, of all the sizes on which you can lay your hands, come first. Moose is the densest of the large antler but shed racks from healthy elk and caribou will do fine. Whitetails and mule deer racks are very dense. Half of my billet knapping is done with an average sized whitetail billet.

The billets you see in the photo give an idea as to shape, size, and useful variety. The quality of antler varies a bit between species and also varies within the species depending upon the health of the animal. Shed antler, when not subjected to excessive moisture, is the best bet. When cutting racks from dead animals, leave the skull bone attached. Rounding the crown portion gives the billet its strongest shape. Irregularly-shaped billets are difficult to use, especially when you need uniform feedback during the learning stage.

With hammerstones, again you'll want to gather a large selection of various sizes and grades. A knapping hammerstone should have toughness, hardness, and the ability to absorb and diffuse excessive shock. Sandstones work very well on obsidians and the weaker flints. When you work the tougher flints, rhyolites, and cherts you'll want a tougher grade of sandstone or a slightly rotted diabase, gneiss, or comparable stone. A good hammerstone contains a mineral constituent as hard or harder than your knapping material, usually crystalline quartz fragments that are cemented together partially by a softer mineral. Each small poorly cemented mineral bond acts as a little shock absorber, helping to diffuse excess shock. The harder minerals in the hammerstone tend to bite into a

Flintknapper's tool kit. Top to bottom, antler billets, hammerstones varying in both weight and hardness, leather knee pad, antler tine pressure flaker, three sizes of Ishi sticks with bottom one showing length of copper rod inserts, leather palm pads with thumb holes, folded buckskin pad, common file, and, most important, eye protection.

core, preform, or biface which allows the contact period to be extended, thus pushing off a flake rather than simply crushing the edge of the platform.

For primary spalling, or cracking of large masses, you often need to use a very tough and hard stone that can take abuse. River-smoothed boulders can be subjected to such abuse as their rounded shape defuses force around their surface.

Pressure flaking tools are usually antler or copper tipped, although anything with the right attributes can be used. In regions where native copper was

Two views of two hammerstones. The left one is ancient while the right one is modern. The modern knapper had never seen the prehistoric one, yet wear patterns from extended use show remarkable similarities.

281

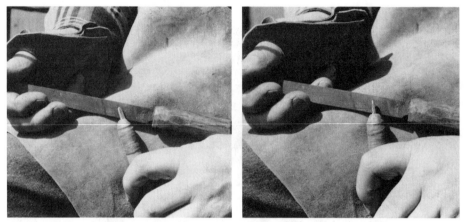

Occasionally use the file to maintain this shape of the copper flakertip as you work.

abundant, as in the copper ranges of Michigan, tools for flintknapping were manufactured of hammered copper rods set in wood handles. *The Archeology of New York State* by William Ritchie shows a photo and artist's reconstruction of a prehistoric double pointed flaking tool of copper with an engraved handle of wood bound together with cordage. In *Ancient Man in the New World* Marie Wormington included an illustration of a copper rod of a style most knappers use today. The last truly "wild" Native American, Ishi, used a long stick with a soft iron tip. Where copper was unavailable even by trade, deer antler served admirably. Saw off a tine, round the cut end smooth, and use it hand held. For heavier work, taper the butt end to fit a fishtail splice in a strong wood stick. After glueing and binding it you will have a leverage tool that will flake any flint. These are affectionately called "Ishi Sticks" by today's knappers in honor of the man who first introduced them.

Abrading stones are used to strengthen platforms. Any shape and size that suits your fancy will work, as long as the abrading stone is as hard or harder than the stone you're knapping. It must also be gritty. Some folks keep a large block beside them and rub the preform against it, while I prefer a little sandstone pebble. A wheel from a bench grinder is readily available and works well.

Knapping pads for knee and palm are to protect your body. No one has found anything that works better than leather.

Copper hardens from use or by hammering. Files, abrading stones or hammers can be used to reform pressure flaking tips. When using soft drawn copper a hammer works well for reforming and strengthening tips. Overly brittle copper can be annealed (softened) by reheating to a low red heat. Remove the copper from the wooden or antler handle before annealing.

Punches can be of great help, especially when you've gotten yourself into a tight spot where only a precision blow can re-edge a blunt platform, though it's difficult to get a flake to carry very far using a punch. Again, antler tines rounded off at the striking butt or copper work very well.

Archeologist-flintknapper Jack Cresson typifies a comfortable working position, seat slightly higher than knees.

WORK SAFELY

Before you jump into knapping, consider the risks to life and limb and take some effort to reduce them. The most obvious risk is that the material you'll be breaking invariably produces very sharp chips and splinters. Although minor cuts to the hands are almost unavoidable, wear leather gloves and pads until you know what to expect. After decades of knapping, I still wear gloves for high risk procedures. I've found it allows me to concentrate on what I want to do to the stone rather than worrying about what the stone is going to do to me.

Eye protection cannot be over-stressed! One stray chip can ruin an eye in an instant. Warn others who are watching to wear eye protection or to keep a safe distance. There is an amusing description of how Ishi dislodged stray chips from his eye by folding his eyelid back and slapping himself silly. I use to time shutting my eyes with my estimate of chip impact until a number of delayed ricochets educated me. Now if I had only watched more B-Rated Westerns I would have known all about ricocheting objects. **Always wear eye protection!**

The knapping of finely-grained stone produces fragments that range in size from flakes all the way down to molecules, where it's classed as a gas for safety purposes. These minute stone fragments rise as a cloud during knapping. The larger visible dust settles in a few minutes, but the invisible gaseous-sized particles float in the air for many hours and when inhaled do potentially harmful things to lungs. Work outside where a breeze or a fan can blow it away. If inside, rig an exhaust fan and work next to it. During the winter, I work next to the draft of a wood stove. Shake out your "infested" knapping clothes before entering living quarters.

Use of the Ishi stick, with the end held under one arm, allows you to "lean" into the flake with more control. Even greater pressure can be brought to bear by placing the backs of the hands on the inside of the knees, then pushing the knees together.

There are many synthetic materials available to knappers these days. Few were produced with the knapper in mind and certainly weren't concocted to have them broken into gas sized dust to be inhaled. Synthetic boules of crystalline material are widely produced for the semi conductor market. Many are dangerous and some deadly when pulverized, then inhaled, during flaking. Avoid them.

Heat treating certain flints has the potential for producing and releasing harmful chemical fumes. Some stone types contain mercury, lead, arsenic, chromium and other dangerous elements locked in a myriad of natural compounds just waiting for unsuspecting flintknappers to play alchemist and transmute them into deadly fumes in the home kiln or stove. If you must heat treat, rig up a good ventilation system. After heat treating, knap the stone with care and good ventilation, as many harmful compounds aren't destroyed by kiln heat.

THE MECHANICS OF FRACTURE
or
HOW ROCKS BREAK

Making stone arrowheads evolved from acquired and passed on skills that have been traced back for well over one million years. It's certainly older than the "oldest profession" by a good measure. Being an acquired skill, it requires much thinking, practice, and patience — plus a good deal of physical coordination.

About twenty thousand years ago, when the bow is thought to have been first developed, society was well along into the specialized craftsmen system. As each of us today is better suited for certain tasks, so it was during primeval archery times. Arrowhead making was, and is, just another craft to be learned, but one that can be frustrating to master without coaching. To make stone points you're going to have to really want to learn.

In many of the ancient trades set up as Guild Systems, the old masters never told novice or journeymen their trade secrets; they expected their students to steal them. On the face of it, it may seem rather odd, but experience and time have shown that information is wasted on those not receptive to it. Now I'm certainly not going to hide trade secrets here, so I want you to pay attention to all the little detailed bits and pieces as the difference between success and failure rides on all of them. Mastering stone point making will require that you break a lot of rocks, as the majority of it can only be learned through experience.

People are different; they learn in different ways. Some folks need complex theory and instruction while others just watch and copy. Being of the type that needs an understanding of what's going on in the stone and how my technique interacts with it, I found that a lot of unusual phenomena I picked up earlier in observed bits and pieces became quite useful later on when I was trying to understand fracture.

For those of you bored to death with abstract physics, go ahead and take a nap (or knap through this), but don't wonder later why your arrowheads are coming out more like errorheads. Because our ancient ancestors did not fully engage their brains before knapping stone, it took almost a million years for them to get good at it. Twenty thousand years ago, with the grey matter fully in gear, they produced some stone work that only a handful of today's masters can duplicate. And the number of flintknappers today, with the world population being what it is, are probably not too far off the number of knappers alive say twenty thousand years ago. Those that think it out fully and practice get very good. Those that don't, won't.

One particular incident I observed years ago proved critical in my later understanding of fracture. I was a Buck Sgt. in the Army and only nineteen years old. Our Field First Sgt. was a huge, powerful, Master Sgt. There came a time when he felt he had to deflate the ego of another N.C.O. The Field First decided on an egg fight between them to prove to the Company that he was top dog. He maintained that "Red", as the other N.C.O. was known, couldn't break a chicken egg between his hands as long as the Field First got to place it just right using some "voodoo" influence. Red took up the challenge in an instant, and though he made an exemplary effort with sweat and throbbing veins as testimony, that

little egg with its voodoo charm would not break. Then the Field First stepped in and lifted the curse by turning the egg sideways in Red's hands. It splattered everywhere as the Field First explained the physics of compressive strength in an arch, or the equivalent of two, three dimensional arches placed base to base.

Heavy stuff for a nineteen year old. It raised the egg to a new level of standing in my book of wonders.

Many years later a friend showed me a batch of adzes from Guatemala and I immediately remembered "The Egg". The Mayan adze makers knew about the compressive strength of arches as the adzes were elongated chicken eggs with sharp bits. Frank Lloyd Wright knew, too. His "radically" tapered support columns incorporated the same principle.

Hertzian Cones result when BB's strike glass (courtesy Are Tsirk).

What all of this has to do with flintknapping is that the egg is, in reality, a Hertzian Cone. To easily see a Hertzian Cone just walk by glass store fronts within easy BB gun range of kids with idle hands. Little holes on the outside, scooped out wide cones of missing glass on the inside. With a few minor exceptions, these scars of Hertzian Cone fractures display all the information you'll need to get you started in controlled fracture.

Grab a handful of dry sand, salt or sugar and slowly pour it on a flat surface. A low cone appears. It's just like using building blocks as a kid. Each successive row in a pyramid stack supports one block less until you wind up with just one at the top. Try building up a square wall, then press your finger downwards on the center block, putting your wall under compression, then start removing blocks while it's under this load. Those not located in the compressive pyramid will slip out easily as they are not held by force. When you double this shape by butting two pyramids together at the wide base (called a bipyramid), you transmit the compressive force from one small point out to a wide margin then back to another small point but the compressive force must be applied to both narrow ends. The high Roman Arch is a good example of the basic principal. This is how The Egg came about. Millions of years of natural selection weeded out all egg shapes that could not absorb the "clunk" of being dropped on other nest mates to be. Those with poor form died. Those with good form survived.

On the other hand, our window pane Hertzian Cone shows that the compressive force was released rather than absorbed. Plate glass is highly polished and can withstand a lot of bending. When struck hard enough in a small area, a tiny bowl of depression occurs, and when that force overwhelms its elastic strength a ring crack occurs and a cone pops out. Keeping a mental picture in your mind of this flared out Hertzian Cone and a "just right" angle of striking the core will help you a great deal in learning the fundamentals of flintknapping.

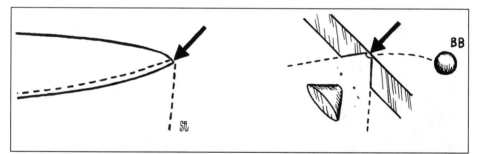

Note how angle of platform and striking angle are the same for both materials. This is an important clue for setting up platforms during flintknapping.

Here we may as well address the story (will it never die!) of arrowheads being made by heating flint, then dripping water on it. Recently, I was at our local flea market and engaged an old gentleman in casual conversation about some arrowheads he had displayed in his case. While I examined two of them, one of a Kentucky type flint, the other a tough quartzite, he repeated the tale of watching an old Indian in Tennessee chip'em out using fire to heat the "flint" (he said

Unusual examples of intact Hertzian Cones in stone resulting from flintknapping.

the quartzite took more heat!), then dripping water on'em with a straw. If you try this yourself you'll only get steam by dripping water on the heated core and rubble if you douse it in water. I've never heard anyone but an Anglo-Saxon repeat this story with conviction, and am beginning to believe it's a red herring let out by old guild masters from the gunflint era to protect their craft secrets.

Heat treating of certain flints, which will be covered a bit later, alters their micro structure and turns strong tough flints into shiny weak ones. Since we are concerned with producing strong, tough arrowheads you should use heat treating only where it's absolutely needed. Rather than spending time figuring out ways to make weaker pretty points, you should be figuring out ways to make them of stronger stone.

Let's assume you have a fine nodular piece of good arrowhead grade stone

Author's twelve year old son, Danny, demonstrates bipolar flaking. While most of the resulting flakes are only good for Abo type cutting tasks, you usually produce enough arrowhead flake blanks to make it worthwhile.

that's remarkably similar in shape to a softball. You would like to extract a flake for making an arrowhead from it.

There are at least three and a half ways to do this. No, that's not a typo. You can diamond saw it into slabs but that doesn't count at this stage. Your options are: (1) Bipolar Splitting (2) Free Hand Spalling (3) De-capping and (3 1/2) Combination of (1) & (2).

(1) Bipolar splitting is accomplished by holding your stone upright on a hard, tough, heavy stone anvil and, with a degree of force only learned through practice, striking directly on its top, straight down towards the anvil. Both egg and anvil should be free of rotted cortex which would rob energy. The ideal result will be a splitting in two of your egg. In most cases a sheet of stone, slightly curved, splits from one side. If bipolar forces are equal, both ends of this sheet will retain fracture initiation scars. Many times the fracture will be initiated wholly from either the hammer or anvil end. While both ends of your flake will most likely be crushed to some degree, the side edges are often quite sharp. This is one of the oldest flintknapping techniques and seems to be almost instinctive in humans.

(2) Free-hand spalling is done by gripping an end of the egg in one hand and using a hammerstone of similar weight in the other, striking flakes off the projecting end.

(3) De-capping involves striking the narrow end to remove it, leaving a fairly flat platform which can then be struck to take flakes down the sides. Those illus-

An egg-shaped nodule of Mid-west Hornstone is an exercise in de-capping and blade production, and illustrates the striking angle and platform angle. There are two arrowheads in each elongated flake and you can, with experience and luck, draw close to a dozen blades from each core.

trated were made with a sandstone hammer on carefully prepared platforms while the core was well supported in the hands.

(3 1/2) This combination of (1) & (2) doesn't have a formal name as yet, so I'll call it the Kalin method after Jeff Kalin who was the first knapper I knew who used it. Jeff is another first rate knapper who is an accomplished "Prehistoric Technician" — as modern primitive skills experts are formally called. He, like "FlintJack" Cresson, work in the stone that prehistoric folks used, which is often hard but very durable. Jeff places a small hammerstone in his palm and wedges the core firmly against it. The core is then struck at an angle somewhat between

a bipolar and free-hand style. This technique produces very usable flakes out of all knappable stone.

Other methods of reducing your nodule is to throw it against a hard rock or a hard rock against it. While a poor technique on small stones, it is sometimes the only way to crack very large ones. The Australian Aborigines used a technique where they sometimes held the core in their hands and struck it against an anvil stone. They also managed to shock anthropologists by cracking overly large quartzite cores by wedging a fulcrum underneath them then building a fire and sitting back to watch heat and gravity split them in half.

STRATEGIES AND TECHNIQUES

The shape of your stone as nature provides it or as you may get it after processing from a dealer will dictate the method used in reducing it to form.

In every batch of stone there usually are a few pieces of superior grade and/or color. These scarce fancy pieces almost invariably wind up in the hands of the inexperienced, suffering a horrible fate. Later, as the stone's destroyer masters his craft he looks back with sorrow at what he ruined. Set those beauties aside and don't touch them until you know you're worthy. You will never regret heeding this advice.

Some of the more common shapes are:

Nodules and Cobbles. Nodules form in seabeds and in gas pockets in rock while cobbles usually form from irregular rock fragments ground to shape through mechanical agencies.

Plates are flattish lenses of stone which have been laid down between other stone, injected into seams, or molecularly invaded and replaced existing stone. Also plate glass and sawn slabs of stone.

Spalls can be frost spalls, heat spalls, fracture spalls and knapped spalls. Bifaces; biconvex preforms knapped on both faces to reduce waste and shipping costs.

Blocks. Rectangular to squarish shape, usually six sides with some angles approaching 90 degrees.

Of these forms, blocks provide the best shape for producing flakes of a size, form and quantity for arrowhead making. Nodules and cobbles, of sufficient size (no smaller than a softball), are next best. Plates, slabs and spalls are fine if you can obtain them in sizes just a little larger than arrowhead size. Very large plates can be spalled to produce starting flakes but you must use care and follow a strategy that will shape the plate into a symmetrical biconvex form or risk it breaking. Plates, slabs and spalls too small to provide useful sized flakes by spalling, but overly large for arrowheads, are best suited for knives and spearheads. Trade them or save them for later use when you'll need knife and spear preforms.

Core Types
Blocks — Nodules and Cobbles — Thick Plates

In this procedure you use a hammerstone to strike off a flake. Examine your block of stone and find a surface with minimal irregularities. If the surface is coated with a soft cortex of material, peck and grind away this soft stuff until

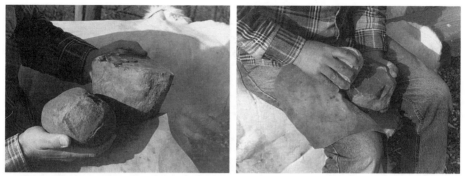

A nodule of stone split in half by nature is a good starting block. Weathered greenstone hammer is smaller but denser and weighs the same.

A few trial swings with no force allows you to judge contact spot and adjust angles where needed.

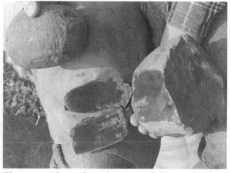

There were lots of good, strong flakes in this fine Tennessee stone.

Flakes taken from a block in the beginning contain cortex and have rough shape. But flakes improve as core shape improves, as seen by flake resting on core. Note penny at lower right for size comparison.

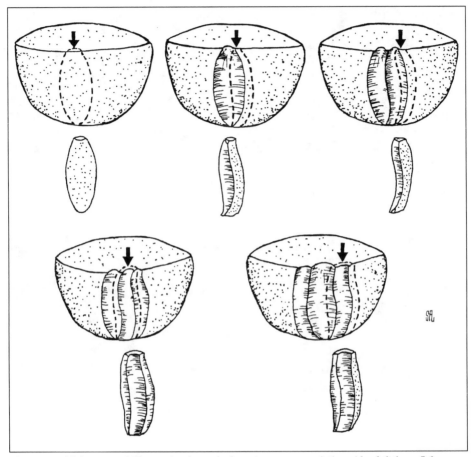

Sequence of flake removal illustrating how platform is set up on existing ridge left from flake scars, so the force of striking blow follows the ridge.

you reveal the harder stone under it. The intersecting face of the stone to your striking platform would ideally be 90 degrees but anything less than 90 degrees down to say around 65 degrees will work. Rasp off any overhang using your abrader or the face of your hammerstone. Grind the edge of this platform thoroughly as it will help strengthen it and help hold the flake together as it comes off. Support the core well with your hand and leg holding it so that it resists movement while being struck but at the same time is cushioned by your hold. It is critical to allow room for proper follow-through with your hammerstone swing. Remember not to hit at the platform but through it. If your core is large enough and shaped so that it can be firmly anchored in the ground, try it that way but allow room for follow-through. If the core is allowed to move too much when the fracture starts, the flake will either snap in two or the core split.

Something like 95% of the energy delivered must be used to depress the stone at the platform enough to overwhelm its ability to remain intact. Once a crack opens the fracture happens quickly. Try imagining that the last 5% of energy is used to pry off the flake. Where the fracture travels is dictated by the angle of the blow in relationship to the core, the contour of the core surface which affects the strength or weakness of the back of the flake, how long the hammerstone stays in contact, and at what angle it strikes the platform. Although in essence you're banging two rocks together, understanding the process will allow you to adjust your tools and technique in order to achieve more control. The length, width, and thickness of an ideal flake should encase the envisioned arrowhead. Any excess curvature of the flake is wasted stone. Once you have taken a few flakes you'll notice ridges between the scalloped center area of the flake scar on your core. If you prepare a platform directly behind one of these ridges, the fracture will have a tendency to follow the ridge. The higher these ridges protrude from the core the more narrow the flake will be. By placing the platform between two of these ridges you can widen the drawn flake while keeping it straight. This is an old technique first developed by Neanderthal people. Learn and practice it until you can produce flakes of your desired shape.

Nodules and Cobbles

Again, examine your stone and remove any overly soft cortex as you would with blocks. Because the core surface is curved, find the best starting spot by carefully examining and estimating where that 90 degree to 65 degree angle can be found. As you take flakes from this core, try to maintain an oval to circular shape around its circumference. Any irregularities in shape weaken it. If ridges between flakes become too pronounced, causing an irregular topography, use a smaller hammerstone to remove only the highest points of these ridges. Any investment of time and effort made here to smooth the back of your planned flake will be paid back in the ease with which you'll be able to remove pressure flakes later. *Good flakes make good arrowheads.*

Plates and Slabs

These are often the most challenging cores from which to remove flakes. If you have a choice set them back and don't waste them until you've gained experience with easier to master forms. If you're forced to use them, examine the

A challenging plate of Texas stone.   *A platform is ground with sandstone …*

... then moose antler billet pops off irregular flake.

The core is flipped over and another platform prepared with the sandstone. May be an arrowhead in one of those flakes.

Continue the process by working around the core's periphery, taking flakes from both faces.

The core's edge after it has been worked.

This strong platform will be struck just to the right of the shadowline.

The resulting flake. While this flake is a bit large for pressure flaking into an arrowhead, note that the core has now become a biface and will soon produce even better flakes for arrowhead blanks.

plate and envision a large biconvex lens-shaped biface lying inside it. You'll want to flake this plate into that shape as it will then gain sufficient strength to allow many flakes to be removed without its breaking. Many of the larger bifaces found in archeological context are in fact flake cores that, after their flake potential was exhausted, became bifacial hand axes, knives, spears, saws and such.

Any end or projection of your plate should be worked first unless it has very bad angles from which to start. A projecting mass from the main core receives vibrations that are amplified at that spot. When the stone bends from these vibrations beyond its tensile strength, it breaks. Find a weak corner and take small flakes from each side. One on one side, then one from the concavity left by the first one but towards the opposite face. Work back and forth along the squarish edge with a light hammer, leaving a sinuous edge. This process is called **alternate flaking.** Perform this around the entire circumference. Where the edge still projects beyond your envisioned large bifacial lens, repeat the alternate flaking two or more times until your biface core becomes symmetrical. These primary flakes will be for the most part chunky at the platform end, thin at the other. Once you've edged the core you're now ready to prepare individual platforms for flakes. Hammerstone flaking will require steep, high angle, strong platforms, while billet flaking will require lower, less strong platforms. Flakes produced with the billet have a tendency to be wider and thinner while

Compare this block core to the plate core. They both work and you can mix and match different billets and hammerstones to either one as the need arises.

hammerstone flakes tend to have more thickness. As a general rule you'll need a big, heavy billet to remove flakes of sufficient thickness for arrowheads. Hammerstones work better here, and by paying close attention before and after the process you can adjust the platform and impact spot to produce flakes of a desired thickness. Always keep in mind that the fracture of brittle stone is subject to a high degree of failure. As you gain experience your success ratio will increase.

Short of having an experienced coach work with you, try this method for obtaining feedback on your successes and failures. During the mid-seventies I was trying to work out a fluting system where long flakes were taken off both faces of an advanced stage preform, as it was practiced in various forms throughout North America for almost a millennia. My attempts were erratic until I developed a system to provide me with positive feedback. Once I had prepared my platform and decided upon my strategy, I used a pencil, chalk or felt pen to draw an outline of where I thought the flake would release. For encouragement I soon started drawing two sets of outlines. One was small and represented the minimal sized flake I thought would release while the other was considerably larger representing the envisioned maximum size. Before removing the flake I would clean up my ground cloth for catching debris. This allowed me to recover the flake or fragments and re-attach them to the preform. By studying where the flake detached relative to where I predicted it would, I could then tell where my success and failures occurred. This process of having to stop, analyze, outline and clean up between each flake will be frustrating at first as most folks want to get on with making something. But by slowing down and thinking about what's happening you will be provided with rich rewards by improving your knapping skills.

PRESSURE FLAKING

Once a suitable blank is obtained, the actual arrowhead is produced by a technique known as **pressure flaking.** Rather than striking the stone to remove a flake, as with percussion flaking, pressure flaking is the prying and pushing off of smaller flakes with a hand-held more sharply-pointed tool. This technique can only produce relatively small flakes, though with much more control and precision. Remember that the flakes and platforms are worked in the same way as with percussion flaking, only in miniature.

Refer to the photographs for suggested holding positions. Poor working position prohibits one from using the body's naturally designed system of being able to apply maximum force with minimal effort and physical control over movement. Bad form causes injury to tendons as well. A seating arrangement that puts the seat of your pants a little higher than your normal seating height will allow you to bend forward and place the back of each wrist to the inside of each leg. With your Ishi stick firmly held in one hand, its opposite end tucked under your arm, and your flake gripped tightly against leather palm pads in the other hand, you can now use the full strength of your legs, wrists, arms, and back to concentrate all force through the tip of the flaker while controlling an opposite resistive force with the other. Think of it as a human vise and use the military analogy of never attacking an enemy force without possessing an over-

After flaking notches on either side of a long blade, lay a stick under it and break its back with a sharp snap of the Ishi stick, yielding two arrowhead blanks instead of one.

Alternately pressure flaking the periphery of the starting flake.

whelming force yourself. With the potential of having massive force you can now use your flaker to carefully produce platforms and through finesse, press and pry flakes off with control. Refer to the various photos of platforms and suggested angles for your alignment of flaker and preform.

One of the most critical aspects of pressure and percussion flaking is the surface contour or topography of each face of the stone you're flaking. Most starting flakes are curved, so your task is to remove flakes from the inside curved ends of one side while removing flakes from the center of the curved back of the opposite face. Furthermore, you need to maintain a reasonably ovate outline to your preform as you flake it into shape. Most everyone has a tendency

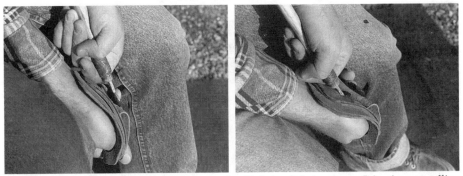

Using platforms high up on the face opposite the side being flaked prevents flakes from travelling too far into a shallow depression where the arrowhead is already thin enough. When you want longer flakes, lower the platform towards the side of the point being flaked and use the Ishi stick to push in along the flake's expected line of travel.

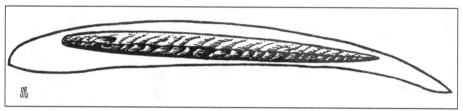

Most flakes have some degree of curve from the side view which must be removed to yield a straight arrowhead.

to flake the thing into an arrowhead shape too quickly, especially so if you have an audience.

Practice and learn by yourself or with a more experienced coach. Often the best coach is someone who is just a step ahead of you in experience. Sometimes the overly experienced are too far removed from beginners to realize that the student needs basic information first.

As you work your preform down to size, concentrate on thinning and shaping the base first, then work on the tip. Again the urge will be to take overly large flakes from the middle area first. But this, because of the excessive mass there, will cause flakes to terminate in steps which are squarish ledges caused by the flake snapping when it was overloaded during the prying phase of pressure flaking. *Rather than trying to make an arrowhead, concentrate on making good flakes. If you do that, an arrowhead just "happens" as a result.*

A biface flake core, right, can provide many arrowheads before it is exhausted. Arrowhead is re-attached exactly where it lay in the core before its extraction with a sandstone hammer. Earlier fluted point makers used virtually the same technique.

Your greatest successes will come if you follow what the ancient knappers were doing. They didn't just invent the biface knowing that its low convex cross section with ovate outline and sharp edges would make a terrifically strong, sharp, and useful tool whether used as a hand axe a million years ago or in miniature form mounted on a straight stick as an arrowhead. The basic form of the hand axe, knife, spearhead and arrowhead came about as a natural by-product of taking flakes from cores from both faces, hence the term, biface. At first they were interested more in the flakes, but over time the well-shaped cores left from better flake removal procedures found favor among folks with ingenious minds.

Some cultures found the core biface more useful than the flakes although this interpretation is highly biased because few archeologists have devoted the time to study flake tools. The lesson in this is that an arrowhead is the byproduct of good flake removal technique. As you work your preform, study it carefully before taking each flake to determine if it will be a successful one. Often you will need to remove a number of very minute flakes in adjusting the surface contour to assure the larger flake will be successful. You need to practice patience and follow my rule: I will take no flake before its time. It may be corny, but you will remember it.

Setting up platforms on the edge of previous flake scars yields longer flakes and leaves a sharp, sinuous edge unsurpassed for hunting.

Shaped arrowhead. While this one exhibits nice flake scars, the dull remnant of platforms must be sharpened before it's finally worthy of being called a hunting point.

Flakes taken somewhat at a diagonal to the point's intended direction of use have less of a tendency to step and hinge fracture (break off prematurely) than ones taken straight in from the side. Somewhat like hiking up a mountain following a zig-zag course, it may be a longer route to follow but you won't run out of steam trying to force yourself up a steep ridge.

The flake with which you begin usually has a bit of an arc when viewed from the side. When pressure flaking, it is necessary to straighten the side-view by removing material which falls outside of the intended arrowhead. Keep in mind that during this phase of pressure flaking you are not only straightening the blank, but shaping and thinning the arrowhead, as well. Not a simple process, and once you've tried it a new and profound respect for all of the "primitives" who have gone before will begin to surface.

SHARPENING THE ARROWHEAD

Every aspect of an Archery System works towards the goal of delivering the point of the arrow — whether it be a stunning blunt, barbed fishpoint, or a copy of an ancient stone type — to a precise spot. The arrowhead is the business end of the weapon but is no more important than the string, arrow, or bow itself. Keep in mind a well-placed medium quality arrowhead will kill far better than a perfect razor-sharp one which misses.

A thin point is inferior to a thick one as long as their edge sharpness is identical. Stone's greatest strength is in compression while weakest in tension. Thin points break easily while thick ones don't. The difference in penetration lies not so much in thickness-thinness ratios but in their sharpness. Producing a sharp edge requires that you to be able to make a special type of platform that leaves a sharp edge upon flake removal rather than the remnants of a dulled platform. You need not be overly concerned with it until your arrowhead is shaped, and you reach the final sequence of flake removal.

Start at the tip of one edge. You'll be flaking towards the base at a slight diagonal. Use the tip of the flaker and lightly scrape a few minute flakes downwards and towards the direction you're planning to take the flake. If the platform is too high up on the opposite face, you will need to backflake a little to move your platform more towards the cross-section centerline, but then be sure to scrape a few tiny flakes towards the intended flake's direction. What you're doing is stacking the back of the platform up with little micro flakes which strengthen it and allows you to flake from it. Avoid any platform grinding here as it would over-strengthen the platform and make it too difficult to remove a flake. Rely on your scraping. Your first flake should leave a scalloped indentation in your preform with a very sharp edge. Turn the point over and from the bottom edge of this scar repeat the initial process. Avoid scraping into the sharp area except at the lower edge. This next flake will leave another sharp scalloped edge adjacent to the first. Depending upon how well you managed to shape your preform, you should be producing a sharp sinuous edge with little or no platform remnants. If you've managed to do this on your first few attempts, immediately place yourself in the master craftsmen category and congratulate yourself generously. Knapping and bowmaking have at least one thing in common, they both take years to master, but you can produce a workable item early on and then practice to produce improvements.

Your first attempts at this may produce an irregular edge too asymmetrical for use. To reshape it without major re-chipping, place the point flat on a clean piece of leather on your knee or a bench. Using your Ishi stick or a little nibbler, press the flaker's tip into the edge and scrape a few minute chips downwards before popping off a flake in the same direction. Flip the point over and repeat the process wherever and as often as required. You should be aiming to remove just the projections while keeping the edge sharp. If you try to drive flakes into the point you'll soon discover you can muster little follow through. That's the beauty of this technique. As long as you scrape downwards and push flakes down and off, there is little chance of producing hinge or step fractures.

ARROWHEAD DESIGN AND HAFTING IN WOOD OR CANE SHAFTS

I watched the old man with an intensity bordering on fanaticism as he fashioned the bolt for his crossbow. He tied off the flat, butted nock end to prevent splitting then slit an opening in his bamboo bolt, split earlier from a thick walled piece. He deftly folded a small bamboo leaf into a delta kite shape and slid it through the opening. Now properly "fletched", he placed it on his tiny rosewood crossbow. Its "string" was an intricately split and woven strip of bamboo with node sections along its length. My eyes were drawn to his arrowhead and a feeling of disappointment swept through me. After watching a virtual tour-de-force of primitive skills performed with nothing more than a bush hook and a worn out kitchen knife, this little mountain man wasn't planning to arm his weapon with anything more than a sharpened bamboo stick? I had seen more formidable looking weapons on the end of friction-fire sticks. He casually raised it up like a pistol, aiming at a nearby tree ... thwat ... and it was over. I bolted (pun intended) for the tree and received a lesson in arrowhead design I'll never forget. That little stick was buried deeper than I could comprehend at the time. As I turned to him in disbelief, I saw him grin, a blue sapphire stone set in a gold cap on his tooth gleaming in the sun. I grinned back like the fool I was.

I learned a lot from that lesson although neither of us spoke one word of the other's language. You can learn craft skills through reading, pictures, drawings, and conversation, but nothing beats watching it being performed. Witnessing that hardened sharp bamboo sliver penetrate a tropical hardwood taught me that small sharp objects penetrate better than large, dull ones. Most importantly, I learned to be very wary of absolutes as nature and circumstance offer too many variables.

In choosing an arrowhead design for large game, you'll be restricted by state laws to some extent. These laws were written a long time ago by well-meaning folks with little practical knowledge of the subject. More recently, lobbyists for commercial interests have succeeded in banning all but metal types in some states. Today's contemporary bowhunter carries a quiver of arrow clones useful for one type of game in one type of situation. The "clone hunter" is actually doing the best he can considering his information on the subject is rather limited. On the other hand, the contents of our Stone Age hunter's quiver reflected his thorough knowledge and understanding of various situations. A mixed bag of arrow types with individual names like "he go far", "he no stick in treetops" and "he walk on water" was much more reflective of an archer in tune

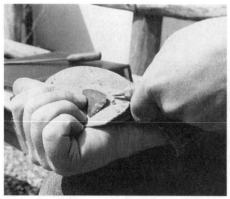

To notch the arrowhead, chip the corner from a triangular-shaped point.

Shape and isolate a platform.

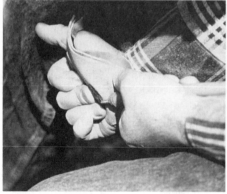

Load pressure into the platform with the pressure flaker, then remove the flake.

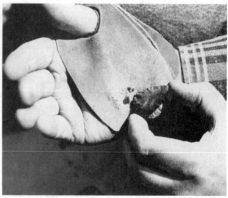

The resulting flake and its scar.

Trim away thin stone at the notch and prepare another platform...

...then remove a flake from the opposite side of the arrowhead.

Continue removing flakes until notch is the desired depth, then finish the notch by carefully nibbling to shape.

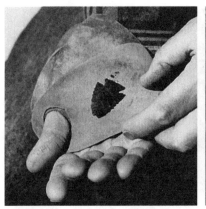

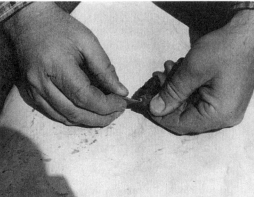

Repeat the process on the other corner.

Use a grinding tool, such as a quartzite flake, to smooth and dull the notch so the sinew binding will not be cut.

with reality. Very few stone tipped arrows have been recovered from archeological sites relative to those armed with bone, antler, wood, scale, tooth, etc. The stone tip was just not that necessary in most hunting situations. Because stone points are so durable, through time they tend to accumulate and give a false picture of the past. Trying to tell whether a stone point was an arrowhead, spearhead, dart point, knife (and many stone knives were tiny) saw, reamer, drill, scraper, awl, root splitter, food dicer, etc., is a biased process.

Grind the base in the same way.

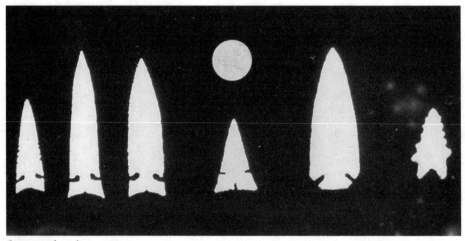

Some notch styles.

Before you start your point, decide whether it's for hunting or not. If for hunting it should be of legal size and shape. Some states require a minimum width and no barbs. If you're making a replica of a certain type, use it as a template and study its chipping pattern, angle, and width to thickness ratio. If you're fortunate enough to examine the workshop debris left from the original manufacture you'll have the chance to see, frozen in time, the various steps the ancient craftsmen followed.

In this case we'll consider a typical arrowhead. It should have optimum sharpness, possess a low biconvex cross section, be made of the toughest stone you can master, have a weight compatible with your archery system, be symmetrical in all aspects, be shaped at its base to fit your hafting system, and be permanently engraved for reasons of ethics and pride. Engraving a maker's mark on your points is a way of insuring that your creation will be recognized for modern work instead of ancient. Inexpensive diamond scribers are widely offered for sale in a number of markets. I mark everything I make with the full knowledge that some day it's all going to be scattered across and beneath the land. I like to think that each one is a miniature tombstone to mark my passing. Let's not forget the flintknappers rule: He who dies having made the greatest number of marked, quality arrowheads, wins!

Consider your arrowshaft diameter as compared to your point's width where it will be hafted. The photos will give some suggestions but there are no hard and fast rules here. If your point is stemmed or notched, make it slightly wider than the shaft. As the sinew/glue mix shrinks, it produces as strong a bond as possible within the component's ability. Oval, triangular, and other wide types should get a wrapping of sinew where possible. Any extra binding that doesn't make the haft too thick is useful. Dulling the hafting areas on a stone point with sandstone was, and is, a good practice to prevent cutting the sinew binding.

The only way to find out how well you have done the job of hafting is to test the points. I stay in touch with stone point users and listen to their experiences

Shaft of Viburnum and Tallahatta Silicified Sandstone (quartzite-like stone) used to mount the arrowhead.

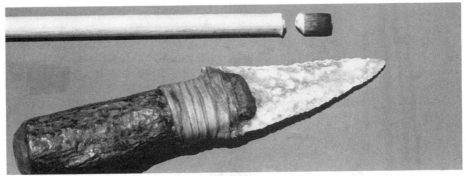

Use knife to saw a flat surface on hafting end of shaft.

The hafted blade was used to saw the initial slot while the arrow was gripped in the soft cedar clamp.

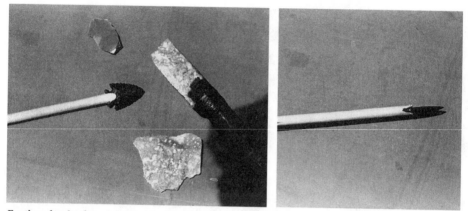

Further slot depth and shaping is done with a simple flake, followed by minor whittling of the shaft tip in order to assure a smooth, even fit.

closely, then incorporate their advice into my latest Mark 17 Model. Armed with this state of the art knowledge and a quiver full of new concepts, I test a batch on various targets to see the results, then modify the next batch in search of the perfect point-shaft-arrow combo in my new Mark 18 Model.

After destroying countless points, I've gleaned these observations for your consideration. The cross-section of the arrowshaft and arrowhead should be a smooth transition from stone to resin to wood to glue to sinew to finish coat in

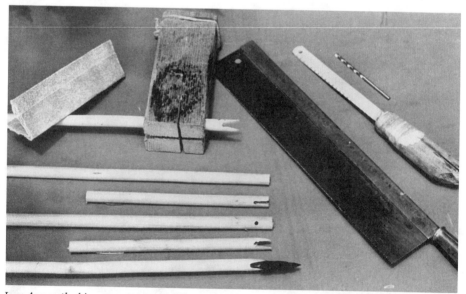

Iron Age method incorporates pre-drilling and sawing to the drill hole followed by custom sanding of the haft area to fit the point. Glued or taped together hacksaw blades can also be used to fashion the slot.

Implements for making pitch. Clockwise, from bottom left; greenstone sculpting flake, copper spatula set in bone (both used for shaping spruce gum resin), metal lid containing rock dust and fiber for fillers, rolled out resin sticks. At center is a small stone oil lamp for melting resin. Coffee can with holes in bottom is placed over oil lamp or alcohol burner to heat resin in small tin can on top.

that order. Although sinew and hide glue-bound stone points work, they work less efficiently than ones that use a layer of spruce gum, pitch or bitumen between the stone and wood. In dry weather hide glue continues shrinking along with the sinew and soon breaks free of the stone. Those with a layer of slightly plastic bonding material remain tight regardless of weather, save in the case of excessive soaking. Spruce gum can be made from any conifer pitch by carefully cooking off its moisture and most of the turpentine-like fluids in a double boiler. Old dry resin blobs from scarred trees can be re-dissolved in turpentine then processed like fresh sap. Use the finished product like any hot-melt resin. The sinew, hide glue, resin and wood of the arrow become, in effect, the ferrule of the point. The stone point should be heated over low heat to drive out moisture. Heat the notched arrow tip, then drip hot resin on the point's base and insert it in the notch. Re-heat both and spin balance it, making adjustments and shimming with wood slivers as needed. Use a hot knife or, for true primitives, a copper spatula or stone flake to sculpt and remove excess resin. Bind with glue-soaked sinew as illustrated and let dry. The shrinking sinew causes resin to ooze out of the haft and form little blobs. Pop them off with your thumbnail and rub the area vigorously to remelt and smooth the resin. Crushed rock dust and

Point set in notch with resin, now ready for a coat of warm hide glue.

shredded plant fibers can be added to the resin to give it body and impart more flexible strength. A coat of your favorite arrow finish completes the project.

Points break when they hit objects at any angle other than straight on, and sometimes break even then. A properly balanced and tuned archery system should deliver your arrow as straight and as quickly as possible. All stone-tipped arrows surviving straight on shots were thoroughly bound with sinew and had a reinforced wrapping beneath the point's base that extended 3/8 to 1/2 inch up the shaft. This yielded maximum strength without impeding penetration.

Cane or bamboo shafts using wood foreshafts must have similar reinforcements where the foreshaft is set into the cane. The area to be bound must be

Shaft has been blackened to show the almost invisible sinew, applied over the hide glue. This illustrates the lashing where the last 1/4" or so of sinew wrapping also goes over a loop of cord, in this case twisted sinew. When the last bit of sinew wrapping is reached, pass it through the loop and pull the loop out, which pulls the sinew "tail" under the wrapping and leaves a no-knot binding which can't come loose. The loop should always be pulled forward to force the lashing tight against the point's base.

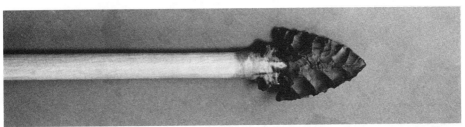

Finished. Once the glue has dried enough not to be tacky it can be burnished smooth with antler, bone, or fingernail.

The smoother the taper the better the penetration.

thoroughly sanded or scraped to remove the waxy coating prior to gluing. Needless to say, your cane shaft should already be fully dried and straightened before you start hafting. To accomplish this in a satisfactory manner, treat the subject of shaft selection the same way you would for bow staves or hunting areas: with a good deal of research, scouting, and high-grading. There are

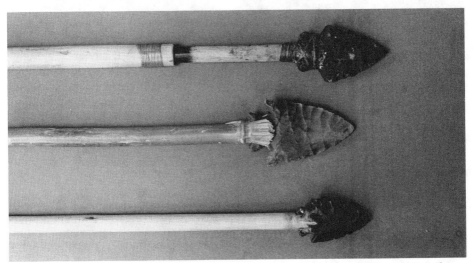

Top, point mounted in hardwood foreshaft set in cane arrow. Another possibility, center, is the "smash and haft" technique; green cane smashed to a fibrous bundle (boil seasoned cane to soften) then mounted in the normal way.

Examples of hafted points of green Normanskill Chert from the Hudson Valley, N.Y. Note nickel for size comparison.

Left to right; locust foreshaft in cane by Steve Watts, N.C., Mid-Atlantic Levanna point in arrowwood shaft by Jack Cresson, N.J., contemporary Ishi-style point of TV tube glass by Barney DeSimone, CA., replica of early Archaic type using Onondaga Chert by Kirk Dreier, MD.

Sacrificial arrows.

Every arrow which failed to strike straight-on caused the point to snap. Those which stuck straight but were weakly hafted also had problems. A wide variety of fletching styles was used.

numerous varieties of cane found world-wide with roughly a dozen types in the U.S.A., depending upon which book you use. Widely employed in prehistoric times, the River Cane of the South has been found in archeological sites as arrows.

A variety of ornamental bamboos have been imported and are thriving in many areas. Japanese Arrow Bamboo, which is most likely the finest natural arrow material available, is now common throughout the Middle Atlantic States. Like all bamboos or canes, it sends up shoots in various diameters depending upon its biological program and the prevailing environmental conditions. Most first year shoots are thin-walled, full of water, and a bit weak if cut too early in the growing season. If left alone for another year's additional growth, which takes place on the inside, the walls of the bamboo stiffen enough for arrowshaft material.

These factors vary so much that you must test each batch individually. I'll cut a few canes which are promising in appearance and use a snapped-flake scraper to shave off the waxy bark-like coating. This is followed by a thorough scrubbing with horsetail rushes, sand, and an old rag or steel wool. Two weeks in full sun is usually enough drying time after the scraping and scouring. Excessive branching or swelling at the nodes is whittled down, then each section between nodes gently heated and slowly straightened. After cooling these "between joint" areas, each node is heated and straightened individually. Once straight and cool, the shafts are spine tested and marked. A batch of similarly sized and aged cane can then be cut to provide good arrowshafts of similar weight and strength.

Guess which point had too little sinew binding behind the point. The one at top with the split shaft.

Point stuck in seasoned elm log. Shaft split and was driven forward into log. Author's note: use more sinew binding, especially when hunting seasoned elms.

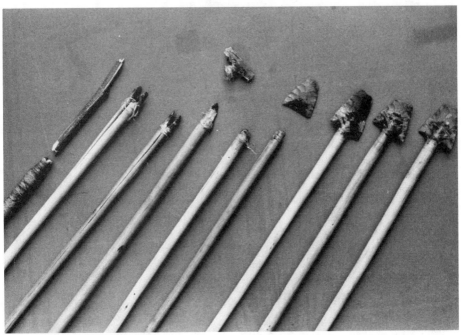

Selected points which broke. All arrows shot from a 50# white ash flatbow, 67" long, at twenty paces. Left to right - The wood point is hackberry, which shattered upon impact. Points with too little sinew binding split the shafts behind the arrowhead. Points without resin in the haft sometimes shed their sinew-hide glue lashing as in the examples at center. Points at right snapped off when arrows did not fly perfectly true.

FORGET TRADITION, I JUST WANT TO MAKE AN ARROWHEAD

As a kid, I — along with maybe half the other adventurous ones in the neighborhood — tried my hand at stone point-making. This was before the days of child psychiatrists with demeaning labels such as "hyperactive sibling with nonconforming social tendencies". Heh, we knew what we wanted to be when we grew up: Savages. The writings of Earnest Thompson Seton, Ben Hunt and the sage advice on cereal boxes by Straight Arrow became our intellectual well to be drawn from whenever we needed inspiration. The lack of good instruction about chipping flint points didn't hamper our efforts, we used roofing slate and a combination of grinding on concrete slabs, punching with nails, and nibbling with wire cutters. Bows made of split green hickory saplings with the bark left on propelled giant ragweed stem arrows with split cedar shake foreshafts at amazingly slow speeds. They were crude to extremes but effectively held the rabbit population in check around our grandfather's Victory Garden.

Since good, sound, practical knowledge of how to chip flint was unavailable to me, I stuffed the need to know in the back of my mind and relied on real life experiences to gather the needed information.

After decades of learning and practicing, it became ever more evident that to

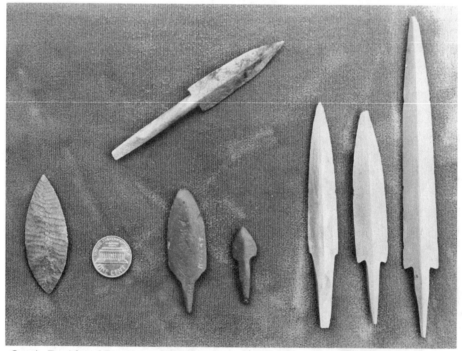

Certain Danish and Egyptian cultures have been well studied concerning their ground pre-form industry but this cast, left of penny, of an Afghanistan point shows other folks were on to it, as well. The two dark ground slate points, right of penny, are old Korean arrowheads. The rest are prehistoric ground slate dart or spearheads, thought to have been used in hunting marine mammals.

A ten-inch diamond saw with trimmed slab and ground preform.

Author's grinding setup. Greenstone bowmaking tools are for Atlantic flatbows, seen at right in mulberry, hickory, and ash.

rely upon just old traditional ways took a near fanatical approach for which most people had no time. They just wanted the finished points. By-passing a couple million years of tradition is an unforgivable sin to some, but almost a necessity to those without extra time to spend learning.

During the Neolithic and Early Bronze Age, a number of cultures began grinding their knapped-out preforms prior to the final chipping stage. A perfectly symmetrical and smooth preform allows superb chipping after a bit of practice. Compared to the ancient way, this method takes very little skill and can be mastered much sooner. You can still follow the old way of going through all the knapping stages before hand grinding or you can bypass that million plus years of sweat and skill and get a diamond saw and wet power grinder. Even poorly knapped preforms can be quickly ground to perfect shape using a hand-held wet Carborundum stone.

If you lack experience in pressure flaking I suggest you stick to obsidian, glass, opal, and the highly heat treated varieties of the flint family as they are much easier to pressure flake and allow you to produce some amazing items.

Either buy sawn slabs through lapidary shops and knapping suppliers or saw your own. Use indelible aluminum or gold colored felt paint pens to trace or outline your point's shape and rough saw it to shape. I start with slabs 1/8" to 3/16" thicker than I want the preform to be as I'll grind that much away. Your preform will lose about 1/4" around its edge as well but this amount varies with the type of platform used and your skills at flaking. It is wise to practice on some trial blanks of inferior shape.

There are three types of preform edges from which to choose. These edges will be the pressure platform where the flakes will start. First, they can be sharp, forming an equal alignment of both faces coming to the edge. Second, they can be beveled to one face which is flaked first, then the bevel reground to the other face which is flaked next, followed by alternate counter-flaking to form the cutting edge. Lastly, the edge can be nearly square to both faces. This platform requires it be ground with a slightly course wheel which leaves a fairly rough surface on the platform, providing bite or a foothold for your pressure flaker to grab.

All pressure flaking is a combination of inward shearing type force together with a follow through of outward prying force. An all inward force produces a step or hinge fracture, while an all prying force produces a short popped out chip. The skill lies in balancing these two forces such that the flake travels the desired distance in the chosen direction at a reasonable depth. Refer to the previous section on pressure flaking for an explanation on one suggested holding position. Any position that works for you is the right one. Take the time to experiment and do your homework before frustrating yourself by attempting Grand Master pieces.

The palm of your hand is cupped with a significant depression when the fingers are curled. If you place your preform flat across it, only the tip and base of your preform will make contact. When pressure is applied to the preform's edge, as in flaking, you're duplicating, in slow motion, a Karate type blow and risk snapping your piece in two. Fill in the depression in your hand with leather or develop a holding position that avoids bending and straining the preform.

Remember the Egg and how much compressive force it can take, and design your hold to put the edge of your preform in compression.

Make trial blanks from any scrap pieces of glass, natural or otherwise that do not make the grade for potentially finished items. If it's good enough for finished items you won't treat it as a trial and will only waste time and effort attempting to make points rather than developing technique. I can't emphasize this point strongly enough. Make up a batch of trial tip sections on overly curved spalls, then after practice chipping, regrind to a new trial shape altering your platform angle or preform convexity for another attempt. Do the same for base areas and mid-sections.

The overall shape of your preform is critical. It should not be wider than your holding technique's ability to control. Follow-through with your pressure flaker should travel the same curvature as your preform convexity. Don't attempt two-inch-wide points in your initial learning phase. Stick to three quarters or one inch. As you get the hang of it, start widening the preform one quarter inch at a time. When you start having real problems taking flakes, stop and fully evaluate your preform shape (convexity), platform type, and the holding technique you're using.

The preform should be slightly thinner at its tip and either uniform in thickness the rest of the way or with a very small decrease in thickness towards the base where it will be hafted. Any variance from a perfectly smooth even surface on your preform will cause flake scars to dip and be irregular. As with flakes, good preforms make good points.

Too fine a grinding surface will strengthen stone. Pick a grinding grit surface that works for your technique. Most grinding stones are manufactured in standard grit sizes. 220 grit is a popular size although I use an even courser diamond grit of near 125 for a lot of my work. Courser grit stones are less forgiving during grinding and require some practice to prevent chipping of the preform. Ask your lapidary dealer or a member of your local Rock & Mineral Club if you can

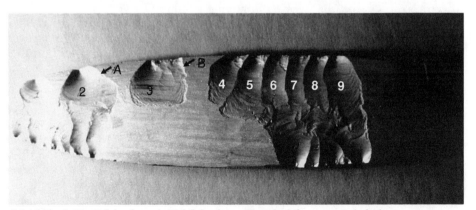

A trial blank. No. 2 flake shows initial flake shape. No. 3 had the unwanted platform remnant as seen at "A" chipped away to make a new platform. The next flake will be taken at "B". If flaked sequentially in this manner, parallel flake scars such as (at top right), 4,5,6,7,8, and 9 can be obtained. Random flaking as shown at bottom right leaves an irregular flake pattern.

While this is possibly more suited to taking Wooly Rhinoceros, you can chip smaller ones to suit your needs. The smaller and very narrow width points with skinny flake scars will hide many mistakes. Try them first.

try out some different grit stones to find one that works for you prior to investing in the wrong one.

The size of your pressure flaker tip, along with the chosen depth into the platform it contacts, will dictate the size and width of your flake. Balance the two to remove flakes of a size you want. This type of sequential flaking requires that you pay close attention to repetitive action; do everything the same way each time. Your skill will be brought out when you make a mistake — like taking an overly deep and wide flake which requires compensation with the next flake. The first flake taken is a typical flake. The next flake taken beside it will overlap the first scar to some degree. How much of the first flake scar you remove is up to you. Typically one third to one half is overlapped. If you make a mistake with a too deep & too wide flake next to a series of very uniform ones, you don't want to jump back to very perfect ones leaving a glaring wide one as testimony to your error. Correct the error by removing another flake just a little narrower and shallower than your mistake but a bit wider than your normal good flake scars. Then repeat the process of diminishing flake size over a few flakes until you're back to normal. Almost every point made this way is a series of minor corrections. Really horrendous mistakes are treated by regrinding the entire side of one face where the mistake was made and reflaking.

Again, as with old-time techniques, flaking at a slight diagonal is easier, and less difficulties occur. Taking flakes straight in, and getting two sets of flake series on one face to meet in the middle with uniform width and alignment is the most difficult, especially on thin pieces. Called collateral flaking, this was practiced by early man in the new world, evidenced by Eden points with thick diamond cross-sections. Many flintknappers attempt it because of the challenge, but I suggest you work on diagonal flaking until the technique is completely mastered.

Using carefully ground preforms, those with only a moderate level of knapping skill can quickly begin turning out exquisite points.

The "Ronco Chip-A-Matic" is another modern method which horrifies many traditional knappers, but allows the beginner to fashion effective points in short

The arrowhead at left and the Dalton-style knife at bottom, both of strong flint, were flaked in the old traditional manner. They lie on top of two obsidian knives made from ground preforms. Chipping from ground blanks is to flintknapping what painting by the numbers is to art.

order. Martin Tillett, Staff Naturalist at the Owens Science Center in Maryland, brought one of these devices to one of our Experimental Archeology Workshops in Virginia. Some of the more conservative archeologists were aghast and would have run him off if he wasn't so big and burly. Martin understood and practiced knapping in various old traditional ways, but needed a way to get kids to complete a project in a limited time frame. I'll let him tell you about it in his own words: "This board is a variation of a similar device I saw in use at a rock and mineral show. The person using it at the time said he saw the board in a book but didn't recall the title or author. I guess it is best described as a "rock shop arrowhead maker". At any rate it is simple and I have had students as young as nine make points using it with little difficulty.

I used 2 pieces of 3/4" plywood, 2-8" pieces of copper tubing, some glue and nails. The copper tubing is hammered flat on one end and cut and spread out on the other end. This allows the tubes to be sandwiched between the plywood (Don't flatten the top end of the tubes with a hammer until they are sandwiched and positioned between the boards). I cut the corners on the top piece of plywood to allow a space for the C-clamps to hold the board to a table, desk or bench. This also helps keep the clamps out of the way. The top board also has 2 holes drilled the diameter of the copper tubing. Once everything is assembled I

The Roncomatic. Copper tube is split and fastened to bottom of the board. Top end of tube is hammered flat.

cut a piece of carpet to go over the board and around the copper tubing. This keeps the hands comfortable when pressing a glass blank against the tube.

I usually use whatever flat pieces of glass I have available. I have purchased some black and purple glass at a stained-glass supply store. This makes the point look either more authentic (obsidian) or like a craft project if a more unusual color is used. Kids either go for an authentic appearance or the gawdy costume jewelry look.

I use a glass cutter to etch a triangle on the selected glass and then a tile breaking tool to snap the triangle out of the larger glass. Students are required to wear leather gloves, eye protection and a lab apron.

The idea is to press the flat/squared edge against the copper tube then tilt the glass upwards while maintaining pressure against the copper tubing. (Wide tube/wide flake, narrow tube/narrow flakes) When the flakes pop off, they usually fly back into the face of the person using the device. *Eye protection is a must!* I usually have to comb my beard afterwards to get out all of the shards or debitage. With a little practice, one can easily learn how to control the size of the flakes you want to take off. Once you have completed one side you turn the blank over and do the other side. A piece of emery cloth is needed to occasionally rough up the copper tube to give more bite on the glass. Kids need to do this

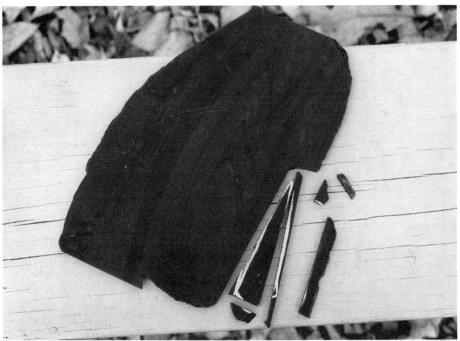

Marked blank is sawn from an obsidian slab.

The edge of the blank is pressed firmly into the copper tube, then the near side tilted upward.
Large or small flakes result from heavy or light pressure. Eye protection is mandatory.

A ten minute point, requiring another fifteen minutes of careful retouching to sharpen the edge. A deer will never know how it was made. Is this the wave of the future in knapping? Not likely, but remember there is no law or ruled carved anywhere on how arrowheads should be knapped.

step more often. They have more instances where the glass blank slips without taking a flake off. This slipping tends to smooth the tubing surface.

For notching and very small flakes, you use the flattened top of the copper tubing. Again, pressing the now flaked object against the flattened tubing and pressing and tilting down or up cuts into the glass. This allows for shaping the point and making the notches or tangs.

Most of the students attend the class hoping that they will obtain a "real" artifact. The ethical end of collecting artifacts is discussed and flintknapping and reproductions of artifacts are considered as alternatives to collecting limited archeological resources. Most students are happy and satisfied with the "rock shop arrowhead", and some have copied the device and have later shown me examples of their efforts."

The points produced with this method have dull crushed edges which satisfies the requirements of keeping sharp objects away from devious minded kids.

Putting a razor-plus edge on them is accomplished using the alternate flaking and re-edging technique previously described in the pressure flaking section.

Although ground-out preforms or the cheat & chip points may not satisfy hard-core traditionalists, the game you take with them sure won't know.

HEAT TREATING FLINT: STAR WARS TECHNOLOGY AT WORK

The lore surrounding the heat treating of certain crypto- and micro-crystalline and fibrous silicas has drawn many knappers into heat treating almost every piece of stone they get their hands on. That the process improves the ease with which the stone can be flaked is indisputable. That the process visually improves the stone is indisputable. That it also considerably weakens the stone is indisputable. Exactly what takes place in the stone to cause this is, however, highly disputable and is the subject of an ongoing series of disagreements. It appears to involve static ionic transfer of length-slow chalcedony pseudomorphs from low order chrystobolite to 11th dimensionally instable flux paramorphs of dense star matter. Gosh, I sure hope I got all that right. Did I mention the part about anti-gravity influence on the negative super strings? Well anyway, that should be close as I read all the pertinent articles about it.

In other words, none of the explanations prove anything at present, but the bottom line is that heat treating does work.

Again, only use heat treating when you have a knappable stone that is very uniform in quality but is just too grainy and strong to flake with control. Remove a few spalls or flakes for testing. The thicker the spall the more chance for failure during heat treating. When all other factors are equal, stone that has been thoroughly dried out will survive the process best. Set your spalls or cores in the sun or in an oven so that temperatures can reach 125 to 200 degrees —

Tough and grainy grade of Flint Run Jasper. It was too tough for pressure flaking so it was heat treated, which reddened the exterior.

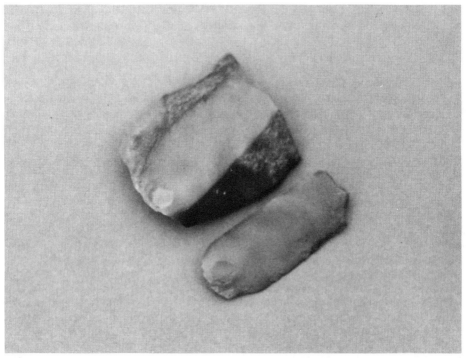

Flake taken after heat treating reveals the now creamy-smooth texture of the stone. Like all witchcraft this should be used judiciously, on stone which cannot otherwise be worked.

you don't want them to reach the boiling point. Thick cores can take weeks to completely dry out. One quarter inch spalls can dry out in an hour in an oven at 190 degrees. While your stone is drying, work on your heat treating set-up. Stone such as novaculite from Arkansas (used untreated as oil stones for sharpening knives) requires temperatures in the neighborhood of 900 degrees to alter, hence a kiln rather than a stove is required. Most jaspers, cherts, agates, and chalcedony can be treated while many of the N.Y. flints and prase along with the Mid-West nodular stone known as hornstone doesn't require or tolerate heating. All of the well known varieties of Texas stone respond well to heating along with much of the stone along the Middle to South Atlantic Piedmont and Coastal Plain. These can be heated in your stove or outside in a cooker or beneath a campfire.

"Arrowhead Fred" Bollinger is truly a legend among knappers not only for his ability to knap out excellent arrowheads with his one arm but also for his photographic skills and tall-tale rendering. This Missourian developed a practical stone cooker out of an old cast-iron bath tub elevated on steel poles and a system of laying a few inches of sand around the stone to buffer it from excessive heat. A wood fire is maintained under the tub as well as on top of the tub where a few inches of sand is also present. Once the fire is well under way, the top of the tub is covered with a heavy sheet of metal (in Fred's set-up, an old truck hood). This prevents an unexpected rainstorm from destroying a critically hot and therefore fragile load of stone. Fred points out that the fire follows the underside of the tub and produces its greatest heat at the sloped end away from the drain plug end. Stone needing more heat is packed there. A day in the cooker with occasional stokings, followed by a day or more to cool down after the firing is done, turns out smooth glassy stone of pleasing color.

Archeologist Michael Johnson from Fairfax, VA., cooks his stone by digging out a fire pit and burying jasper right in the dirt beneath the fire. The amount of buffering dirt is adjusted to the dampness of the earth, the estimate of how much heat will be required, and the size and duration of the fire. Takes some trial and error, but gives excellent results in a most traditional manner.

Larry Kinsella from Southern Illinois held a flint cook out in his backyard for friends. He used a backhoe to dig a rectangular trench a couple of feet deep by maybe ten by fifteen feet across. He then threw in three to five tons of Crescent chert (give or take a ton) and covered them with a foot or so of dirt. A few cords of wood on top were set ablaze, followed by periodic stoking throughout the night. I do remember hearing some explosions now and then, but the better part of the flint came out fine. When you're treating stone by the ton, different rules apply — such as it takes several days to cool down.

For the home oven cooker heating slabs of Brazilian Agate or spalls and chips of stone, your biggest problem will be the mess of stone shards that invariably fly about when something doesn't go as perfectly as planned. Negotiate an "I'll clean up the mess afterwards" clause into your oven-use agreement with whomever controls it (for some reason, females seem especially over sensitive to getting chunks of flint in the casserole). A double layer of aluminum foil encasing your cooking hoard helps control exploding stone. Some folks bury the stone in a buffer of sand or clean kitty litter (it better be clean or you may not want to use the oven again!).

Each type of flint requires a different altering temperature. Most alter in the 350 to 550 degree range. Stone requiring high temperatures can usually be altered in lower heat but over a much longer time span, sometime an additional day or two.

Conduct trials with poorly shaped flakes that still represent the general size and thickness of your better shaped ones. Mark each one with its description in India Ink as most change color and are then difficult to recognize. Your first trial should shoot for 350 degrees. Start the temperature at just below 200 degrees for at least two hours to drive off any latent moisture, then up the temperature 25 degrees to 50 degrees each hour until you reach 350 degrees. Hold the temperature at 350 degrees a few hours then bring the temperature back down 50 degrees an hour. Once the oven temperature falls to around 200 degrees, the core of the stone will still be very hot and expanded. If cooler outside air is allowed in and hits the stones casing, you'll hear cracking and know then that you should not have peeked. Leave the oven door closed, and if you used a good layer of sand or litter as a heat buffer, go to bed and sleep soundly knowing all is well with your stone.

In the morning, dig it out and take notes on which stone did what. Take flakes from each, and compare each to unaltered samples of the same variety. Those showing little change should go back in the oven for another trial at 375 degrees for an additional few hours. Be sure to raise and lower the temperatures in slow increments as before, use a buffer, and allow an overnight cooling period. Repeat the entire process as many times and at as high a temperature as is needed until you get the results you want. When the stone suddenly weakens to cracker strength, you've over-reached the technological limits of this phenomenon.

✧ ✧ ✧

Though knapping your own points takes some time, and above all perseverance, if you stick to it and don't fall prey to the modern malady of instant gratification you'll eventually even learn to read flintwork from primeval times. In the words of a contemporary Hawaiian Craftsman, you will "Learn from those who no longer speak".

PASSING THE TORCH

Jim Hamm

It's easy for me to remember the exact time that the *Bowyer's Bibles* began. Jay Massey, John Strunk, and I were sitting beneath a pine tree. Late into the Michigan night we exchanged bowmaking ideas, pet theories, and disasters. Though I had met these men only the afternoon before, they could have been my oldest friends. For hours, we spoke passionately about our wooden bows while the rest of the camp slept. And it was there, in the middle of a July night in 1988, that the toxophilic spark which had lain dormant for so long was fanned.

Before that time, the flames of natural archery had flickered and all but died from their heyday in the 1940's. The wooden bows and pioneering adventures of the Thompson brothers, Ishi, Saxton Pope and Arthur Young had been almost forgotten beneath the deluge of fiberglass and compound bows of the last forty years. Jay, John, and I had labored in our own limited world, making discoveries — and mistakes — in solitude and silence by the agonizing trial and error method. The first fifteen bows I made broke before ever launching an arrow. In retrospect, if I'd had any trace of sense I would have given up, though it would have been about as easy to give up breathing. Some deep-seated need compelled us all to make wooden bows, as against all reason we toiled alone, like moles burrowing underground.

And then, the three of us were invited to the archery tournament in Michigan to present a program on wooden bows. I knew of Jay from his books and from occasional correspondence, and John by reputation. Though I approached meeting these fellow bowyers with anticipation, there was, I confess, an undercurrent of misgiving. A mole always blinks as he approaches the light, unsure of what the new perspective will bring.

The concern was wasted, it turned out, for five minutes after meeting we were chattering happily away, oblivious to our surroundings, totally immersed in our mutual love for wooden bows.

I found Jay Massey a soft-spoken, articulate man, but if one peered closer, beneath the calm exterior, the hint of granite could be detected underneath. This demeanor is evident in others who are very good at what they do: martial arts experts, airline pilots, Special Forces veterans, men who carry no trace of a chip on their shoulder because they know they have nothing left to prove. Guiding and outfitting in the Alaskan wilderness, Jay's profession, tended to select for soft-spoken ability, since the experience either left a man exceedingly competent or dead.

John Strunk, too, was a modest, generous man, patient to a fault. His kindness and patience are reflected in his bows, which can only be described as art —

yew and horn and rawhide the medium instead of canvas and paint and brush-es. Though the last thing I needed was another bow, I quickly struck a deal to acquire one of John's masterpieces, which hangs on my wall to this day. He was a high-school woodworking shop teacher by day, and occasionally helped a student make a bow. A geologic age ago when I was in high school, with natural archery just beginning its life-long assault on my sanity, I would have *walked* from Texas to Oregon to take one of his classes.

At the tournament, we discovered hundreds of enthusiastic fiberglass longbow shooters, but fewer than a dozen wooden bows, including our own, in the entire camp. Our evening program was received politely enough by the fiberglass devotees, I suppose, but the real treat for us was talking late into the night, every night.

We left for home with our bowmaking flames burning brighter than ever. Afterwards, we kept in touch, exchanging raw materials such as bow staves or relating our latest bowmaking breakthroughs — or just plain breaks.

The meeting had greater repercussions it turned out, since it seemed to somehow act as the critical mass for the handful of wooden bow enthusiasts who had weathered the decades-long mechanical archery storm. Within a few months others became part of the loose-knit network — remarkable artist Steve Allely, Bert Grayson, bowyer and archery historian, Jay and Joe St. Charles, whose father, Glenn, was one of the founding members of the Pope and Young Club, Al Herrin, who kept alive the archery traditions of his Cherokee people, bowyers and gifted flintknappers Errett Callahan and Scott Silsby, along with old-time bowyers Cliff Coe, Bill Crawford, Harry Drake, Frank Garske, Gilman Keasey, Wally Miles, and Carney Saupitty, all of whom had for years been infected with the natural archery virus — and who had toiled in virtual isolation.

As the next summer tournament in Michigan drew near, we faithful decided to once again make the pilgrimage. And it was there that we met two men, whom we had been corresponding with for months, who would help steer traditional archery into uncharted waters.

Paul Comstock was literally the mild-mannered reporter, a professional newspaperman, who has now become a toxophilic Superman. He was the first to insist that elm, ash, and hickory, the "white woods", could be made into first-rate bows if they were made long enough and wide enough. Jay, John, and I, being thoroughly steeped in the "Osage and yew were the only true bow woods" school of thought, were at first skeptical, but intrigued. Paul's excellent elm bows proved that he was onto something, though at the time none of us were sure exactly what. The prevailing theory was that some woods, such as Osage, magically "recover" faster than others, and Paul's bow design was somehow affecting the recovery rate of his bows.

We also met Tim Baker, whom Paul's book had hooked on white wood archery the year before, and found him to have a badger's tenacity for solving problems and perpetual curiosity, ideal attributes for someone determined to fill the gaping holes in bow design theory. He generated ideas at 100 MPH, with gusts to 150. Few people lasted more than a round or two with him in a friendly verbal boxing match, but his remarkable intellect was perfectly tempered by a laser-like wit which he aimed, mercifully, mostly at himself. In time, however, we would discover that Tim possessed far more subtle but even more valuable assets — refreshing honesty and unbendable integrity.

At the tournament, we were all somewhat surprised at the increased interest in wooden bows. Perhaps thirty participants used self bows, primarily John Strunk's yew longbows, but other bowyers such as Chuck Boelter demonstrated his flawless static recurves, or Dean Torges, a professional woodworker, who shot with his nicely finished Osage orange bows.

We all found the freewheeling exchange of ideas about bowmaking invaluable. Before, we had been like the blind men describing the elephant, each of us with one part of the puzzle but no clear picture of the whole. Perhaps Paul put it best, when he said that anyone who has made five successful bows knows something that no one else knows. By comparing notes and bouncing ideas from each other, we were able, in a very short time, to greatly expand our bowmaking knowledge beyond anything we had ever experienced.

It was this gathering which formally initiated the writing project which was to become the *Traditional Bowyer's Bibles*. If a tiny group of us meeting informally over one weekend could be so enlightened, we felt the same type of exchange in book form with an expanded number of authors writing on his (or now in the case of Gabriela, her) particular area of expertise might prove useful.

Little did we know.

With chapters assigned for the first volume, we quickly found that having to write down our bowmaking techniques compelled us to clarify and distill our thinking. Theories were one thing, but there was no room for ambivalence or half-baked ideas on the written page, especially with the hyper-sensitive critics — each other — that our chapters would have to satisfy before ever reaching print. This writing-induced focusing led to months of bowmaking for testing, thorough review of existing archery texts, still more tests, and, most importantly, marathon-like long-distance discussions (read arguments) about the different facets of bowmaking with which we grappled.

Tim was the first to grab "The Truth" and shake it by the throat with his design and performance revelations. He proved, against all historical written and oral bowmaking tenets (and against my increasingly feeble arguments that Osage was somehow sacred), that there was no magic in any individual species or stave of wood. The magic was all in the design and the amount of energy it stored, the design being simply adapted to accommodate the species of wood.

Paul, too, put on his cape and leaped tall dogma with his quick-drying technique for staves. We were all surprised to learn that wood did not have to season for years, as "civilized" bowyers for the last few centuries had thought, but could be dried in a matter of weeks.

As ideas bounced from one writer to another and began to solidify, other subjects came in for closer scrutiny: bow finishes, strings, recurves, lumber bows, glue, tillering. In fact, I had finished the tillering chapter for Volume 1 — it was tied up with a big red bow — when Tim and I got into an unrelated argument about the stresses on thick versus thin pieces of wood. After weeks of friendly wrangling, the original premise had been transformed into a revolutionary new tillering technique. The tillering chapter, representing months of work, had to be scrapped and almost entirely re-written. I mention this incident not only to illustrate the metamorphosis which took place in our thinking during the writing of the books, but also because this is about the only argument that I can ever remember winning with Tim.

The books which resulted from this full-contact give and take were, quite frankly, a surprise to us all. The process of co-writing and editing the books has increased my overall knowledge and grasp of archery principles by three or four times, at least. The bows I now fashion have improved accordingly, and I feel sure the other contributors would express similar sentiments.

At the latest traditional archery tournament in Michigan after Volume 2 had been out for a few months, it was evident to Jay, Tim, Paul, and I (John was teaching a bowmaking class on the West Coast and couldn't attend) that the embers of natural archery, which had almost faded into oblivion, had been stoked into roaring flames once again. We saw hundreds of shooters with wooden bows who had taken up the torch — self bows, sinew-backed bows, flax-backed bows, recurves, lumber bows, pyramid bows, short bows, long bows, and best of all, kid's bows. Fully a third of the participants carried hand-made wooden weapons, an unforgettable spectacle for the four of us.

One young man stopped by to show us his new Osage orange self bow. Well-designed, perfectly tillered, and beautifully finished, the weapon displayed the bowyer's complete grasp of the art, especially since a massive hole graced the center of the upper limb. Place the tip of your thumb and forefinger together and you'll have an idea of the size and shape of the cavity right in the working section of the bow. The four of us examined it in wonder, noticing how the pin knots were carefully worked on the back, settling our hands around the comfortable leather grip, and pointing out the marvelous workmanship dealing with the awesome hole in the limb, how the sides widened and the bow was subtly thicker to compensate for the flaw.

Jay finally asked the man, "How long have you been making bows?"

"Oh, I just started a couple of months ago," the bowyer said with a smile, "this is my fourth one."

In perfect unison, all of our mouths fell open.

"Incredible," I managed to sputter.

Paul shook his head in wonder.

The bowmaker shrugged his shoulders, "I just read the books and did what you guys said. I didn't have any problems."

Tim cleared his throat. "Evidently," he said, with the beginnings of a grin, "by writing the books we've rendered ourselves irrelevant."

The torch had clearly passed to the fledgling bowyer.

✧ ✧ ✧

Maybe a hundred years from now some curious young man will be poking through his great-grandfather's books, packed away in a dusty attic for a generation or two, and stumble across faded copies of *The Traditional Bowyer's Bibles*. Innocently thumbing through them he, too, will be infected across the years by the natural archery virus, and his life will be changed, as ours and countless others stretching back into the mists of history had been long before. Some inner drive which he doesn't yet fully understand will compel him to cut a tree and try making his own wooden bow.

And the torch, in its turn, will have passed to him.

APPENDICES

GLOSSARY

Back: The side of the bow facing the target.

Backing: A material on the back of the bow, usually applied to prevent fracture.

Belly: The side of the bow facing the archer.

Billet: In modern usage, a short piece of wood that will be used to make a bow limb, or half of a bow spliced at the handle.

Brace Height: How high the bowstring is from the strung bow. Usually measured from the string to the bow's back next to the arrow plate.

Cast: How far a bow shoots an arrow.

Check: A crack-like opening in the wood that follows the grain, usually caused by the drying process.

Chrysal: In the old definition, a section of a bow's belly showing a number of small and faint compression fractures, usually caused by some error in construction.

Compression: What happens to the belly of the bow when bent. The belly of a drawn bow is acually shorter, due to compression, than when the bow is unstrung.

Deflex: Any curved or angular bending of the bow limbs toward the belly side.

Diffuse-porous Hardwoods: Trees in which the yearly growth rings are sometimes difficult to identify because the wood is more homogeneous than the soft/hard layers exhibited in ring-porous trees. Examples are maple and poplar.

Fistmele: An old term for brace height. The fistmele was usually measured from the string to the belly side of the handle, and checked by placing a closed fist on the handle and extending the thumb toward the string.

Fret: In the old definitions, a large chrysal. A fret poses a greater risk of breaking the bow compared to most smaller chrysals.

Heartwood: The dark section of interior wood in many trees, lying under the sapwood. In most hardwoods, the heartwood is brown. In yew, it is pink or red. In Osage orange, it is yellow or orange.

Nock: On a bow, the grooves, shoulders, or added tips of horn which hold the bowstring to the limb tips. On an arrow, the notch which accepts the bowstring.

Reflex: Any curved or angular bending of the bow limbs toward the back side.

Ring-porous hardwood: Trees in which each annual ring is composed of a soft porous layer, or spring wood, and harder layer, or late wood. These alternating layers are what show as the rings on the end of a cut log. Examples are Osage orange, mulberry, ash, elm, hickory and oak.

Sapwood: White wood which lies under the inner bark on almost every species of tree.

Self bow: In the strict old definition, an unbacked wooden bow made from a single piece of wood. Today, self bow is used to mean any unbacked wooden bow, whether made from one or two pieces of wood.

Set: Failure of any elastic material to resume its original shape because of being bent or stretched. On a wooden bow, set is deflex caused by compression of the bow's belly. If the tips of a bow's limbs are an inch farther to the belly side than the back of the handle, the bow is said to have an inch of set.

Setback: Natural or manufactured reflex in a wooden bow or stave, usually measured by comparing how much farther the limb tips are toward the back side compared to the back of the handle.

Sinew: Animal tendon.

Softwood: Coniferous, cone-bearing trees with yearly growth rings much like ring porous hardwoods. The spring growth of conifers, however, generally has more integrity and strength than the spring growth of ring porous trees. Examples are yew, cedar, juniper, pine, and fir.

Splice: Joining two halves of a wooden bow at the handle, using matching saw cuts and glue.

Stave: In the modern usage, a long piece of wood used to make a bow.

String follow: The same as "set." Often used as "follows the string."

Tension: What happens to the back of a bow when bent. The back of a drawn bow is actually slightly longer, or stretched, than when the bow is unstrung.

Tiller: As a verb, the process of making a wooden bow curve correctly by tapering the limbs in width, thickness, or both. As a noun, the condition of the curve in the limb of a bent bow.

White wood: Trees made up mostly of white sapwood, with the resulting bow made up mostly or entirely of white sapwood. White woods include ash, birch, elm, hickory, oak, and others.

BIBLIOGRAPHY

BOOKS

Allely, Steve, Baker, Tim, Comstock, Paul, et. al., *The Traditional Bowyer's Bible, Volume 1 and Volume 2*, Bois d'Arc Press, Azle, TX, 1992, 1993.

Ascham, Roger, *Toxophilus; The School of Shooting*, 1544.

Bear, Fred, *Fred Bear's Field Notes*, Fred Bear Sports Club Press, 1976.

Budge, E.W.W., *A History of Ethiopia: Nubia and Abyssinia*, Anthropological Publications, Oosterhout, N.B., The Netherlands.

Catlin, George, *Letters and Notes on the Manners, Customs, and Conditions of North American Indians*, London, 1844.

Comstock, Paul, *The Bent Stick; Making and Using Wooden Hunting Bows*, Delaware, OH, 1988.

Crowther, S.A., *Journal of an Expedition up the Niger and Tshadda Rivers*, Frank Cass, London, 1854/1970.

Dodge, Lt. Col. Richard, *Plains of the Great West*, New York, 1877.

Duff, James, *Bows and Arrows*, The MacMillan Company, New York, 1944.

Dusgate, R.H., *The Conquest of Northern Nigeria*, Frank Cass, London, 1985.

Elmer, Robert P., *Archery*, Penn Publishing Co., Philadelphia, PA, 1926.
— *Target Archery*, Alfred A. Knopf, New York, 1946.

Ewers, John C., *The Horse in Blackfoot Indian Culture*, Smithsonian Institution Press, Washington, D.C., 1955.

Ford, Daryll, *The Peoples of the Niger-Benue Confluence*, International African Institute, London, 1955.

Gunn, H. and Conant, E.P., *Peoples of the Middle Niger Region, Northern Nigeria,* International African Institute, London, 1957.

Hamm, Jim, *Bows and Arrows of the Native Americans,* Bois d'Arc Press, Azle, TX, 1989.

Hansard, George Agar, *The Book of Archery,* Henry G. Bohn, London, 1841.

Hardin, Dr. Stephen, *The Texas Rangers,* Osprey Publishing, London, 1991.

Hardy, Robert, *Longbow, A Social and Military History,* Bois d'Arc Press, Azle, TX, 1993.

Herodotus, *The Histories,* Translated by Aubery de Selincourt, Penguin Books, London.

Hickman, C.N., Nagler, Forrest, and Klopsteg, Paul E., *Archery: The Technical Side,* National Field Archery Association, 1947.

Hunt, W. Ben, and Metz, John J., *The Flatbow,* Bruce Publishing Co., New York, 1940.

Hussaini, I., *The History of the Ebira People,* Olowu Publishers, Lokoja, 1986.

Journal and Notices of the Native Missionaries, The Niger Expedition of 1857-1859, London, Dawson of Pall Mall, 1968.

Klopsteg, Paul E., *Turkish Archery and the Composite Bow,* Evanston, IL, 1934.

Massey, Jay, *The Bowyer's Craft,* Bear Paw Publications, Girdwood, AK, 1987.
  — *The Book of Primitive Archery,* Bear Paw Publications, Girdwood, AK, 1990.

McDougall, John, *Forest, Lake, and Prairie,* Toronto, 1910.

McGregor, L. and Oldfield, R.A.K., *Narratives of an Expedition into the Interior of Africa,* Frank Cass, London, 1854/1970.

Markham, Gervais, *The Art of Archerie,* 1634.

Nagler, Forrest, *Archery — An Engineering View,* 1946.

Parker, W.B., *Through Unexplored Texas,* Hayes and Zell, Philadelphia, 1856.

Pope, Saxton, *A Study of Bows and Arrows,* University of California Press, Berkeley, CA, 1923.
  — *Hunting With the Bow and Arrow,* G.P. Putnam's Sons, New York, 1925.
  — *The Adventurous Bowmen,* G.P. Putnam's Sons, New York, 1926.

Powell, Father Peter John, *People of the Sacred Mountain — A History of the Northern Cheyenne Chiefs and Warrior Societies 1830-1879*, Harper and Row, San Francisco.

Ritchie, William A., *The Archeology of New York State*, The Natural History Press, Garden City, NY, 1969.

Russell, Osborne, *Journal of a Trapper*, University of Nebraska Press, 1914/1965.

Shane, Adolph, *Archery Tackle*, Bois d'Arc Press, Azle, TX, 1936/1990.

Snowden, F.M., *Before Colour Prejudice: The Ancient View of Blacks*, Harvard University Press, Cambridge, MA, 1983.

Stemmler, L.E., *The Essentials of Archery*, New York, 1953.

Temple, C.L., *Notes on the Tribes, Provinces of Northern Nigeria*, London, 1965.

Thompson, Maurice, *The Witchery of Archery*, 1878.

Wormington, H. M., *Ancient Man in North America*, Denver Museum of Natural History, Denver, CO, 1957.

PERIODICALS

Barr, Thomas P., *Arrow Wounds*, Kansas Anthropological Association, May, 1968.

Boots, J.L., *Korean Weapons and Armor*, 1932 supplement to North China Branch of Proceedings of the Royal Asiatic Society.

Clark, J.G.D., *Neolithic Bows from Somerset, England, and the Prehistory of Archery in Northwestern Europe*, Proceedings of the Prehistoric Society for 1963 — Vol. XXIX.

Eliott, Lt. Col. Milan E., *Technique of the Oriental Release*, Archery, Dec, 1962.

Hamlin, Cmdr. H.S. Jr., *The Korean Bow*, Archery, July, 1948.

Mason, Otis T., *North American Bows, Arrows, and Quivers*, Smithsonian Institution Annual Report, 1893.

Ohiare, J., *The Royal Niger Company: The Impact of European Activities on the Communities of the Lower Benue, 1884-1897*, annual conference of the Historical Society of Nigeria, Bayero University, 1988.

TABLES OF CONTENTS

INDEX